Great Oboists on Music and Musicianship

Great Oboists on Music and Musicianship

MICHELE L. FIALA AND MARTIN SCHURING

with

LAURA SMITH

OXFORD
UNIVERSITY PRESS

Oxford University Press is a department of the University of Oxford. It furthers the University's objective of excellence in research, scholarship, and education by publishing worldwide. Oxford is a registered trade mark of Oxford University Press in the UK and certain other countries.

Published in the United States of America by Oxford University Press
198 Madison Avenue, New York, NY 10016, United States of America.

Library of Congress Cataloging-in-Publication Data
Names: Fiala, Michele L., interviewer. | Schuring, Martin, interviewer.
Title: Great oboists on music and musicianship /
[interviews by] Michele L. Fiala and Martin Schuring ; with Laura Smith.
Description: New York : Oxford University Press, 2021. |
Includes bibliographical references and index.
Identifiers: LCCN 2020020009 (print) | LCCN 2020020010 (ebook) |
ISBN 9780190915094 (hardback) | ISBN 9780190915100 (paperback) |
ISBN 9780190915124 (epub)
Subjects: LCSH: Oboe players—Interviews. | Oboe—Performance. |
Music—Interpretation (Phrasing, dynamics, etc.)
Classification: LCC MT360 .G74 2020 (print) | LCC MT360 (ebook) |
DDC 788.5/20922 [B]—dc23
LC record available at https://lccn.loc.gov/2020020009
LC ebook record available at https://lccn.loc.gov/2020020010

1 3 5 7 9 8 6 4 2

Paperback printed by Marquis, Canada
Hardback printed by Bridgeport National Bindery, Inc., United States of America

Contents

Preface

This book was conceived in 2008 at the Grand Teton Music Festival when the two coauthors discussed the number of oboists who had not written or been interviewed about their teaching and musical ideas. We chose as a model the seminal Jerome Hines *Great Singers on Great Singing* volume published in 1982. We wanted to make the interviews useful beyond the sphere of oboists and thus we decided to focus on musical and pedagogical ideals instead of more transient details such as equipment. We decided that we would vary the questions depending on the person's career and interests. We created a list of famous oboists and started the process of interviewing as many as possible. It wasn't possible to be comprehensive. Some interviews didn't work out with scheduling/geography, etc. Nevertheless, we are thrilled to be able to represent the artists in this book who are wonderful musicians who have helped to further our field.

After interviewing each subject, we transcribed the interviews and edited out the "question-answer" format to create a flow of prose that would be enjoyable to read. We arranged recurring themes under subject headings within each chapter to make them easy for the reader to locate. We worked closely with each subject to revise, represent accurately, and to showcase the personality of each artist. Nevertheless, ideas change with experience, so this represents only a snapshot of these great musicians at the time of writing. We hope that you will enjoy reading this volume and will learn as much from it as we have learned in the process of writing.

Acknowledgments

I gratefully acknowledge each of our interview subjects for their generosity with their time and expertise. They made this project fun and inspiring. I am very grateful to Laura Smith for her invaluable help in formatting and indexing. I thank my former students who helped with transcription, including Erin Goad, Kristen Urbanski, and the aforementioned Laura Smith. Steven Stamer helped with typesetting musical examples and Kate Erlewine with images. From Oxford University Press, I extend gratitude to Suzanne Ryan and Sean Decker. Finally, I'm grateful to my son Scott, without whose patience this book would not have come to fruition—as an infant, he napped in my lap through countless hours of typing!

—Michele Fiala

1

Neil Black

Neil Black was an internationally known oboist and a professor at London's Guildhall School of Music and Drama. Black attended Oxford University and earned a degree in history. Three years after finishing at Oxford, he became principal oboist for the London Philharmonic Orchestra. Later in his career, he became the principal oboist for the Academy of St. Martin in the Fields and the English Chamber Orchestra. Black performed as a soloist and chamber musician around the world and appeared at the Marlboro, Sarasota, and Spoleto USA festivals. In 1989 he was awarded the appointment Officer of the Most Excellent Order of the British Empire by the Queen of England. This interview was conducted by Martin Schuring and Michele Fiala in Birmingham, England, at the 2009 International Double Reed Society Conference. Black died in 2016.

Early Career

I started life in this city [Birmingham]. I attended lessons from the lady who was the principal oboist here because this was wartime—1943. The men were away at fighting and so this was one of the only chances for ladies to get positions in orchestras, which had mostly been a male preserve to that point. A lot of ladies played the oboe at this time because of [Léon] Goossens and his tremendous charisma and attractiveness. My teacher was one of these and so I had a lot of care and attention from her for the valuable years from eleven to thirteen.

I began with the oboe because my father played the flute and he said, "You want something more expressive than this." There happened to be this lady playing who was a very nice lady and the clarinets were to be seen in the public house—the bar—and the horn players were a little bit the same so my mother thought it would be suitable for young Neil to go to this lady.

Great Oboists on Music and Musicianship. Michele L. Fiala and Martin Schuring, Oxford University Press (2021). © Oxford University Press. DOI: 10.1093/oso/9780190915094.001.0001.

And that's why I'm an oboist. They were not musicians, my parents, but they could see that their boy needed to try it. They said, "Go and see and try it; if it doesn't work, we'll talk again. Go to Oxford to get a history degree or some sort of degree first so that you'll be able to do other things." I thought that was totally fair and I had a lot of amateur playing at Oxford University, where they had me playing all the time really. So I was so lucky to have my parents.

Later, I'm going to Oxford University where I could have had lessons but I mostly didn't, but there was one man whose playing caught my imagination and he was called Terence MacDonagh. He was [Sir Thomas] Beecham's principal oboist [in the Royal Philharmonic Orchestra] and I wanted to go to the Royal College of Music and study with him—he was a professor. So I wrote to them and they said, "You could come to the Royal College but we can't guarantee which of our professors you'd go to." I thought, "This is no good." And a friend of a friend said, "You should go to Mr. MacDonagh and tell him I said he's got to give you lessons." So I went to him and he accepted me and I had six lessons. He was a man always on edge—he had electrical treatment for his mental state—he was the worst person to live with oboe reeds and the uncertainties of our instrument. He had a terrible time himself so he'd give vast pleasure to other people with his playing. And he gave me these lessons: two of them were marvelous, two were goodish, and two were terrible where he hardly said a word, just looked miserable. And then he said, "You should ring the contractor (I think that's what you call it in the States—we call them fixers), ring the fixer of the Royal Philharmonic," which is his orchestra, "and tell him that I said you were to be booked as an extra." So I found myself in an orchestra with the finest woodwind section in the country as an educational player coming in and I said, "Mr. MacDonagh, when is my next lesson?" He said, "You're a colleague now. I don't teach colleagues." And that was the end of my musical training. I think the result of that is that you become a student all your life and you never stop learning. That astounding Mozart concerto that I heard last night from Ortega [Spanish oboist Ramón Ortega Quero], that was a lesson too. I've been learning a lot about reeds recently so you never do stop.

Reeds

On entering the profession, I felt I had to make my reeds because I couldn't take the uncertainty of waiting for these little packages through the post;

I would rather sit up all night before a concert to make a reed than have this uncertainty. So I started. In those days there was one little book—a notebook, handwritten: Evelyn's little book of oboe reed making which was by Evelyn [Rothwell] Barbirolli. Her husband had been conductor of the Houston, Texas, Symphony Orchestra and she had learned something about reed making from the principal oboist of the time. But that was all that was known because the players here—the top players—just did not make their own reeds. It wasn't like this wonderful well-organized, international reed making. It was just a few people who were out of work who made them often very slipshod—there was one really good maker that would make them for Léon Goossens—but it was so hit or miss, that whole business. The oboes didn't work very well; the polished standards of today were completely unknown in those days, so everyone had to find their own level. You could go right through the Royal College of Music and never be taught anything about how to make or scrape a reed.

I'm sure that the professors managed to make their reeds work but they didn't teach me reed making because they knew so little about it themselves if I be honest. Certainly our great players—MacDonagh, who I spoke of, and Goossens, who were the sort of kingpins of the time—never made a reed in their lives. When I was in the National Youth Orchestra, which is something I left out, Goossens came and did a couple of days of master classes with us and I wanted my reeds scraped and he turned his back on me to scrape them and I thought, "Wow, this is professional secrecy." And someone later told me, "He turned his back on you because he didn't have any idea what he was doing and he didn't want you to see." Honestly, just like that. And at the very, very end I made Goossens's reeds for him when his wonderful supply that he'd gotten during the war ran out. And by then, he was asking for the thinnest of the thin because he was about 80.

The way in which reeds are made today in Britain is very different from how we used to make them when I started. There's much more emphasis on the central spine and the shape of the tip has changed as well. It used to be more or less even across the reed and now there's far more of a crescent. I never thought that the American scrape could be made to sound, forgive me saying so, un-American because the way you've developed—from my memories of Harold Gomberg, who I knew, and Ray Still, the playing has changed so much. The generation that you represent, I would have thought that you couldn't make the sort of sound that is now currently in America with a long-scrape reed but it's quite clear you can. Particularly in terms of flexibility, subtlety, nuance, and so on. Every time that an American orchestra visited England there was at least one sort of criticism, equally balanced by criticism of English players when they came to America. It was a well-known thing but the papers always used to point out, "If it were not for the thin oboe sound we associate with British orchestras, I would have enjoyed this concert." Honestly, it went that far and the sound to me is a subject I don't like to get into but I do notice that the reeds have changed phenomenally.

I go to Sarasota every year and have done [so] for the last fifteen years, and in that time the playing of the young people, who are *top* young people—we get them from Curtis, and New England Conservatory, and Indiana, and UCLA and so on. There's say six oboists chosen from about forty-six CDs—there's been an enormous change there. And almost equally in our country—we've gone to more of a European style than to a more insular British style.

Tone

I have never talked a lot about tone because I think, if we see two sopranos—one large and one a smaller-sized soprano—you don't expect them to make the same sound. When we hear Pinchas Zukerman and we hear Gidon Kremer—two violinists who have totally different sounds—we as wind players aren't thinking, "Oh, Pinchas Zukerman's sound is so full, Gidon Kremer can sound scratchy." What we're thinking about is how they use this equipment to make music and that is the thing that I am always concentrated on. I'm absolutely delighted to see that Hansjörg Schellenberger, who I admire very much, has written somewhere almost exactly the same thing and echoed this thought that I've had all my life. We concentrate as oboes too much on the tone and don't realize if it is the best vehicle for expression that you have with your physique. All our lip structures are different and everything is different—we shouldn't be talking about one-size-fits-all for this or that nationality or even the so-called Euro sound, which is talked about so much where the borders have disappeared in Europe—we can get to Paris almost quicker than we can get to Manchester so there is no reason to have national styles. There aren't national styles. They're just disappearing every day.

The thing that seems to be central is that you are a singer with a misplaced larynx. Instead of there [points to his throat] it's slipped a bit here [indicates an oboe]. But the fact remains that, whereas a singer has to rely entirely on their body, the resonance is here, the resonance is everywhere, you have the additional advantage of having an oboe. But to so many people, and nearly every student that I hear, the oboe is actually getting in the way of their beautiful singing. And even though they haven't had a singing lesson in their life they can probably sing a phrase more musically than they can play it on the oboe. It's all about singing or dancing. That's all the music is about to me. I feel that those are the basics—without that, you can't be a wonderful oboe player and all the players I admire have that quality. Heinz [Holliger]—although he has not had good press in America—if he's playing a Schumann piece, he has such control of the instrument that his musical imagination can shine through every phrase he plays, whereas someone of the size of Lothar Koch wouldn't make a sound like Heinz. Heinz is a skinny fellow—and Koch was enormous, strong—so you would expect them to produce different sounds. A lot of young ladies, some of them quite small, in England, felt that unless they could make the Berlin Philharmonic sound that they'd failed as oboists and there was no way physically that they could make a sound like Koch. They weren't built like that, why should they? I think the important thing is to match your reed making to your physique.

Technique

The whole question of the possession of technique is to have freedom—to let your musical imagination speak. The liberation of having a good technique allows you to play things because that's what you want to do rather than because that's what you have to do. But, there are people who build up a fantastic freedom then have nothing to say. I'm not interested in them as an oboist and I don't feel the public is. They just say, "Oh, that's very fast isn't it?" But then, every flute player, third-rate flute player, can play very fast, so to the public there's nothing amazing. To us it is amazing because we know how hard the oboe is to play, technically—with complete technical control. But it [technique] is only the means to the end and I'm interested in the end.

On Playing in Different Settings

The biggest change for me was between playing in symphony orchestras and chamber orchestras. We were in a very good chamber orchestra—the English Chamber Orchestra—and we were so lucky with our directors.

We were totally being inspired by the likes of our eight years with Daniel Barenboim and then cycles with Murray Perahia and these wonderful musicians to associate with. I played the Bach double with [Isaac] Stern, [Pinchas] Zukerman, [Ferdinand] Helman, [Yehudi] Menuhin all in one year and would have played with my favorite of all, David Oistrakh, but he died on the way to the concert, which was a great tragedy. But the fact is, with all this luxury, what I want to tell you about playing in chamber orchestras is that it's much less demanding as an oboist than it is playing in a symphony orchestra. Apart from the odd *Tombeau de Couperin*, Pulcinella [suite by Stravinsky], perhaps "The Silken Ladder" [overture by Rossini], there are not pieces in the repertoire that make tremendous technical demands for the first thing. The second thing is, in a symphony orchestra, you have to play so quietly but you also have to play so loudly. If you play loud in a chamber orchestra, the director immediately damps you down because you are too powerful for the string players. When it says piano, it's usually solo so you play it a little bit louder so in the end, your level is mezzo piano to mezzo forte. If you play a real true forte you are too loud for a chamber orchestra and if you play piano and it says so, somebody will want to hear more oboe because you are, for a brief time, a soloist in a Mozart piano concerto. Woodwind players, when they have their moments, have to play like soloists and it almost certainly says piano. So, in the end you don't have to worry too much about the extremes and also bottom notes. I almost neglected bottom notes because how often in the Mozart/Haydn repertoire do you actually play anything lower than a D? No C♯ to worry about because they all knew C♯ sounded foul on those instruments. Bach never wrote a C♯ in the bottom for an oboe, I don't think. Even the d'amore they realized that when he wrote a C♯, and it was the d'amore playing, he'd have a terrible sound. So, he didn't write Bs either. Anyway, I would say that I found that liberating that I wasn't trying to make reeds where you had to crawl around the bottom and when I stopped playing in chamber orchestra and I was freelance playing, which has been since about 1998, I found out I had to be much more critical about my reed making in case I play in a symphony orchestra one day. But, obviously when you've then changed to solo playing you have to have a bigger range and I was doing that playing in the middle of the chamber orchestra. So, in the twenty-eight years I was with them and the five years with [the Academy of] St. Martin in the Fields, I don't think I had to concern myself too much about changing reed styles for different jobs.

On Being a Soloist

As the young man last night [Ramón Ortega Quero] showed me so well—
you have to possess the whole. He certainly possessed the whole last night in
his attitude and he looked as if he'd paid the mortgage off as well. Fantastic!
But, I think all that has to be put on. If you're naturally not a person who
feels that they're very interesting, for the moment you're on the stage, you
have to *look* as if you're interesting. You've got to walk on meaning something and in a chamber orchestra you can remain quite a soloist. That's why
someone like [François] Leleux has taken to the Chamber Orchestra of
Europe rather than playing in the Bavarian Radio Orchestra. I'm sure that
his temperament is better suited for being a chamber orchestra player because he is quite flamboyant. Jonathan Kelly is another person that I have
enormous respect for. He also has played a lot in the European Chamber
Orchestra as well as the Berlin Philharmonic. The life suited me (and my
shortcomings, too) very well because I'd never had a flashy technique in
any way and Mozart/Haydn didn't write particularly flashily for the oboe,
so the fact that I started really as a jumped-up amateur, I've been studying
ever since.

While practicing, a little bird should be sitting on your shoulder and every
time you think, "Ah, I didn't do that badly," it would say, "Ah, but what about
the tuning of that top note and what about this and what about that," and that
little critical bird would never go away until the moment of the performance
where you sweep it away and say, "Right. I've done the work the best I can.
This is as good as I am now. Bird is gone. I'm going to generously give." There's
a thing here. We don't talk about doing performances; we talk about giving
performances. To give a performance is like giving a gift to someone and the
generosity of that gift is part of the whole thing, so I don't think it's completely
a matter of semantics saying I gave a performance to a small audience or to a
live audience at an event. I try to go on the feeling that they aren't waiting for
me to split a bottom note—that they actually want to be entertained. I *want*
to entertain them, so we have a great bond. And this attitude of performance
should be reduced to simple things like that.

Let's say I'm beginning the Strauss slow movement—that lovely long
tune—I'm thinking of where am I going to, for instance [singing] now
that B♭ there [singing] is part of the end of the first half of the phrase but
it doesn't stop there it [singing] because it's going on as well and I'm sort of
thinking of shapes and phrasing two shapes. But I'm trying not to let it be

too technical because I want to clear the decks for just singing and a singer doesn't think, "I'm singing." She does have words to help her. I say her because we're a soprano. Strauss writes for us like a soprano voice and he had a lifetime love for the soprano voice. That's why he writes such beautiful tunes for us. To try to get a sense of stillness—I'm thinking of atmosphere. I'm thinking of the atmosphere I'm trying to bring to that piece and that the first movement isn't a bad display of finger waggling but it is the feeling of an old man whose world has crashed around him. His favorite opera house is in ruins; it's old Germany. The cultured Germany he knew is no more. Every time before I play the Strauss concerto, which was about 65 or 70 times and I've still got one to do this year actually, I listen to my record of the *Four Last Songs* written at the same time—Lisa della Casa and the Vienna Philharmonic is one of my very, very favorite records. I don't think I've played the Strauss concerto without hearing that record within the last two days before playing it. The Strauss was often a monthly event for me but it never got routine because it's such a personal testament of a great composer who's been through everything and is now looking back on his lifetime and suddenly *Rosenkavalier* waltzes just flip past. This is the atmosphere I'm trying to send out and create when I begin to play the Strauss. So often, I hear students and young people playing the long notes a bit boring without a sense that there are three phrases that grow out from the beginning one right after the other.

There are so many other factors that get in the way—people wanting great success in the world, people who are battered down by one bad critic—it's like steering a ship between a rock and a hard place. You have to find that way through and not be distracted by all the things. Just keep to your own and to your path. Don't allow yourself to be distracted. There's a career thing that can get in people's way and I think if a career is not open to you because you simply do not have the talent, you have to awaken to that one day. I know people who are never happy in a job because there's always another job just a little bit higher up the scale—they're miserable because they can't get to it or because somebody else got their job. I once played in an orchestra where, and forgive this expression, the second oboist was fingering my parts. I thought, "My God," you know that's a very unhappy person. That person wants to be sitting where I am and that's not a very good attitude to have whether you're a second oboe or anything else. I try to get rid of all that sort of rubbish and just get down to the simple thing of giving somebody something as beautiful as you can make it.

Role Models

One of the people that I have learnt enormously from is Murray Perahia. That is a man who is totally dedicated to music and is utterly self-critical and he pays you the compliment of being equally critical about you. He goes through so much self-criticism that it sometimes weighs him down in rehearsal and then he's done his work and in the performance, he rises above it superbly. Some of my greatest memories are with him. With Daniel [Barenboim], everything is new, everything is extemporized. You fear in every concert that you don't know what he's going to do—whether we're going to make a new chord that we've never made before—you make it with him and he winks at you. It's a wonderful feeling of music being made. Murray is made with fantastic preparation and self-criticism. So, those are two different ways of approaching performance. David Oistrakh was to me one of the aristocrats of music. I played the Brahms Concerto and the Beethoven with him in my early days with the London Philharmonic and I so looked forward to playing that piece with him. That was a great, great sadness to me in every way when he died in Holland [in 1974].

Among oboists—well, there are so many—but today, I listen with the greatest enthusiasm to the pupils of Maurice Bourgue. What might be almost my favorite excerpt I have on my little talk [a presentation he was to give about the history of oboe playing in the 20th century] is of him playing Schumann *Abendlied*. He's done so much good: from Diana Doherty in Australia to Jonathan Kelly and [François] Leleux and many others who spread this wonderful feeling that it's easy to play with a great sound and wonderful technique. The Paris Conservatoire School generally I think has been such a hotbed, dating right back to the times when so many of the American orchestras had French players. Before Tabuteau, even, you had [Georges] Longy and [Henri] de Busscher (de Busscher was, I think, from Belgium) and Fernand Gillet in Boston. I have always felt that there is so much coming from the Paris Conservatoire and a lot of players, particularly from the Far East, come to Germany now but either of those countries is a wonderful place to study and I study their players with great humility and a desire to learn.

One of the singers I worked with a lot was Richard Lewis. He was with the Bach Aria Group in New York with Robert Bloom and when he came back to England as he did later on, he wanted to keep doing some of that with his wife, who is a mezzo-soprano. I got great pleasure from playing Bach with him. He organized something along the same lines in England in a much smaller way and I enjoyed that tremendously and got to know him well. I was talking earlier about how we should model ourselves on singers—they have a sense of purity. I actually enjoyed the singing of Kathleen Battle when she came to us. There were problems but they were not to do with her voice at all; she was absolutely gorgeous. We had Kiri Te Kanawa where we did a lot with her and the very rich thing for the oboist was the *Songs of the Auvergne*; she did them all with us. Enormously open parts and including a great cadenza for the oboist and our record of that was the first time we met up with the man who was going to be our conductor in chief who was Jeffrey Tate. He'd been a repetiteur at the opera house.

We did *Figaro* and *Don Giovanni* with Daniel Barenboim in Edinburgh at festivals. We did two years of *Giovanni* and two years of *Figaro* and the singing was absolutely top class featuring Fischer-Dieskau and other people. I never forget those and I was learning from what I heard on the stage all the time. One of the things I would say to students is, however advanced you are, never stop learning. Never, ever, stop learning.

On Teaching

Where I feel teaching is difficult for me—although I do encourage people and I do try to make them play like good musicians—is by not having had the personal experience, background, of being trained, I haven't really got a great idea of how you do it. I had been Professor of the Royal Academy of Music until I gave it up because I did too much touring and they had an age limit so when the age limit came up, I moved to the Guildhall who didn't have an age limit. I've had private pupils on and off but I much prefer to get advanced players coming along with a concerto or an audition to do, the certain pieces that they want to study. To take someone for four years starting with Ferling studies to passing out with fantastic and difficult Lamorlettes and Gillets and things at the other end—I often felt really that I wasn't doing as good a job as I could.

I have found my way through keeping an open mind—not allowing myself to be clouded by prejudice or "you've got to do this" or "you've got to do that," and reducing it to simple things. "How would you sing it? Put the oboe down. Sing that phrase. Do you notice where it went? Do you notice what the most intense note was? Now pick up the oboe and do it again." So often that improves it just like that and we haven't really said anything except listen to yourself. Listen to what you're doing. [Pablo] Casals said, "take an ear off and put it at the other end of the studio" to hear what that sounds like to someone else—not what's going on inside your head.

Reminiscence

I've had many, many funny experiences but one of them was playing the Strauss in the Queen Elizabeth Hall. It was already a very awkward concert because someone had, on a motorcycle, run over the cor anglais player's car and killed himself so she arrived terribly late and terribly flustered. It was actually Celia Nicklin. And the Strauss concerto was delayed. We put a string piece in while she came and then she arrived. We were all a bit out-of-ordinary feeling and I was just about to start playing when there was a shuffle and a streaking figure came and sat at the end of my bell and it was Heinz [Holliger]. He'd come. It was so funny because afterwards when we'd finished he came out to see me and he said, "Why did you play C♯ instead of C natural in that last movement?" Dear man.

I don't really learn from Heinz because I think he's such a phenomenon of nature that you can't learn from that. We used to do *Trittico* by [Antal] Dorati. We toured it and of course I wasn't in it so I would watch and the oboe d'amore and the English horn were all sitting there one after the other and he never ever tried the reed or anything. He just picked it up and played it. There was never water anywhere and I thought, "No, this is . . . he's just lucky, isn't he?" [Laughter] He would play in the draftiest churches in the world and never anything. He just got on with it. Or I'd be chatting away in the band room and we'd be talking about something and then we'd hear applause from the end of the piece before and he would start putting his oboe together still talking about what we were talking about, a couple tweaks on the reed, bang it in and walk out and play the Strauss or the Martinů or whatever it was without any sort of preparation or anything—you're dealing with a phenomenon of nature there. That was a lovely friendship to have and it survived. I've had contact with a lot of absolutely wonderful musicians. Looking back on my time, it's been such a complete treat doing my hobby. It never got to really feel like a profession until sometime in the London Philharmonic when you go along to a children's concert at 9:30 in a cinema—two thousand children—and they've put a pad down in front of you of simple popular classics. I was a young man of twenty-six and this pad would be put down in front of some bagpipes or something—some pieces you'd heard of but didn't really know and you had to play them there and then without rehearsal. That was when I felt, "Am I going to sink or swim in this professional world?" But mostly it's just been a complete treat. I'm allowed to do what I like.

2

Maurice Bourgue

Maurice Bourgue is a French oboist, chamber musician, composer, and orchestra conductor. He studied at the Conservatoire National Supérieur de Musique de Paris, where he took oboe classes led by Étienne Baudo and chamber music classes from Fernand Oubradous. He was awarded first prize for the oboe in 1958 followed by the first prize for chamber music in 1959. He went on to win the following major international competitions: Geneva 1963, Birmingham 1965, Munich 1967, Prague 1968, and Budapest 1970. Bourgue was hired by Charles Munch in 1967 for the Orchestre de Paris, where he remained the oboe soloist until 1979. He has also performed solo under several prestigious orchestra conductors (Claudio Abbado, Daniel Barenboim, Riccardo Chailly, John Eliot Gardiner), and began working as an orchestra conductor himself in France and abroad. Since 1972, he has been devoting a large proportion of his time to chamber music with the eponymous octet he founded, comprising musicians from the Orchestre de Paris, with which he has recorded several albums. As the musical director for the Académie Internationale de Musique de Chambre Sándor Végh, Bourgue continues to teach at the conservatories in Paris and Geneva and in the master classes he runs in Budapest, London, Lausanne, Moscow, Oslo, Jerusalem, and Kyoto. Bourgue additionally has recorded a great number of award-winning albums. This interview was conducted by Michele Fiala via email in October 2018.

Many thanks for the translation by Adrienne Hayes Demirelli.

Early Career

At nine, my father, who was a clarinetist, asked me to choose an instrument. Since I couldn't decide, he turned on the radio and said, "You will listen to this

Great Oboists on Music and Musicianship. Michele L. Fiala and Martin Schuring, Oxford University Press (2021).

orchestra and listen well to all the instruments," and I chose the oboe. I do not know the oboist to whom I owe this gift. I have never regretted this choice, despite all the torments one encounters while learning this instrument.

Until I was thirteen, the instrument and music were quite foreign to me, up until the day I was asked to play in the orchestra. After the first chords of the trumpets in the Magnificat by J. S. Bach, I had an emotional breakthrough that made me question: "That's music, then?" That's what made me decide to be a musician. Music and oboe have been, since that day, always together.

Competitions

The first obligation for an international competition is to remain true to oneself and to defend, as one's own life, one's concept in each work and to follow the path that your instinct maps out for you. On the other hand, preparation for such a test must be done technically, just as an Olympian prepares. You must first have a strong mind capable of resisting all forms of interruption of your concentration. The key to all this lies in the mastery of breathing, the corner-stone of your balance, among many other things.

Multi-Faceted Career

Of course, there is a difference of approach between chamber music, orchestral, and solo work. What matters is to clarify these three situations. Which work demands the highest technical level? A refined sound? Or is the most musically convincing? And presents the clearest understanding of the text you are defending? It is my point of view that solo work is the best because there you are alone and you cannot hide. All other situations flow from this one. So if you master this one, you master all the others.

National Styles

I have never been a strong advocate of schools because I believe in only one aesthetic criterion: beauty. Even then we must define: what is beauty? From a sonic point of view, a beautiful sound is a round sound that must project into space. On the oboe, I have only this means to convey my feelings, my emotions, and all kinds of external circumstances. I must be able to vary the color of this beauty to be elastic, fluctuating, totally at the service of my creativity. It is not necessarily bright or dark, but consistent with the color that I hear. If that is what you mean when speaking of the French style then we agree. But today, as in architecture, sounds around the world are similar and have the tendency to become uniform and lose their personal color.

Articulation, also, has its importance, which is why the lightness of this sound must be preserved. All this combines and harmonizes a set of elements in perfect balance. I also believe in the direct relationship that exists between the sound and the language of any country, a deep-rooted relationship that one produces when singing, for example, and it is this relationship that has always fascinated me.

What can I tell you about the evolution of the French style? National styles have faded away and are following the trend of globalization just like lukewarm water that has lost its original taste. One only has to see what's happening to Camembert [a famous French cheese], which has lost all its taste because of the stupid laws of Europe which now pasteurizes the whole process of fermentation.

Memorable Performances

I remember a dress rehearsal in Grenoble where I played the Mozart concerto with a German conductor who was quite bad and I was completely discouraged as to how the evening concert would turn out. We replayed the slow movement and I said to myself, "Repeat it again and we'll go to sleep to forget this all." Then something wonderful happened that I cannot explain. The music transformed into something beyond my wish; it was not me who was playing but I was being guided by something throughout the entire musical process. I had finally let go after losing all hope of making a beautiful concert and now the music was free from any hindrance. It was miraculous. Did the orchestra feel this difference too? I do not know but I was moved deeply after this experience.

Advice

I have applied this principle all my life: ask yourself the real questions, and you will have the right solutions because your intuition is the best of the masters.

3

Nicholas Daniel

Nicholas Daniel became known as an oboe soloist after winning the BBC Young Musician of the Year award at the age of eighteen. He has performed and conducted around the world and was awarded the Queen's Medal for Music. His many recordings have earned recognitions like the BBC Music Magazine Premiere Award in 2016. He is the professor of oboe at the Musikhochschule, Trossingen, artistic associate and founder member of the Britten Sinfonia, and artistic director of the Leicester International Festival. This interview was conducted by Michele Fiala and Martin Schuring backstage in the Birmingham Town Hall before Daniel's performance at the 2009 International Double Reed Society conference.

On Teaching Students to Connect with the Audience

It's an approach to teaching which is about the end result of concertizing. It's very easy to be a professional student and to end up slightly institutionalized and it's disturbing. People should take the time they need to study but I try to turn every lesson into a performance and my students get very, very nervous playing for me, I suppose because they respect me. But not because I shout at them because I absolutely don't. But I think they feel this performance thing and I say, "Look, listen, I want you to perform this even if it's an etude or a scale. I want you to play that as if you were playing to somebody in the next room. Project!" There are tricks I use like I'll actually walk up to somebody and I'll squeeze their earlobe and I'll say, "I'm just borrowing your ear." And I take it and I give it to different members of the audience and I say, "Now, you are now listening to yourself from this person's point of view and then this person." And the ear goes around the audience and they get used to doing that. Then you take it back to them and say, "Ok you can have it back now," and if they're prepared to play with you then that works quite well. Another

Great Oboists on Music and Musicianship. Michele L. Fiala and Martin Schuring, Oxford University Press (2021).
© Oxford University Press. DOI: 10.1093/oso/9780190915094.001.0001.

thing that works very well is eyes. Eyes and ears are absolutely central to it. You can penetrate into an audience too much with your eyes. I certainly used to do that when I was young. I remember somebody writing to me after I'd played the Poulenc Sonata in London and saying, "It was so intense it was as if we'd done something wrong." And I thought, well it's actually not too bad for the Poulenc to have that feeling of Catholic guilt in the last movement. It's all about that. He said himself that it was a piece of religious music. But it made me wonder. So I train them to play with their eyes over the audience somewhere quite general, not into one specific place or person. There are lots of very good acting techniques that I've picked up from reading about the actors' studio and from working with animateurs on education work.

If you ask the audience to lift up their hands when they feel the person's made eye contact with them, then if you've got a big audience, you can actually sweep your eyes over an audience and you get a Mexican wave of hands going. There will always be one stubborn person that you have to kind of really look at really closely who says, "I'm not putting my hand up until I really felt their eyes bore into my head." I try and get the audience to be kind in that situation but that takes away the fear of communicating.

It's only fear: people don't want to go to the audience because they're terrified of what the audience is going to say or think. Or what they think they're going to think. And so I say, "You're worried about what I think that you think that they think that you're going to think that they think that you think." And they just go, "Ok, it's funny, I realize."

I personally feel that there's an energetic aspect to this. Benjamin Britten talked about what he called the Holy Triangle of composer-performer-audience. And I think there is another aspect to it because I think there is inspiration-composer-performer-audience. Who knows where the ideas come from for a composer but somehow they have an idea. Then they have their technique to develop those ideas. Our job is to be something in between the composer and the audience which actually interprets the composers' wishes and understands the style—often using archeology, as some music is well over 300 years old. I remember when Steve Hammer did the Britten Metamorphoses on a Yamaha DX7 Wind Synthesizer and said it was just as authentic as playing Baroque music on the modern oboe. It's hilarious! He's quite right. But, in a way our job is as actors and our job is not to impose but to use all the information we have about a piece, to let it come through us. This is the important thing for me is that the music comes through me not from me.

On Fidelity to the Composer

It's my first priority; I feel strongly. I sometimes get very creative students and we've all had things like that. They're either very troubled or they've got an incredible, creative imagination. I always encourage those students to take up painting or sculpture or composing or maybe jazz because jazz is much more creative than performing a piece of Mozart.

There are times, even in Classical [repertoire], where ornamentation is definitely possible. You wouldn't hear even a late Mozart piano concerto from any major pianist without a certain amount of ornamentation. Because we only have one Mozart oboe concerto, people tend to be quite purist about it, particularly as people learn it for orchestral auditions, which is a death to any piece. I think we should have a campaign to have the Mozart banned from orchestral auditions and they should all listen to Dittersdorf or attributed Haydn or some other piece than our beloved Mozart concerto. Why does it have to be that? Why does the other piece they have to hack through have to be the Strauss? There are other pieces that you can play that demonstrate much more than those pieces.

Anyway, Janet Craxton, my teacher, was absolutely rigid about that [fidelity to the composer]. And my teaching very much goes from the harmonic basis. I'm not only taking the instructions from the composer because that could be a little "*comme ci, comme ça.*" With early Poulenc, metronome marks are hysterical and well over the top. Later Poulenc, he's actually much more thoughtful about the metronome marks. That's just one aspect, metronome marks. It doesn't always have to be absolutely authentic because composers—I've been working with Thea Musgrave—she always says, "Oh, that is much too fast." I say, "Well, that's what you wrote," and she says, "I know but you don't want to worry about that." I say, "Well I do, a bit!" [Laughs]

Harmonies and Interpretation

The way I teach phrasing is to absolutely connect it to what the harmonies say. And if the music is atonal, I'm still seeking where the harmonic stress is. I don't think there's a good composer who doesn't write using harmonic stress and release in some way. Even if it's very linear like Isang Yun and a solo piece—for instance the glissandos in Piri are all about rising tension and sort of strange, bizarre movements. But when I'm teaching a piece of Handel or Mozart or anything, my phrasing is absolutely connected to the harmonic stress and release. That's really important for me and I find it's a way that I get peace with myself. Because the responsibility sometimes of playing great music is big and we have to find a way of being able to deal with it. If you can say to yourself, "Well you know, the composer did this in this way—wrote this harmony in a certain way for us to bring it out," you get this feeling of, "Ah, well that must be what it is."

Problem Solving

It's so interesting the comparison between medicine and music—there always seems to be a big similarity and I've always tried to figure out, "What are the similarities between doctors and musicians?" It's basically because we're problem solving. When you're learning a new piece, you're trying to work out the best way to play. You're trying to understand the style, be able to produce it. Doctors try to find out what's wrong. We're trying to find out why what we're doing is wrong. Why is it wrong? Why is it not working? Either because our muscles don't know it, because we haven't understood the harmonic basis of it, or we don't know the style well enough and we need to read around the subject, as it were, like actors do. Then you can actually say to yourself, "Ok, it's possible that I've got a valid interpretation." I'm very, very self-questioning. And I've learned that there really isn't such a thing as confidence. It doesn't really exist. You can pretend to an audience and to yourself you're confident. And you can be used to the concert situation. But in the end you are absolutely naked on the stage. And I doubt myself all the time but then if I feel that I've understood a piece from the inside out harmonically, with the analysis. . . . I mean not analysis of myself, analysis of the music—that's another subject [Laughter]—an important one. But then I feel like I can relax, I can really sink into the piece, into the character of the piece. And I think that it is very much an actor's approach and that there's a mystical approach to it too. It's a bit like the way in which healers work—on an energetic level. The people I know who work in that area say it's very important, that if you're healing people and you're just giving of yourself, you'll burn out so quickly. But if you imagine it coming through you, then it actually does refresh you. And I see many very musical students with a lot to say who play too much from themselves and don't just let the music pass through. Then the audience gets a feeling of being included rather than being something that's burning the performer on the way out. And then, funny enough, you get someone like Rostropovich who burnt every candle at every end that there was to burn and still somehow managed to be amazing. But the energy of that man was just extraordinary.

Letting Music Come through You

Basically what happened to me in this respect was not through any oboe teaching; it was through an amazing Alexander technique teacher I was working with called Jean Gibson who was a pupil of Alexander himself, and she taught many of us of my age in London. She was as old as the hills. One day I was in a group session with her in her gym and she put her knee in the middle of my back and pulled my shoulders towards her and there was this enormous crunching sound, like the way a chiropractor might work on you. I had an extraordinary reaction to it and I seemed to watch the reaction happen almost from outside. First of all I cried a lot for about five minutes and I was inconsolable. And then I fell asleep on the floor, sort of fetal. When I came round I was just sitting in a chair and I said, "I don't know what just happened." She said, "I've been waiting, ever since I've known you, to do that and this was the right moment." And she said, "You don't have to use your own energy when you perform. It can come through you. It can refresh you as it goes through." I thought, well I guess I could try that.

Next concert I had was Mozart's Twenty-fifth Symphony, the early G minor symphony, which is the opening music to the film *Amadeus*. And it's very *Sturm und Drang*: big, dramatic opening and then all of a sudden the oboe does this melody in whole notes. Semibreves—the round white ones. [Laughter] We call them semibreves. This melody is very simple, G D E♭ F♯ G, G B♭ C♯ D, and I thought OK, I'm going to try this and I'm just going to let it go and I'm just going to play the notes. I'm going to try to phrase it really well; I'm going to use appropriate style, appropriate vibrato; I'm going to try to play really in tune. I'm just going to let it come through me. And I tried it and I thought, oh God that was awful; it was really boring. I thought, oh dear. Joy, my wife, was in the audience for that concert and she was playing in the second half. And she ran up to me and said, "What did you do?" I hadn't told her anything about it. I said, "What do you mean?" She said, "That first solo. What did you do? And she said it was as if a ghost had entered the room."

And I said, "Well what I did was actually I did nothing." And she said, "Well you must do it some more." [Laughter]

It was a fabulous lesson. There are certain composers—like with Italian music, it's very, very plain and simple melodies, like Bellini. I think with Italian music there is a certain amount of the performer's ego written into the music. We're talking about the "id." The Italian composers wrote for the prima donnas, for the divas, and there's an element in the music left for them to do, same as with ornamentation. But when I've conducted Beethoven symphonies, which I've done recently, if you try to compete with Beethoven's ego, you're just going to burn. Burn, baby, burn. Because you can't and it's the same with Mozart. Unless you are listening from outside it very slightly, you can't actually do what he asks which is listen to him. Mozart of all composers has the strongest voice in your ear. You can play a Mozart phrase and go, "Oh that was alright," and then you play the next phrase and you die a thousand deaths. And Mozart goes, "There you go! You're not so good after all." He tells you so clearly what you want and all you do all the time is compare yourself as imperfect to his perfection. You know what that feels like as performers when you're playing Mozart. He talks to you all the time in your head; this horrendous, self-critical voice is [Laughter] is Mozart's voice actually! But if you can somehow step outside it then I think it's possible to get a more bird's-eye view.

There's a dreadful, dreadful, dreadful book (but there's some very interesting parts in it) by Janet Baker who was a great British mezzo-soprano, one of our really great artists. I was lucky enough, actually, at the end of her career to do some recordings with her. We recorded Berlioz's "Nuits d'été" and Brahms's Alto Rhapsody and some other things. It's a horrendous book because it's so full of her importance. It's called *Full Circle* and it's a diary of her last year. She had great hauteur, you know great grandeur. And yet somewhere in this book there's a great moment of illumination, where she describes her performing process; she describes working with a healer who told her she was using far too much of her energy and that she was going to burn out unless she stepped back and let the music come through her. And the way she describes it is absolutely fascinating; it's really worth reading this awful book for that one passage. Of course, the healer knew about that because that's the way healing energy works. It's a similar place it comes from.

What I've learned to do, gradually, is to be a slightly outside participant so that all of the basics—it's like when you're typing. You have the home keys and you always return. You know that if you're basically in the right place and you're in the right place mentally, you can stray here or there away from what is perfect as long as you can come back to it and you can be in that right place again. Some pieces more than others, I will feel a participant in. But now I have the technique, emotional technique as it were, to be able to stay outside it always. If I'm playing Classical period music I'm always very, very conscious of keeping the "me" out of it. And what happens in that situation is that your ears become sort of hypertronic X-men ears—supercharged hearing. You hear everything in such a different way because you're not so involved in being emotional. When I'm teaching it I'm making people use their ears and their eyes in a different way.

One fascinating thing is when you play music for the first time, often if you're moved by it, it's very hard to be outside it. There were two examples and one was when I was working to conduct Shostakovich's Fourteenth Symphony, which is all about death basically. My father was suddenly diagnosed with what ended up being terminal cancer and I was going into these rehearsals with Cambridge University Chamber Orchestra and I couldn't face the piece at all because I couldn't deal with the emotions that were being discussed. Basically I had to go back and learn the piece— score reading it myself—I had to go back and spend another three days going back to the piece and entering the emotional aspect of it again and somehow familiarizing myself with it in a kind of psychotherapeutic way actually, because that's what you do with therapy. You face yourself with your problems over and over and over again until they become less relevant. And then you can get outside it and you can have some circumspection to it.

A similar thing is true with John Woolrich's oboe concerto which is a piece that was written for me that I'm very, very, very proud of. It's a massive piece. A thirty-minute concerto with three oboes and a soprano saxophone, so kind of a gang of five on the stage with me and it's a huge orchestra with three horns, triple woodwinds, contrabass clarinet.... Massive ... I think six percussionists in all playing post-industrial percussion instruments—lorry springs, tin cans, all very dry. There are timpani and there's a Verdi bass drum and huge tam-tams and a waterphone. There were things in Woolrich's life at that time that conspired for him to write a truly great piece at that moment just as I wanted one and I was very proud because I pounced at the right moment to make it happen. I heard a piece that he had written and I could just sense there was an awesome, awesome storm in his music. And I thought: I want that storm. That storm has got to be mine. That storm has got to be for the oboe. That piece that's coming, I could sense it rising in him. I'd known him for quite a long time—for ten years I'd known him. He'd written some other lovely things—delicate, fine, mysterious, beautiful, wistful things. And then this thing started and I said, "Right, it's the time. I want you to write this concerto." Kenyon, who was running the proms at the time, said, "Actually we'd very much like John to write a concerto for you. What do you think?" And I said, "Absolutely yes. Let's do it."

John was completely non-collaborative about it; he just wrote. I got it in the post. I was so excited. We rehearsed it for the first time two days before the world premiere, which is always what happens. You get these incredible occasions. It's a prom where there's a thousand people standing in front of you who've paid five pounds for a ticket. They have five and a half thousand people in the outer hall. Last year I did the Elliott Carter concerto to five and a half thousand people because they put Beethoven [Fifth Symphony] in the second half so they all came for the Beethoven. And they all heard Elliott Carter in the first half as well so it was wonderful to do that. But at the first [Woolrich] rehearsal—there's this one place in the piece where basically it's a sort of snuff movie, the piece. There's this ceremonial kind of horror thing and I thank God that the oboe doesn't play in that part because the first time I heard it, it was impossible to listen to it without being moved. I just thought oh my God, how am I going to stand on the stage of the Albert Hall and not weep at this music, particularly as I had to play something so hard afterwards where the oboe comes back in with the opening theme and just drifts around like a lost feather in the breeze and then gradually everybody stops and the oboist is left with what you could call a mobile, which is basically a repetitive phrase which just keeps going around and around and around. I say it's a snuff movie because the orchestra goes "Bang, Bang" at the end with the most horrendous shock and basically snuffs out the oboe. It's very hard, that last part. You're quite tired after playing thirty minutes up to that point and it's completely unaccompanied the last two minutes of the piece with this mobile just rustling in the breeze around you. So you have to be really ready to play that and you have to be not blubbing. Again I used the same process. I went home and I went into the music over and over and over again trying to access why it was upsetting me so much and why it was so moving. I think it was in part because there were aspects of John's life at this time that he basically wrote into the piece—a really, really sad, tragic situation. And there was the fact that his whole energy as a composer had risen to that point and this was the culmination of it.

It is a truly great piece and I think it'll stand the test of time and I'm so pleased we were able to record it. We recorded it in one three-hour session. There was a fire in the recording studio the day we were supposed to have two sessions to record it, and the BBC Orchestra (who we recorded it with), the manager said, "Right, what are you doing tomorrow?" And I said, "Oh my God, I have a live broadcast in the evening." He said, "Well, I can give you the orchestra in the morning if you want . . . if you want to do this." And I said, "Let's do it." So we did it and it was hard but it was great. The concert in the evening probably suffered a bit.

Skills for a Solo Career

You need to be able to play the game. I've talked about egolessness, which I think is actually essential to being a good musician, but you need to be able to be an entertainer as well. You have to understand what good programming is. You have to understand our repertoire. And you have to understand the needs of any given audience on any given occasion. I've found for instance in America that they're much less accepting of arrangements—the same in Germany. Britain and France tend to be more laissez-faire about that kind of thing. In our debut at the Frick Collection in New York with the quintet when we wanted to play the Mason Jones version of *Tombeau de Couperin*, the lovely lady there, Joyce Bodig, who I adore, said, "We don't have arrangements here." And I said, "Joyce, listen. . . ." She talked about it with her board and staff. It got that serious. And then she said, "Well, tell me why you think you should." And I said, "First of all, because the piece was originally written for piano and then Ravel arranged it himself. This is basically like we play the wind parts from the orchestra." And she said, "Ok, since it's you, I'll let you do it." Actually she loved it. But there's a lot of resistance to it because there's a lot of purism which is for good reasons, comes from a good point of view. Same in Germany, they are very much less accepting than they are of original pieces so that slightly limits us.

If you are playing in a small music society and you've got your kind of, "Oh I have to play my Stockhausen or something or other here . . . this is something I need to do." No you don't do that there. What you do is you maybe play something which has got a bit of a tang in it, like some living music. But you give them something of what they want and you extend and you push their boundaries a bit. You have to understand about pacing yourself in terms of timing in a concert, particularly recitals and general music things. You have to understand what works with the ear. I don't like to have piano solos actually in your recital—I think they've come to hear a duo. But in these days I often put in a piece of English horn or oboe d'amore as well to change up the timbre. I very often will not start with Baroque and progress through the periods. I'll very often start with Bach and end with Bach and go straight into contemporary music after and before. Having said I don't start with Baroque, actually Bach for me has become more and more central to my life and I realize the relevance of Bach more and more. So we just love to play Bach, particularly with piano but also with harpsichord.

I think also about how you present yourself. Some people have it easier and I think there are enormous dangers involved because there's the whole aspect of the incredibly superficial nature of much of the recorded artists one gets to hear. Record companies and major managers have a lot to answer for because they're choosing people for how they look when actually the primary thing they'll be doing is recording. The most times people will hear them play is either over a radio or on a CD. These days with things like YouTube there's much more openness and the video is becoming much more common on computers and stuff so the visual aspect of it is important. But, if there's a choice between someone who plays amazingly and doesn't look as good as somebody else who plays quite well, they'll always choose the pretty one. So you've got to make the best of yourself. Particularly the oboe, it looks unfortunate when you play, so you've got to use your eyes because you have to allow the audience to see into who you are via your eyes. That rule is very good for breaking as well. If you want to close your eyes for a certain part of the piece that's also absolutely fine. That gives a kind of rapt, centered quality to what you do. Interestingly enough, in meditation recently I've noticed that people are talking more and more about meditating with eyes open, whereas the traditional way was with eyes closed and the thinking behind that is that we should be meditating so that it has an outward effect as well. That was what of course the Maharishi Mahesh Yogi talked about—"healing the world"—you know the man who taught the Beatles to meditate . . . got them off LSD for a while.

To return, you've got to try and look really good so that people really want to look at you. They want to be entranced by it. They want to know that you're not uncomfortable, that you're at ease with yourself, that you want to be there, that you're having a good time doing it. I get a bit disturbed when people say, "You look as though you're having so much fun." I'm not sure that's good. I try to let myself go onstage, to "go with the flow" to a certain extent, just as long as I'm sure that my center is where I want it to be. Then I feel as though I can move from there.

You've got to understand, in terms of playing solo, about the materials that you need to have. There's a very fine boundary between producing stuff for promoters and audiences that's too professional looking and not professional looking enough. I do quite a lot of promotion. I have a festival and I have a lunchtime series. I get sent hundreds and hundreds of brochures in the post every year. I have boxes and boxes of stuff to look through. And anything that looks too slick, my experience is that it's actually just not worth bothering with. The performers will be probably be fairly shallow; they probably got some money from someone to throw it all together. Something that looks clear, calmly done, classy—that I'll spend a bit more time looking into because if I listened to every CD I was sent, I'd be spending my whole life listening to CDs for one twelve-lunchtime concert series. It's just not practical. The stuff that comes with the photocopied sheet and not very good photograph or you notice somehow or other that they're 65 and their photograph says 21. You're kidding yourself and you're not going to kid me. So having fairly reasonable photographs with something that looks animated and connected with the audience or something very dramatic. It's important to have something up-to-date and arty if you want to but not too arty. Make a connection; think who your audience is. I get very, very frustrated when people print biographies of me that are a thousand years ago that talk about me going to Indiana University to teach. That sort of thing really bothers me but you have to try and control that. Having good availability of things like a website—the internet is absolutely essential to many people's research into you. Having a YouTube presence, which I've had for just over a year now, has been really great. The first thing I put on was the Britten's Metamorphoses that went on to George Caird's Britten Metamorphoses DVD with this incredible, incredible book, beautifully researched. I think it's amazingly well done. George and I are going to do some more research and performance like that with an even more interactive DVD, possibly to Britten repertoire. He's raising the funds to do the research. I think that will be great.

Vocal Music and the Oboe

There's an absolutely unbelievable video from 1982—peak Kiri Te Kanawa—from the Met of the trio from *Rosenkavalier*. Unless you understand that music, you cannot play the oboe concerto. Unless you know Strauss is an opera composer, you can't possibly know why he wrote that melody as he did in the slow movement. So, all you do is you go to YouTube and you just bang it on, there it is. When I first went to Indiana, I remember talking about the Mozart Oboe Quartet, about Ländler, and about Austrian folk music to a Chinese student who just went, "Huh?" And I said OK, let's see if I can find something. I typed into a search engine about Austrian folk music, about Ländler and lederhosen and all kinds of stuff, and I had some interesting sites coming up for that, which wasn't quite what I expected . . . but I found very quickly video footage of people dancing in the mountains outside Munich from about 1912. So sweet. He went, "Oooooooh, I see. [singing]" And I said, "Yeah, that's exactly it." The internet is so useful from that point of view. There are some incredible things on YouTube from people like Casals and you can see Britten and Pears doing *Winterreise*—you can get lost in it. We used to get lost in the internet and now I just get lost in YouTube. It's amazing really.

Commissioning New Music

If you're interested in new music, and I think there's no point trying to be a solo oboist without being interested in new music, nurturing relationships with composers is so important because it's a really a hard life being a composer. There are very few composers in the world who only earn a living through composing. Mostly they teach or they conduct or they drive a taxi, who knows. [Laughter] I make it one of my missions in life is to befriend composers who I'm interested in and show great interest in and develop an understanding of their work and eventually ask them to write something. Sometimes you can make friends with them very quickly. Other times, particularly with well-known composers, it takes time.

James MacMillan is a composer who I like very much, who's one of our leading composers and in a very particular kind of way he can be very tonal. I've done lots of work with him. I've also played other music under him. We played some Galina Ustvolskaya, this extraordinary Russian, who has just died actually. She was a pupil of Shostakovich and she was a religious minimalist of the most grim, wonderfully grim, bare, brutal music. Jimmy, despite the fact that her music is a million miles from who he is, he just loves her music because it's very real. So I've done Ustvolskaya with him conducting and there's a piece for two oboes, eight violins, piano, and percussion. There's another piece for trumpet, trombone, a bass who recites the Lord's Prayer, oboe, and coffin played with meat hammers, or a big wooden box but everybody sees it's supposed to be a coffin. It's desperate stuff but Jimmy really loves it and I do too. And then I was asked to play his English horn concerto which is called "The World's Ransoming," which was commissioned by Christine Pendrill; I was asked to play that with him last year in Poland. The cor anglais concerto is just stunning. It's all about Maundy Thursday; it's just a beautiful piece. At the same time we did some work with him with the Britten Sinfonia. I asked him to be composer-in-residence for my festival in Leicester, got to know him really well . . . as well as you can with Jimmy because he's quite shy. And then the Britten Sinfonia offered him a commission for whatever he wanted to write and he said, "Actually I'd like to write a concerto for Nick." So next year I'm doing the world premiere of a concerto and this hall here [in Birmingham] is co-commissioning it as well. This is really important because he's a major composer and he's really happy with what he's writing at the moment. It's going to be quite a charming lovely piece, not very heavy duty which I'm really pleased about because his music is at its best when it's being really beautiful.

If you can befriend composers and just let them believe in you then I think that's a really important aspect. And then you have to program them really carefully and you have to work hard with getting the money for these commissions and it's not always possible to pay for it yourself. I have put money from my own pocket into getting music in the past and that's a very good way to use your money.

You cannot be a solo oboist without playing new music; therefore, you have to get the composers to trust you. Actually one very interesting composer who lives in New York who's writing for me, Huang Ruo, is writing a solo piece for viola and oboe and he's absolutely way out there. It'll be very, very, very hard, very virtuosic. I'm playing with Richard O'Neill, the Korean viola player who I think is so fantastic.

I definitely don't say yes to everything, but I generally say yes to a good composer writing a new piece because you can be disappointed some of the time but most of the time you won't be.

Expect the Unexpected

One composer, one very famous composer, Oliver Knussen, wrote a piece—
a memorial piece for Janet Craxton. I did this concert in memory of Janet
Craxton when she'd been dead for ten years; I thought we needed to remember her life. And it was I think eleven or twelve composers wrote pieces
for that one concert. Oliver Knussen's piece arrived through what was in
those days a fax machine at two in the morning. He then phoned and asked
us to play it for him over the phone. It's a beautiful piece for English horn and
clarinet called *Elegiac Arabesques*. It's absolutely beautiful. And he worked on
it with us for 45 minutes on speakerphone. That's pretty extreme. You can't
time manage that.

Another thing that happened with James MacMillan is, his piece called
In Angustiis is a memorial piece for 9/11 and there are several versions of it.
I downloaded it from Boosey and Hawkes's website and it was just one page.
I paid twelve pounds for it, which I thought was a bit steep for a download.
He was up in my festival in Leicester. I got to the day of the performance
which was a lunchtime concert; I was playing the piece. And I said, "Hey
Jimmy, can I play that piece for you now—that *In Augustiis* piece?" "Oh yes,
that'll be nice Nick." I said, "It's very short. It won't take long. It's only one
page." "One page, Nick?" And I said, "Yeah." "It may be a wee bit more than
that." And I said, "What are you saying?" He said, "Well I'm not sure. I better
go make a phone call to Boosey and Hawkes." So Boosey and Hawkes faxed
the other six pages over. I learned it in an hour, with the composer watching
me practice it. Which included him developing the piece at the same time
and actually me working in a whole new technique I've never seen written
down, with blowing across the reed and getting whistle tones. I've never seen
that technique described but you could call it Aeolian oboe because that's
what Aeolian harp is, just the wind through the strings. You know how you
can hear whistle tones in the flute? The reed does that; not a very good reed
does it better! Very easy, in other words. So that included that developing the
piece time because there were three or four places where he said, "I would
like you to take longer. It sounds wonderful this noise you're making here."
And I was going, "Oh my God, oh my God. The concert's in fifteen minutes!"

There was one very good piece that was written for me by Simon
Bainbridge that was a double concerto for my wife and I. Simon Bainbridge
won the Grawemeyer Prize with his work for mezzo-soprano, bassoon, and
orchestra which is on Primo Levi's poetry and he's a very, very good British

composer and his style was going through a real sea change in the time he was writing this double concerto for us. It was daily phone calls, huge amounts of hand holding, alcohol, cups of tea; it was really like therapy. It was months of it going on. "I feel as though I've written something not good—I'm really not sure." "Simon, I think it'll be great. Just keep it. I'll come around the middle of next week. I'm free to come over again." John Woolrich, a composer I'd just mentioned, was also giving him tips on the piece at the same time and he said he was getting daily phone calls too. It was a time when his music was evolving from something a little lighter to something much more serious. It was a difficult time like a sort of adolescence for him.

Other composers, like John Tavener, has written now these pieces "Kaleidoscopes," the big piece, "Songs of the Sky," and the first piece he wrote for me was for oboe, countertenor, eight violins, eight violas, and I recorded it with viols, a consort of viols. It's called "The Hidden Face" and it's exquisitely beautiful. Just came through the letterbox. It's actually very, very, very hard because it uses Byzantine inflections from Byzantine religious chant which is microtonal and he has very specific ways of wanting it but not of notating it, and I knew what he wanted because I'd heard him demonstrating it before. And then there's this repeating phrase which goes C, top C, top E, top F, top A, G, [sings] and it repeats many, many times through the piece. At the same time, the countertenor is singing [sings the same line] right in the middle of the register where a good countertenor can sing really, really quietly so that you're left going [sings very loudly] at the top of the oboe somewhere and what's more, a lot of it's in rhythmic unison and he writes for the oboe and countertenor to be at opposite sides of the stage. Luckily I did it with Michael Chance, who is just amazing, and we had this understanding together of how we were to do it. But there are lots of microtonal inflections; there were no instructions other than it should sound like Byzantine inflections. No concept that that was a hard thing to have written repeatedly over and over again through a piece for the oboe. What I did was I just sat down with my instrument in my music room and I closed my eyes and I just tried to get that register to be part of my resonance and to find these quarter tone and microtonal inflections that were just natural, sounded very Eastern because he was very strongly Greek Orthodox at this time. In the two more recent pieces he's written, he's left Orthodox and he's left Christianity and moved further East to a sort of Humano-Christo-Buddha-Hindu kind of area. And it's very much more inclusive actually in that respect. This particular thing, I needed to find where this sits. And I found it in the end. I found a place where it sat in my instrument and in that reed on that day. The piece is good and I think of all the recordings I've made, I'm probably proudest of that one. It was partly because the producer really helped us get something special. When you're recording, I find the dynamics between the performer/recording artist and the producer to be very, very, very special and important and I hate producers that say too much. I like producers that wait for the right moment to say one thing that—like a great teacher—just turns it from a stressy moment into something that you can just release. Great producers understand when the moment is right for a great take and they understand the energy and the nature of recording. They also understand that when you're recording it's an act of enormous imagination because there's so many boring recordings out there, it's just unreal. I buy a lot of music and I'm so often disappointed. Great recordings are where you've created the audience in your head, therefore there's an act of creativity in that respect and it's therefore much more tiring than just playing to an audience.

4

Pedro Díaz

Pedro Díaz joined the Metropolitan Opera in 2005 as solo English Horn. He has lectured at the Juilliard School, Manhattan School of Music, Eastman School of Music, Hartt Music School, and Duquesne University. His international appearances include master classes in Panama, Mexico, Canada, Puerto Rico, Leipzig, Berlin, and Italy. A native of Puerto Rico, he received his early musical training in the Escuela Libre de Musica, an esteemed public school for the performing arts. He has performed as a guest artist with the Chicago Symphony and New York Philharmonic, among others. This interview took place in December 2009 with Michele Fiala at Díaz's apartment on the Upper West Side of Manhattan.

Early Life and Career

My parents loved the arts. My brother and I grew up in Spain because when we were very young in Puerto Rico, my father was a writer and an author and he moved to Spain to write a novel. We used to go to concerts a lot. At that time there were no other forms of entertainment, really, just going to concerts and going to the circus. I developed a keen appreciation for the orchestra concerts, and it stayed in the back of my mind. My brother was entering the conservatory in Madrid and he wanted to play the piano, but they made him take a year or two of solfège before he got to play the piano. So he got discouraged and so did I. On our return to Puerto Rico, my brother started in a school for the performing arts, and he chose the horn. Two years later, I came into the school and I just liked the oboe. I heard it in some commercials and TV, and also in the orchestra, and I always liked the sound. And, against my brother's advice and everybody else's advice, I picked the oboe. They said that it was hard and the keys break, and the reed is all messed up, and I just thought, well, I want to play the oboe. I wasn't one of those kids

Great Oboists on Music and Musicianship. Michele L. Fiala and Martin Schuring, Oxford University Press (2021).
© Oxford University Press. DCI: 10.1093/oso/9780190915094.001.0001.

who was forced to play the oboe because there was nobody else that wanted to play. I actually wanted to play the oboe.

I entered the school. I didn't have an instrument. The school had some instruments in a very bad state of disarray and some notes wouldn't come out, but I could play most of the notes and I just played in the orchestra in school, and the band, and one thing led to another. Then there was a youth orchestra and they got a bunch of new instruments that the state bought for the orchestra—nice plastic Bundy oboes—[that] could play all the notes. It was great! So whenever I hear students complain about their oboe, I always remind them of that. If you really want to play, it will show somehow.

I had a teacher at the school for the performing arts, but he was mainly a saxophone player and he taught all of the instruments. He was a little bit limited in what he knew about the oboe, but he actually made a few reeds for me. I also studied with the second oboe player in the Puerto Rico Symphony for one semester, and that was very helpful. My grandfather had some recordings of Harry Shulman and of Helmut Winschermann, and oboists like that, and I listened to those recordings, those LPs, over and over. I wanted so badly to sound like that. In a way, you could say I was a little bit self-taught in the beginning because I just tried to imitate what I heard.

My early career went along swimmingly, but very slowly. There were some triumphs, but mostly I think of it as a big struggle. I didn't get my job in the Met until I was almost forty years old. So, it took a while, although I'm very grateful. I think it was just a succession of things—one thing led to another. From being in high school, getting a scholarship, to studying in Pittsburgh thanks to the American Wind Symphony, studying with the co-principal oboe in the Pittsburgh Symphony, Jim Gorton. And, I played in the youth orchestra in Pittsburgh. I studied with John Mack, also, a little bit. And then, on his advice, I auditioned for Juilliard. After I graduated from school I played in South Africa. But there were always a few years in between where I wasn't doing a lot, just practicing like mad. Like everyone else, I was going to auditions, sometimes without having a real sense of what an audition was, just showing up. I thought it was important to show up.

I thought about changing careers, but there was nothing I could ever think of doing other than playing the oboe. I thought about watch-making, but then I realized I was leaving one dying career for another, so I would just say if you really feel like there's nothing else you can do in life, then hang in there—be creative and be prepared to work at Starbucks or something in the meantime. Work dignifies, no matter what work you do. So just hang in there and do whatever it is that you need to do. You're not going to forget how to play the oboe if you have to work somewhere for a year or two. A lot of people go in and out of music at different stages in their lives. What matters is the intention and the focus.

On Auditions

I have had some "sort of" successes in the past but not nearly as spectac- ular as when you're talking about the Met. Mostly it was failures. I think it had to do with my sense of preparation. It's always been hard for me to pre- pare for it, and I always took auditions thinking, "Oh well, if I don't do well on this one, I guess I'll do okay on the next one." I guess it was some sort of procrastination.

The audition for the Met was my last audition. I told myself, you know, if I don't get a job, this is it. This is going to be it; I'm going to quit. So I think the sense of urgency made me really prepare. But also I was a little bit benefited by the fact that I've already played the Met before, in audition. I was a sem- ifinalist for the second oboe position when Eugene [Izotov] got the job. So I knew what it was going to feel like; I knew what the acoustical requirements were. And I knew the repertoire because I also auditioned when Robert Walters had the job at the Met. So I prepared at least four to five months in advance, and I prepared really well. That was probably my best-prepared audition.

On Becoming an English Horn Player

Interestingly enough, before I got my job at the Met, I was playing principal in the orchestra in Mexico, in Guadalajara, and usually I dismiss it and I say, "Oh no, I'm not an English horn player." But the truth is that I did put in my time. I took some lessons with Tom Stacy; I studied with Lou Rosenblatt; I studied with Felix Kraus—the late Felix Kraus with the Cleveland Orchestra—and also with Harold Smoliar, and I got a lot out of those lessons with them. My first job, in South Africa, was an English horn job. So, I did have the prep- aration to go into an English horn audition knowing what to expect and knowing how to sound like an English horn.

When I was in school, Tom Stacy was teaching English horn, and he actually had English horn majors, something that's very scarce today. I would be a smart aleck and I would go to them and I would say, "What are you doing? You're practicing the same five English horn excerpts for four years. You're not playing any oboe. What are you doing? You're wasting your time. I'm going to come up to an audition; I'm going to borrow an English horn, and I'm going to beat you." And people say, "Yeah, you said it and you did it." But the truth is, I didn't do it. I actually did take English horn lessons. Maybe in the old days, if the trombone player couldn't play high notes anymore, he was moved to the bass trombone section—it was almost like a punishment. Or, if you weren't good enough or if you're not doing a good job, they would move you to the English horn. Maybe it was true sixty years ago, but today, you cannot show up to an English horn audition without knowing your stuff because there are people who are specialists, people who know exactly how to tune this note and that note on the English horn, and how to beat the resistance and the pitch issues. There are specialists.

I can give you a perfect rationalization between what I do when I play oboe and English horn. There is a big difference and you really have to be aware. The more aware you are that you're not playing the oboe when you play the English horn, the more you're going to sound like an English horn. The quality instinctively wants to play high when we grab the English horn after playing the oboe; it wants to go high. You have to be aware that the sound should be broad and relaxed, and it should go down instead of up. It's a much more relaxed way of playing, and everything is slower. I think I write on my website, "Think of oboe in slow motion." So, there are inherent differences, much like the difference between playing the violin and the cello. The strokes of the bow are longer, the vibrato is slower, there need to be more lows in the sound, so when you make your reeds, you have to take into account that you want to put more lows into the sound.

When you play the oboe, you're used to keeping the pitch high enough, because that is the biggest trouble when you play the oboe. It's not high enough; everything needs to be tight and focused, really tight. When you grab an English horn, instinctively, because the ear doesn't recognize the note that you're actually fingering, your body will want to go up, it will want to make the pitch go higher, because it feels like it's playing an oboe even though it's not playing the oboe. So you have to be completely aware that, "This is not an oboe, relax, let the note feel a little bit flat," because it's going to feel flat to your body. It's not the same vibrations. Ideally, you should know exactly what note you're playing every time you play the English horn, what concert pitch. That will be very helpful.

On Phrasing

First, I think about the most mundane thing like functionality—being able to play a phrase according to what the way the composer wrote it. If you just play the music the way the composer wrote it, the music will take care of it-self. But, after that, of course I do think about phrasing; I think about mood and feel. In fact, I try to prepare my music away from the English horn, the oboe. When I learn music, I look at the score, I look at the music, and I ac-tually solfège it in my ear. I try to hear it before I play it, because you get too busy playing the instrument to actually try to understand music at the same time. So I try to get the brain part first, and then I get the muscles going.

If I'm playing Bach, I try to think about the figured bass, the counterpoint. If it's a solo piece I just try to find out as much as I can about the piece. If I'm playing opera, which is what I mostly do, then I try to learn as much as I can about the story. I learn the opera completely when I really find out what's going on onstage.

When I'm teaching, I remind them that music is storytelling, and take phrases and break them down to the common denominator—break phrases down to smaller fragments and practice them that way, whether it's for tech-nical reasons, or they need to learn the phrase better, For instance, a solo like the solo in Mendelssohn's Scottish Symphony [sings], you can break it down so that the student understands much better, in a musical sense, the direction of the phrase. This will help them play the phrase better, fast. [Sings the pas-sage slower, with phrasing demarcations] Then, if you put it all together, it flows. I really believe in finding the note groupings.

On Breathing and Support

I almost always tell my students to blow a little more than they do. I don't have any particular special methods of blowing or air columns or this or that. I just go by whatever works for the student. If it sounds like it's a healthy tone, then I don't really go into the science that much. I don't have any partic-ular exercises, though there are certain methods that I like. I like the Prestini

Esercizi Giornalieri. It's a very rare book, and I bought as many as I could find on the Internet. I found there is a place where they still publish it in Italy but it's hard to find.

I encourage them to practice while making reeds. I think practicing and making reeds should go hand in hand, so the body gets used to a new reed and the reed gets used to the blowing—it should be immediate. You make a reed and after ten minutes you should play on it. And then you can fix it as you go, rather than spending two hours making reeds and then waiting forever to practice, killed by your knife. It gets too separated—you can get out of shape from not playing and then you don't know what to expect from the reed. The more you play a reed, the more you can be discriminating.

On Listening to Singers

I have so much respect for singers. They can do things that we cannot do. We have a lot of flexibility as oboists, but their role is so much bigger and awesome. They have to speak languages, they have to act, and they have to learn the music and there are no keys to press, and you can't change the reed if you don't like the sound of your instrument.

If you get to play in quite a few bel canto operas, a few Bellini operas and even some Verdi, you learn how to phrase differently and how to imitate what the singers do. For example, an aria like the English horn aria in *Otello*. A lot of this aria, you are exchanging with the singer, so you want to mimic the singer as much as you can. Or, we just recently did *The Damnation of Faust*, "D'amour l'ardente flamme," "Burning flame of love"—it's the name of one of the arias—there's imitation, there's counterpoint, question and answer, so I do learn, aspire to do what they do, but I know there is a limit to what we can do. We can never do what they do. They are special.

On Good Ensemble Playing

There are two laws that you really cannot violate. I always tell my students: pitch and rhythm. If you have really good pitch, you can fit in anywhere. And, even if you don't have the rhythm, that's something that can be worked on, that really can be fixed. So, pitch and rhythm. Tone? It's completely subjective. People worry so much about tone that they lose the pitch and the rhythm. I always stress to my students: functionality. Make sure your reed works. Then, you can worry if it sounds good nor not. Dealing with your ear: your ear should work. You should be able to blend with your colleagues; you should be able to get out of the way when you have to. And then you should be able to present yourself when asked, bring yourself forward.

On Teaching and Learning

The fact that you have to demonstrate so much makes it very challenging. It does help your playing. People are addicted to teaching because they feel they need to demonstrate to remember all those basic concepts that we were taught in school by our teachers. I believe that's a reason why we have these schools of playing. It's just students paying honor to their teachers and trying to remember what they teach. Because once your teacher has said something to you, once you graduate, you never forget that; it's amazing. You never forget what your teacher said.

Every year I feel less confident on the oboe because I spend so much time playing the English horn, and I'm teaching oboe at Juilliard, so it's very hard for me to keep both instruments—one of them always suffers. I have to voraciously try to practice as much as I can both instruments and make reeds and keep up with the job and with the teaching, because the students are getting so much better today that it's hard to keep up with them. They're playing pieces that I haven't played; I just tell them that, "Do as I say, not as I do." [Laughing] For you must be better than me! [Laughing] Students must be better than their teachers!

Students have this safety net of being in school where no matter what happens, how they play and this and that, they're not going to get fired or they're not going to die from it. So, it's a very challenging role in life, and I cherish it but at the same time many times I feel like giving it up, because I wonder if there might be better people out there who can teach than me. I always wish I had more time to learn my operas, because I've only been playing for five years, and at the Met there's always new operas to learn, so I make the time.

A Musical Memory

It is playing the St. Matthew Passion in Vermont in Marlboro with Blanche Moyse. In fact, she's still alive. I think she's one hundred and one years old. [Blanche Honegger Moyse, 1909–2011. She was the cousin of Arthur Honegger and daughter-in-law of Marcel Moyce.] At the time she was ninety-five years old or ninety-three years old. They had this New England Bach Festival, and I was playing with Steve Taylor, Allan Vogel, and Mark Hill. We were playing the St. Matthew Passion, and she was conducting by memory. Just the vision of this very old sweet lady conducting by memory in this beautiful barn St. Matthew Passion; everything was so, so sublime that more than half of the orchestra was weeping while we were playing. We just could not believe the experience of playing something like this with someone that knew the piece so well that she could conduct all the way through the piece from memory at the age of ninety-three or ninety-four. It was surreal. It was very, very, very angelical and sublime. Wonderful experience. I think that was the first time I ever felt what it feels like to play while crying. It's a very bizarre experience. Very special.

5

Diana Doherty

Diana Doherty joined the Sydney Symphony Orchestra as principal oboe in 1997, having held the same position with the Symphony Orchestra of Lucerne (1990–1997). She was born in Brisbane and completed her undergraduate studies at the Victorian College of the Arts. In 1985 she won the Other Instruments section of the ABC Instrumental and Vocal Competition and was named Most Outstanding Competitor Overall. In 1989 she completed her postgraduate diploma in Zurich, studying with Thomas Indermühle. Career highlights since then include first prize at the Prague Spring International Music Competition in 1991; being named joint winner of the 1995 Young Concert Artist auditions in New York and subsequent American recital tours; the premiere of Ross Edward's Oboe Concerto (Bird Spirit Dreaming) with the Sydney Symphony Orchestra and Lorin Maazel followed by performances with the New York, Royal Liverpool, and Hong Kong Philharmonic orchestras; and performing concertos written for her by composers such as Graeme Koehne and Allan Zavod. This interview was conducted in December 2017 by Michele Fiala.

Early Career

I grew up in a big noisy household as the last of nine kids. My parents were both doctors and avid music lovers. They played the piano; all of my older siblings played piano and something else at some stage, so you can imagine the noise levels! We didn't have a TV until I was nearly ten (I remember being transfixed by Nadia Comaneci at the Montreal Olympics, in color!), so I guess music was what we all did, if it wasn't homework or playing cricket in the back yard! I started on the violin and piano, and being the annoying youngest sibling, I used to sneak a turn at my older siblings' instruments if I could. I pretty much just wanted to do whatever they did. When an opportunity

Great Oboists on Music and Musicianship. Michele L. Fiala and Martin Schuring, Oxford University Press (2021).
© Oxford University Press. DOI: 10.1093/oso/9780190915094.001.0001.

came up to learn the oboe at school, it turns out we had one in a cupboard somewhere as one of my older brothers had played for a while, and I was allowed to have a go.

A big part of my musical childhood was the Queensland Youth Orchestra—an amazing institution which turned fifty last year. It had a range of ensembles, from junior string ensemble and wind band to three orchestras of different levels, so it provided a whole social network along with instruction and performance opportunities. Being part of that was a big reason why I ended up pursuing a career in music.

On Her International Career

Australia and Switzerland were similar in the sense that there are a number of different influences, and not really a national style. In Australia particularly, I feel like that is a real plus, as we don't feel bound to a tradition but can cherry-pick and combine the elements we like of various styles. I see that as a bit of an Australian mindset, to respect tradition but to put an Aussie spin on it. The biggest difference in style I see is when I teach in North America. There I rely a lot on the students to educate me too, as I'm hesitant to suggest an adjustment in case it disrupts their technical balance. It's fascinating, though!

Warming Up

My goal is to find a balance between effort and ease so that the act of producing a sound feels good, like something you want to keep doing! I go into a kind of meditation, really focus inwards, check that all the elements feel OK—posture, air, resonance, response. Practicing long notes without using your tongue to start notes is a very good place to start. It gives you the opportunity to really examine how you are using your air, how to have just the right balance of pressure and resonance to make the note "want" to sound on its own. Michelangelo apparently said that his angels were hidden in the marble and he had only to uncover them. Maybe we can think of our music like that too, as if it's already in the air and we encourage it to be heard. It's a nice concept to contemplate as you meditate on your long notes, at least.

On Reeds

The reed is a very important part of the balance. I like a reed that responds easily but can also take plenty of air without going wild. That can be a difficult balance to achieve. Often there are reeds that we can adapt to if necessary, but in doing so, some other element gets out of balance, so you know that something has to change: either change reeds or adjust the reed. What I look for is when you can forget the reed and just work on yourself—it doesn't have to be great, just good enough to do the job to a degree where you can make subtle adjustments in your own playing and focus on representing the music as well as possible. I often think that choosing a reed is like choosing a pair of shoes in a shop—they may look great, be affordable, even be quite comfortable, but could you run for the bus if you had to? We have to be quite pragmatic about the choice and leave our hearts out of it in a way. A friend once told me that a weed is just a plant in the wrong place. So maybe a bad reed is just one that you are trying to use in the wrong piece. Put it away and find a different reed better suited to the task at hand. It may well come in handy in a different piece, or when traveling in another climate.

Priorities are intonation, response, and stability. My orchestral position with the Sydney Symphony is my main focus so I have some very clear criteria for reeds to determine whether I can use them in orchestra or not. This is somewhat complicated by the fact that I make my reeds at home, in a small room, but have to imagine how they will behave when I'm onstage in a huge hall with dodgy air-conditioning! So I try to have a "shortlist" of reeds to choose from in context, and swap around in rehearsal.

Advice for Learning Technical Passages

Memorizing. If you can play a difficult passage with your eyes closed, then you know it's locked in. We know how it should sound; we don't need to see it, and you can start very slowly and with a small group of notes and build up from there. Listen to it in your head and work it out in your fingers. It's a whole different brain process. Endless repetition can be problematic in the sense that your brain registers everything, the mistakes and the corrections. If you are going to repeat something, it has to be perfect every time in order for the brain and the muscles to remember it well. Often, I find students don't think they can remember a passage, but they can if they have to, or at least, they can work it out. This boosts their belief in themselves. Even if you never intend to perform the piece from memory, there is something about the process of trying that files it away slightly differently in our brains.

Developing Articulation

I would say that this is a very personal thing, depending on what the student's issues are. I try to invent or adapt exercises for their specific needs. What I would say for everyone is that articulation is not just about the tongue. It's about the connection between air and tongue, having those two things work really well together. We all have such different physiology that there can be no right or wrong way to do it. Finding a balance that achieves what we want to hear and is economical in terms of energy expended is the goal.

Listening Suggestions

Not only oboists! Violinists, singers, pianists, cellists, whoever really inspires you. Oboe is a very limited instrument and we need to be careful of listening only to oboe, as it begins to shape our musicality by its limitedness. We have to dream beyond those limits in order to extend our own abilities.

Humorous Reminiscence

I was playing in an arrangement of "The Blue Danube" for chamber ensemble: string quartet, clarinet, and oboe. The clarinettist and I were reading off the same sheet and he accidentally started by playing the oboe part, which was not transposed. You can imagine how strange it sounded. I totally got the giggles, and it got worse because he continued to play while laughing, which sounded even funnier. Such a talent! You can imagine that I couldn't get a sound out—every time I tried to play I couldn't even form an embouchure. Eventually the piece finished and I had laughed through the whole thing, tears streaming down my face, and I hadn't actually played one note.

6

Elaine Douvas

Elaine Douvas has served as principal oboe of the Metropolitan Opera since 1977 and oboe instructor at the Juilliard School since 1982. She has been an artist/faculty member of the Aspen Music Festival and School since 1997 and teaches at Mannes College of Music and the Bard College Conservatory of Music. Douvas has performed the Strauss Oboe Concerto with the Met Orchestra in Carnegie Hall, James Levine conducting, and Dutilleux's "Les Citations" with the Met Chamber Ensemble. She has participated in hundreds of live broadcasts, DVDs, and studio recordings. Originally from Port Huron, Michigan, Douvas trained at the Cleveland Institute of Music with John Mack and at the Interlochen Arts Academy. Her previous positions include four years as principal oboe of the Atlanta Symphony under Robert Shaw, and several summer seasons as guest principal oboe in the New York Philharmonic, the Grand Teton, Marlboro, Angel Fire, and Bravo! Colorado festivals. For many years she has devoted her spare time to figure skating. This interview was conducted by Michele Fiala at the Juilliard School in May 2009 and was updated in April 2019.

Early Life and Career

It was hard to find classical music in the small town where I grew up. I first heard classical music at ballet class when I was in first grade. It captured my imagination totally. I remember going home and looking through my parents' record collection, which had stacks of 78s of operas that people had given them as wedding presents. It wasn't anything they had listened to, but it looked intriguing to me.

The thing that's different in my background (from many of my students) is that I really loved the music first. A lot of the people took up an instrument when they reached the age to join the band. They found they had some

Great Oboists on Music and Musicianship. Michele L. Fiala and Martin Schuring, Oxford University Press (2021). © Oxford University Press. DOI: 10.1093/oso/9780190915094.001.0001.

success with it so they decided to keep going, but it was more the instrument and the attention that it brought than the actual music. I don't observe in most students the extreme amounts of zeal for the music that I felt. I ask my students to study three recorded examples of a symphonic work, look at the score, acquaint themselves with the context, and prepare as if they had to conduct a wind sectional. To me this is the most fun thing in the world. This isn't work; this is what a musician lives for.

After dance class, I wanted my parents to buy a piano. I was fascinated with the lives of the composers; I read composer biographies like crazy from the time I was in the third grade. One of my hobbies is composer films. I love them and I love the sport of researching how much of the plot is true. My parents let me join a mail-order record club, and I used the public library to check out records. I remember struggling to pick up a Detroit radio station to get more classical music.

There was a guy who lived next door to me who worked in the food service at Interlochen, the national music camp, as a summer job, and I heard about this place that was all music. I wanted to go there desperately. In my little town there were quite a few people who played the piano better than I, and I realized this was not going to be a career for me, so I tried the violin. As a fifth grader, I felt like I was already too late to start the violin. The kids who were good started when they were four. When everyone was joining the band in sixth grade, they made me start with the French horn because they only had one oboe. They weren't going to give it to somebody unless it was going to work out. I played French horn the whole summer, then they gave me the oboe I wanted. I chose it for the no-competition aspect, but I had immediate success with it. Everything just fell in my lap. In a couple of months, I was in the cadet band; in three months, I was in the varsity band. By seventh grade they let me play in the junior college wind ensemble where all of the music instructors and all of the band directors played. It was a stretch for me, but they gave me solos to play with the adult band.

I couldn't understand how you could have talent for one instrument and not another. I didn't understand that each instrument has a particular set of physical aptitudes that is very specific. I lucked out—I picked one that suited my physical aptitudes. So I made my way to Interlochen. I got to go there for two weeks of All-State in eighth grade. I spent three years of high school at the Interlochen Arts Academy boarding school and five summers there. Those three years of high school were just magical, and I got a huge head start. There were eight concert programs each summer and about fifteen programs in each winter season; by the time I got out of high school, I had played most of the standard orchestral works. When I got to college, the Cleveland Institute of Music, I had to switch off with other fine players, so I was really drawing on that high school experience. I got my first job with the Atlanta Symphony when I was twenty-one, and thanks to Interlochen, I could handle the position.

On the Metropolitan Opera and Auditions

I don't think I'd have my job at the Met if it weren't for blind auditions. The Atlanta Symphony was about one-third women. There was nothing unusual about being a woman in the Atlanta Symphony, but the Met at the time only had fourteen women. I expect most of them got in by blind auditions, so I feel lucky about that. The Met is still the only place that keeps the screen up entirely until the end. I believe in this so much.

When listening to auditions, I want to hear total comfort with the instrument—fluency—plus thinking and planning that results in creativity and musicality, and enough authority. You can hear everything you need to know by listening to a person play, and then a new player should have his/her two years of probation as a chance to grow into the job: to understand the conductor's style, to understand the personalities of the people sitting around them. That's what the probation is for. Anything that you would get from looking at the person ends up being political.

On Vocal Style

The sound of the singers rubs off on everyone on the orchestra, and the conductor, James Levine, asks for everything to be as vocal as possible. That to him means no pressure in the tone or in the articulation. Pressure can be a major factor in oboe playing, so you have to find a way that it will not be heard.

My teachers in high school used to say, "Play as singers sing." I had no idea what they were talking about. If I thought of an opera singer, I thought of a tendency to scream and a vibrato as wide as a mile. I was listening with the ears of an amateur; I heard the mannerisms without really understanding what made it great. What I learned about vocal style from playing in the Met is that chiefly we're meant to copy the smoothness (the legato), and that the slurs have shape in them: a slight scoop shape for the upward ones, an arch shape for the downward ones, but you should never let notes fall out or sound like straight-lined connections. The singers can sustain the line beautifully; they don't have any mechanical instrument in their hands to take away from it. And they make a variety of consonant sounds that we should seek to imitate—inflections of speech. Singers exemplify the idea that up is up, and down is down; they make something glorious of the singing top notes; the low register is full of mystery and depth.

The outer registers have a certain tension in them—the high notes are the home run of opera. Although an oboist can just put on the octave key, you still have to create the drama, the suspense, the danger, and the glory in attaining a high note, even though a high note is not that difficult to play on the oboe. And always the lack of pressure in the tone and articulation; it's a hard thing to create the illusion of no pressure on the oboe. You certainly cannot produce a good tone without making pressure.

On Tone Production

Support is not how much you blow. It's how you hold the air from the bottom and the top. It's compressed. I want to do it in a way that no one can hear as a listener, and I want to produce a tone that is layered and complex, not two-dimensional, also buoyant and floating. The difference between "air speed" and "air amount" is something a teacher needs to define. I always heard teachers talk about air speed and it was a nebulous term to me. I understand it now. Air amount is how much you blow. Air speed means you have to narrow the passage, and that creates resistance or backflow—it's as if a river is very wide, and then when the banks come in, the water travels faster. It may even get white water or backflow or turbulence as opposed to a still pool or a wide river that doesn't move. We're talking about funneling the air. That means either the reed is the funnel, the jaws are the funnel, or something else—something involving the back of the tongue. If it's the reed, you do hear pressure. If a person just blows directly at the reed and the reed is used as the point of resistance, it's going to be very difficult to dispel the sound of pressure, especially in the articulation. I feel the same way about the jaws. I would rather oppose my abdominal muscles against an internal place safely away from the reed, so there is no sound of pressure.

I floundered around for a long time to find some musical way of describing this focus that won't mix people up. My best description is borrowed from voice teachers: the beginning of a yawn. I ask people to muster up a yawn. "Is it open or closed?" It is decidedly both; the mouth is open, but there is a place that is almost totally closed, somewhere down the throat. This is the resistance, the back pressure, that opposes the abdominal muscles. Wind up and throat down. I think this is the way a singer supports. Oboists should not throw all their air at the reed; you drink it in, almost inhaling it, as a singer would.

I ask people to think about the shape inside their mouths; they have the ability to create a certain roundness of tone and spaciousness of tone by the space in the mouth. I tell them, "Imagine somebody put a large marble inside your mouth and you don't want to swallow it." That's a good position. But we also don't play in a fixed position—that's the other part of this. We're in flux all the time depending on the dynamic you're playing or whether you're tonguing or slurring. With any technical thing, it's extremely important to speak about the musical result desired rather than to tell somebody, "Put your mouth here; put your stomach here; put your throat here; now try to play." You never get a good result with that. Instead, say, "It sounds bottled up, too tight, or too dead, too dull, or too screamy, spread, or shouted," and ask them to find their own way to it first by ear. If it doesn't work you can make some technical suggestions. Later, you might want to make some technical suggestions so they know what to say to their students.

What I don't want to hear or feel is a waterfall of air driving my tongue at the reed, attacks that explode, articulations that sound thuddy, or that you can't stop a note without getting a tongue noise. These things are important to me: to be able to tongue with very little tongue noise, to be able to stop a note without any tongue noise at the end. The throat is definitely involved in cushioning attacks and ending notes.

Variety of Articulation

To develop a range of articulation, I say to the student, "If you sang that with syllables, would you put an 'm' on that note? Bum-baaahm; deedl-a-dum-bum-bum, deedl-a-dum-bum-bum [opening of the Mozart Quartet]" is totally different than "Dut-daaht, duddl-a-dut-dut-duh duddl-a-dut-dut-duh."

If you would say "m," you must play "m." If you take it apart, it's a bell-tone; it's got a sudden decay; it's a diminuendo. Then you get into the whole idea of how to make a diminuendo. The thing you often hear on the oboe is this very stiff wind and stiff support that sounds, "Dut-daaht, duddl-a-dut-dut," where you can hear a "t" syllable on the ends of the notes, and that isn't vocal at all. Explaining about the "m" syllable and a certain amount of imitation should be enough.

On Playing in an Opera Orchestra versus Symphony Orchestra

One of my colleagues said an opera player is to a symphony player as a distance runner is to a sprinter. Stamina is certainly a huge factor in playing with the opera. Physical stamina with the instrument and concentration stamina also. A person's reed style is dictated by the demands of the job. The main demand of my job is that I mustn't get tired or sore. [Laughing] So stamina is a big difference!

For any piece that has words, if you don't know what you're portraying, you could get the character completely wrong. You must know the words. Especially now that they've got subtitles, everyone in the audience knows what's going on. If you don't do the research to look into this matter, you could play something very incorrectly. That's different from a symphony; there isn't quite so much right and wrong about how you interpret wordless music.

The singers are the stars of the opera. We have our solo parts and our solo moments, but it's more of a teamwork situation. There isn't room for egos-run-wild in the opera pit and that's nice. We're all secondary to the singers, and that has to be okay or else a person would be unhappy in the opera pit. Because we are there for such long hours, and we have a wonderful cafeteria where we congregate for the intermissions, there's a wonderful *esprit de corps* in the Met. It's a very satisfying, bonding experience. There are no special deals in the orchestra—the concertmaster is there just as much, if not more, than the rest of us. That is a morale builder. You don't have to go around feeling that somebody's got a better deal. We're all in it together and I know that everybody else is showing up when they're tired and they have a cold and they've played all day. It helps you, when the going gets rough, to know that everybody else is in the same boat.

On Reeds

When I was first in the Met, I sometimes had to put paper over my teeth to get through the long operas because of the embouchure pressure and teeth marks. I haven't done that for decades. The reed simply cannot make me tired. The sides have to be extremely tight so the high notes can hold themselves up to pitch. The high notes on my reeds basically cannot be played flat with normal embouchure and any kind of a wind stream. They are absolutely held up by the tightness of the sides and the way I've configured the entrance into the tip. I've devised tests on the reed alone to tell me whether I've done this or not, and I try to be as objective as possible. In other words, I don't scrape the reed, put it in the oboe, and see if I can work to get my favorite sound out of it. Instead, I put the reed in the oboe and imagine it's the most perfect reed in the world, and I play it just the way I would play the most perfect reed in the world, then the reed will tell me where it's deficient. I try to be as objective as possible with these tests.

Reed Tests

To test the reed, first play an aspirated attack on the reed. I'm looking for cushion but not fight. I don't want the reed to blurt out where I have to pull it back or cover it up, but I also don't want to be working too hard. I'd like to have it make an attack that I can't miss. Then I would peep on it repeatedly in my normal playing position, both loud and soft, and I'm looking for a lack of tip noise. I don't want to hear extraneous tip noises. I don't want to feel or hear "tip" as a separate element of the reed. I really don't want to hear the reed at all. That's probably everybody's goal, to just be able to think about the music and play comfortably and not be very much aware of the reed. That's where these tests are hopefully going to lead me.

I peep on it in playing position and I'm looking to see if it has a "pitch floor." This is a pitch below which it simply cannot drop. That depends on your oboe. I wouldn't say that the pitch I'm looking for is the same for everybody, but on the setup I play, if I don't get a C peeping in playing position, my high notes are going to be flat. It should feel very awkward and kind of a strain for me to play B [peeping]. If that's the case, then it really is C, I'm being objective, and that's the right place for me. I need the pitch to be stable, but I want it to have a certain measure of flexibility. I will then go from playing position to a glissando off the end of the reed. I push the reed out of my mouth with my lips, and I want it to go a minor third, no more, no less. That's exactly how much flexibility I want it to have. Any more would be work for me to control it, to hold the pitch up, and less than that would be a struggle to get enough range, enough ability to adjust intonation to play with my neighbors. If I don't have enough flexibility to get a minor-third glissando, then I drop the sides of the tip down a little bit until I do. Sometimes people will look at my reeds and think I've carved this as a shape. No. Everything has a reason for it, and I drop the sides as much as I need to get that amount of flexibility and no more.

In terms of holding the high notes up, there needs to be concavity in the profile of the entrance to the tip. Actual concavity. Without that dip, that reverse curve, the high notes don't hold up well and the reed is inefficient. It's difficult to do that much separation and not get tip noise. I usually have to jimmy it around quite a bit to get it just right, to get enough of that dip at the base of the tip, which does so many good things. It not only holds up my notes, it gives so much action and efficiency to the reed that you can get a lot of tone for very little effort. It also permanently deepens the tone and improves the articulation, especially in the low register. Sometimes people think that articulation only comes from the top of the reed but it comes from the bottom of the tip also. Any place on the reed that can do all of those things is a very important spot; we call it "the Magic Spot." But to do it in a way that doesn't give you tip noise is a challenge.

I crow the reed, but the crow is of much less importance to me than the peep in playing position and the amount of glissando. The side effect of having the peep being a C is that the crow is usually a C♯ for me. It depends what oboe you're playing, and I'm playing on a Lorée Royal at the time of the interview in 2009; now playing on a Howarth XL in 2019. The overall length of the reed needs to give you your low-note pitch. We don't want the low notes to be flat.

Have you ever done the experiment out of the Mr. Wizard Science Book where you make a reed out of a soda straw—where you squash it down and clip the sides? And then you cut it and cut it with scissors shorter and shorter, and the shorter the length of that straw the higher the pitch. I'm using a 46 mm tube, and it's going to crow at a higher pitch than a longer reed. That's where it produces the right low note pitch for me. The rest, I manipulate with the scrape, but the overall length gives you the low note pitch.

I test the tip first, which means the high notes first. Then I test the amount of glissando. That would change the length of the tip on the sides as opposed to the length in the middle. The high notes are held up by having something to blow against that's about a millimeter from the end of the reed. It's a working theory, but I think the glissando may be the difference between the length of the tip in the middle versus the length of the tip on the sides. That's the flexibility. But there's nothing more important than the sides being tight because if they aren't tight, the reed is flat from the outset and anything you scrape out of it only makes it flatter. If you can't create sharpness in the reed, then you aren't allowed to scrape, because scraping it makes it flatter.

After the tip and high notes, I play the thumb octave notes, tonguing repeatedly to look for pitch and "outline" (some cohesion that holds the tone together). I scrape the back until the thumb octaves play in tune. I scrape long narrow channels in the back, primarily to reduce the bulk, taking care not to interrupt the spine in the back because that would ruin the pitch stability. I don't scrape the back just to make it "dark." I play A-G-A-G, to see if G is long enough and deep enough. I scrape the back to extend the low register and tune the thumb octave notes. I think of the plateau (aka the heart) as an even reduction of the gouge; no spine and channels there. I leave as much wood as I can in the plateau and approach it with a short transition from the tip. I test the plateau sturdiness by gently closing the reed on the plaque, making sure the plateau never looks "rubbery" in the middle and the four sides close symmetrically.

It's an important part of my teaching job to help people be comfortable on their instrument so that they don't have to think about it. If you're not comfortable on your instrument, how do you think about the music? How do you play in a way that's enjoyable for a listener? We've all been told, "Oh, forget about the reed," but you can't forget the reed if it's malfunctioning on you all the time. It's an extremely important part of my job, helping people figure out their equipment. You can study music with anybody—with a chamber music coach, with a violinist, with a conductor, with your piano accompanist—but if your oboe teacher can't help you be comfortable on your reeds and understand how to make your oboe function the way it's supposed to (with covering and sealing and tuning), who else is going to help you with this? On the highest level, you're trying to teach every student in a way that's unique to the individual. I don't say, "Make your reeds like this because that's the way I make them." I listen and I say, "That sounds sharp," or "It sounds awkward," or "It sounds spread or tippy or grainy," and figure out how to help them.

On Vibrato

Vibrato is different on a woodwind from a string instrument or a voice. I enjoy listening to all the singers at the Met, but it would be a huge mistake to literally imitate a singer's vibrato. One time I was asked to coach the Schumann "Romances" at a flute convention, and it was a pretty interesting experience for me to hear those pieces rendered on the flute. I was thinking, "Why does this sound so strange to me?" The reason was the player was using constant vibrato on every note. I don't think I'd ever really noticed that we as oboists should not vibrate every eighth note. I used to hear conductors telling the violinists, "Vibrate the running passages." If we did that on the oboe, it would sound unbearably flowery. It shouldn't be constant.

A good vibrato should confirm the pitch and not confuse it. I like tuning As to be given with some vibrato because that is the tone that we play with, and I think a good vibrato is like insisting on a pitch. It's reiterating the pitch center again and again. It is easier to hear the pitch on a note with good vibrato than on a straight tone, which can sound denatured and ambiguous.

The vibrato should not ever be bigger than the tone. The vibrato should stay within the tone outline and it should match the volume of the note. When the tone is small, the vibrato should be shimmery, more like moonlight on a lake, and when the tone is loud it becomes more like separate, dramatic throbs. The amplitude has to vary, for sure. Flexibility in the speed is nice too, but the amplitude really has to change with the volume of the note.

Some students have a very fast, quivery vibrato, and when questioned about it, they say they have been told not to move any body part except the throat. When they are given permission to help out, to amplify, with other body parts, such as abdominal muscles and even the mouth, the vibrato becomes more generous and singing. The vibrato motion is similar to coughing; when you cough, you feel it in the entire breathing column, from abdomen to mouth.

I won't say that vibrato is just a pitch change or just an intensity change. You don't want to hear a vibrato that goes above the pitch. I think there is a pitch change, but that wouldn't be the first thing I think of doing in a vibrato. The quality that makes it reiterate the pitch is that is goes slightly below and it returns to that same spot over and over.

One thing that will prevent vibrato from happening is if the throat is too tight. There are many students who have been told that the throat must be incredibly open. If it's forced open stiffly, it can't move and it cannot make the throat vibrato. If the throat is being pressed into service to hike up the pitch on a flat reed, also it won't give you the flexibility to do a vibrato. There are some things that can be too tight, but I don't think you can play with everything loose. You would never get the air compression to vibrate the reed. It should sound as though the player sings the note inside of himself and that you're not really aware of blowing.

Another thing besides focusing on the shape of the mouth that seems to get good results is to tell people to blow toward the bridge of their nose. It sounds like voodoo, but from years of experience, it seems to strike a chord with people. Instead of blowing straight through the reed, straight down the oboe and out the bell, blowing at the bridge of the nose (which is essentially blowing against yourself) gets rid of pressure in the sound.

Figure Skating and Music

The most important positive effect on oboe playing is learning to present myself: the posture, the confidence, the speed, the grace, the control. When playing the oboe, I find it difficult to spare attention for how it looks to the audience. I hope I am building some applicable habits from my years of skating.

There are lots of connections between music and athletics, especially as a teacher. The effort to learn something new gives me a lot of insight into what it's like for somebody to learn something new on the oboe. Sometimes I wonder, "Well, why can't they just get that?" I'm sure my skating teacher wonders the same thing. But you realize you have to break things down into doable bits that will eventually come together into something important. I've learned that from skating. You don't just go out there and do a lutz. It takes a lot of smaller components, unless you want to fall a hundred times, and at my age, you don't want to fall once.

I've skated for a long time. We used to do school figures—fancy figure eights. The first push-off is exactly like making an attack. Things have to be in position, and then it has to make the impression of glide and travel. Even the symmetry of tracing a figure eight is like doing a long tone. It has to be the right size; it has to be the same on the way up as it is on the way down. Then there's the whole issue of balance.

Skating, like ballet dancing, should look absolutely effortless. It should look light and graceful and relaxed, but it's not done by relaxing. Neither is the oboe going to sound relaxed by relaxing. It should look and sound absolutely relaxed, but it is not done by relaxing. I'm fond of saying it's about as relaxed as a ballet dancer. It's controlled by absolutely superb control of opposing muscle groups. That is the case with skating. Most of the time you're achieving balance by having your shoulders go one direction and your hips another. And the more you're able to twist those in opposite directions, that's your balance. It's locked into place and you won't fall. There are a million analogies for that on the oboe. With the reed, with the support—opposition is what gives you balance—upper lip versus lower lip, the way the reed is overlapped, the bottom and the top of the support. In other words, the abdominal muscles versus the focus. The way in which you would play loud and soft, it's all opposition of some type. I love focusing on that while I'm skating. It's completely essential. If you're spaghetti-like and you don't oppose these things, you will fall; that's all there is to it.

On Teaching

I believe in teaching from etudes. I want to do my part to pass on that tradition which was so extremely important to my teacher and my teacher's teacher and I'm sure his teachers going back to the composition of the Barret method or the Ferling oboe method. I'd be sorry if that tradition died away. I like the fact that you can make some universalities in an etude book that will carry over from piece to piece. Learning something new, you need to break it down into small bits. You don't want to be dissecting a masterpiece of music, breaking it down into little bits like that. That should be taken care of way before. I don't want to work on slur-two tongue-two in a Mozart concerto. I'd like to work on that in an etude book, something that isn't really meant to be performed. If it ends up being painstaking and tedious and difficult, the student will not go away with a complex about a piece.

I further think people should study an entire piece of music and throw away their excerpt books. People come in with an excerpt and play it for me and I say, "What's your tempo? Have you ever heard this piece before?" They say, "Oh yes, in a master class." It's obvious when somebody is not acquainted with the context. It's important to study from the score with the idea that you're going to do it so thoroughly that nobody's going to be able to tell if you've played it in an orchestra or not, because you've created for yourself the same in-depth experience as someone who's playing it for five rehearsals and three performances a week. So, ditch the excerpt books. They could be thought of as a travel copy, a travel condensation, but that's certainly not the way to learn a piece.

I desperately want to share everything that I've learned to save other people time. That's one of the best things a teacher can do, to save people time so that they can get there faster and go beyond. We expect the next generation to go beyond.

7

John Ferrillo

John Ferrillo joined the Boston Symphony Orchestra as principal oboe in 2001. From 1986 to 2001 he was principal oboe of the Metropolitan Opera Orchestra. Prior to his appointment at the Metropolitan Opera, Ferrillo was second oboe of the San Francisco Symphony, and was a faculty member at Illinois State University (1979–1981) and West Virginia University (1981–1985). He is a graduate of the Curtis Institute of Music, where he studied with John de Lancie and received his diploma (1978) and artist's certificate (1979). The original interview took place at Boston's Symphony Hall with Michele Fiala in April 2009 and was updated in October 2018.

Early Career

My mother, Estalene, was a musician—an incredibly natural talent, too. Although she had a beautiful touch and sound on the piano, she probably only had half a dozen lessons. The Dye family was a classic Depression-era Illinois farm family—money was limited and work was hard. The family had many gifts, including music; my uncle played the violin, and both my mother and her younger brother played the guitar and sang. My mother has what is still one of the best ears I've witnessed in a musician—she could play anything she heard—if you sat on a piano she'd name every note. She was the first member of a very extended family who attended college, I believe, and was in the first graduating class of Roosevelt University. She became an English teacher and choral director, and, after a few years of teaching went back to Chicago, to Northwestern, and got her master's degree. In these years she developed one musical passion—Brahms—and one curious fixation— the oboe. In playing four-part theory exercises in class, she heard one of her classmates play the oboe, and there began a notion not just that, one day, a child of hers would have the best musical training possible, but that he or she

Great Oboists on Music and Musicianship. Michele L. Fiala and Martin Schuring, Oxford University Press (2021).
© Oxford University Press. DOI: 10.1093/oso/9780190915094.001.0001.

would play the oboe. She has regaled many a student of mine with the story of pointing out, "there's the oboe, Johnny—wouldn't you like to play that?" Well, I can't say it was an imposition; I took to it pretty naturally.

We were an Air Force family after my father was called to active duty in the Air Force in Germany, and I have crystal clear memories as an eight- and nine-year-old of my mother, teaching music appreciation and choral music again, playing drop the needle on pieces like the Brahms Second Piano Concerto. That there's a lot of talk about the importance of education, but I needed no persuasion—I knew it was something I wanted to do. As well, she had superb taste. Our shelves were stocked with Ernest Ansermet recordings of Stravinsky, Ravel, and Debussy with the Orchestre de la Suisse Romande, and I devoured these as a youngster. Of course, there was always Brahms and Beethoven—in particular, a recording of the Beethoven Violin Concerto with [David] Oistrakh is etched in my memory.

On the other side of the family, my father and grandfather were artists— my grandfather, born in Naples, was trained there as a sculptor at the turn of the century, and my father, also gifted, was a cabinetmaker when I was little. They had an interior decorating business with a studio near the United Nations. I have very clear memories of them working on Italianate projects with elaborately decorated mirrors and late 19th-century-style furniture. Although my father's life took a radical turn when he was called up to active duty and subsequent re-education as an engineer, he was, all of his life, brilliant with his hands. I remember John Sr. and my grandpa Ferrillo looking on, knowingly, when they saw me with my first reed tools. There was a funny encounter between him and my first serious oboe teacher, Richard Summers, in which he offered, "I'm pretty good with my hands—can I help make those reeds for him?" Dick just laughed. I had neither my mom's perfect pitch, nor my father's mechanical genius, but clearly I had essential genes gifted to me from both parents that were critical for my career on the oboe.

I am, basically, a Bostonian. My father was transferred to Hanscom AFB, in Bedford, just outside of Boston, and I received the rest of my elementary, middle school, and high school education there. Most importantly, I was a member of the Greater Boston Youth Symphony, and still am surrounded by many friends from that great training orchestra. In fact, I just played Sibelius Second Symphony, and realized that a number of the folks around me learned it at the same time in the same place—senior year in the youth symphony.

My very first oboe teacher was a man named Rod Ferland—he was a terrific saxophone player and doubler. I still bump into Mr. Ferland occasionally.

He subs often with the Pops on saxophone so he's always bragging to his section mates that he launched my career. Richard Summers—who I mentioned previously—studied with Fernand Gillet (who was my predecessor's predecessor's predecessor and who taught until he was about ninety at NEC). Gillet was also the nephew of Tabuteau's teacher, Georges Gillet. Dick was a very accomplished player, and did a huge amount of the freelance playing around Boston—the Ballet, the Opera and, of course, much Pops with Arthur Fiedler, both on English horn and the oboe. Despite the connection with French tradition, he was of a rather different tradition than Curtis, so there was definitely culture shock going there. Although my classmates had all had previous exposure, I was constantly hearing from John de Lancie: "You never heard of that?" "You never did this?" I never heard, for instance, about getting a reed to crow a C. It just sounded like the craziest thing.

I was late starting the oboe. I wanted to start on the oboe, of course, but years ago, youngsters were started on the flute or clarinet, for lack of teachers with reed training. I chose the flute, and my inspirational first teacher was Gwen Powell, later to become the president of the National Flute Association. She was charismatic (and beautiful—I was just starting to notice those things!). Gwen was married to an Air Force engineer, so naturally they were transferred before too long. As she was explaining this to my mother, my mother asked, "are you headed straight to Los Alamos, or are you stopping off at home?" "Stopping off to see family." "Where's family?" "Ottumwa, Iowa." "I've got family there!" In fact, their grandparents were siblings—a stunning coincidence.

After studying the oboe for four years, it was time for college. When I think now of the rigors that high school kids are prepared for today . . . some kids may have been prepared for Curtis (or THE Curtis, as they said), but I just didn't have a clue. I knew that Curtis was a very famous place that was tuition-free. My dad had really wanted me to be an engineer—I was a very good student—but I wanted to be an oboe *player*. Not a music educator, as Mr. Summers sensibly suggested. I wanted to be an oboe player. I knew that but I didn't know anything else about it.

I had bombed other conservatory auditions—I remember, in particular, bombing my Juilliard audition, in a particularly deer-in-the-headlights moment. It was there, by the way, that I met my future classmate, Marty Schuring, who, I must say, had it all going in a way that was both impressive and intimidating. He was not only warming up on the oboe but playing things like Bach's Chromatic Fantasy on the piano. I turned to my teacher the next week—he'd had me do the Mozart concerto—and I said, "I don't think I'm ready to do the Mozart concerto, but I've always loved the Marcello." And he said, "Well, that's sort of an elementary piece, but if you feel strongly about it, why don't you play that?" I did play that at Curtis, and it was a fateful day.

The first notable event was that our car broke not far from the Verrazzano-Narrows Bridge down on Long Island. I was three or four hours late for the audition, and I walked in and this big, tall gentleman seemed very patient about me being late. He wasn't always patient about everything that took place over the next five years, [Laughter] but it was a very genteel experience, and it was an extended audition. They took several oboists that year; he took three people. I'm quite convinced I was last of that group because I was much less accomplished. My peers, Bob Stephenson and Marty [Schuring], were just so much more accomplished at that point, you can't imagine. Mr. de Lancie decided to take a risk on a talented but ignorant outsider. Not that I wasn't probably already an expressive player and probably had the makings, the basics, of a good sound, but I was a project for de Lancie. And I think maybe, occasionally, he had questions about whether it was going to succeed. Curtis was an incredible eye-opener, but that incredibly thorough training, combined that with my real passion for the core Germanic repertoire and healthy dollop of persistence, and . . . I guess I got there.

He was a titan for me, John de Lancie. As cool as a cucumber, and more able to do exactly what he wanted and needed to do at any moment than anybody I've known. By the way, I have the greatest reverence for John Mack, as well, who I studied with as a young adult in my twenties. But when I was a kid at Curtis, there was John de Lancie. He was, at times, quite the boot camp drill instructor. He wanted to toughen us kids up (in his version of Tabuteau's "I want them to fear me more than they would fear any conductor"), and it was often a painful process. He had, however, an incredibly clear idea of what his priorities were musically and mechanically on the oboe. The mechanics were always in service of his musical vision, which was, of course, sort of a time capsule for the Paris Conservatory at the turn of the century, inherited through Tabuteau. Every week you'd go in and he'd be asking for things that were utterly logical: being able to start a note in a certain way, being able to lay out the architecture of something very clearly. You could never argue with his logic. You certainly couldn't argue with the fact that he practiced what he preached. Every time you heard him, it was this vivid display of what he was talking about, and that had as much force as any teaching.

Towards the end of Curtis, another great impetus for my career came when the second oboist of the [Philadelphia] Orchestra, Charlie Morris, was out on sick leave my fourth year. So, from the end of my senior year, my fourth year, for a couple years there were a lot of subbing opportunities in THE Orchestra. I actually played with de Lancie in his last weeks with the Philly orchestra. That was huge for me. It's one thing to go sit and hear a great player every week. That was nothing like sitting next to John de Lancie onstage.

I'm always the first person onstage in the [Boston] Symphony; he was always the first man on the stage in the Academy [of Music]. I remember having a dispute when I first got to Boston; they used to have lectures up until thirty minutes before [the concert] and I fought this (diplomatically) to make sure that I could get out there forty-five minutes before. But I remember, if you got there an hour before a Philly concert, he was out there, making the reeds for that evening's concert.

When I began studying, in a certain sense I was a silly kid—certainly naive. I don't think I was ever an arrogant kid. I had a very healthy respect for my inadequacies [Laughter] and that was reinforced by my teacher! I had been taught in a very academic way to question, "Is it possible to think of it this way rather than that way?" This "on the one hand and on the other hand . . ." was NOT the Curtis way. John de Lancie wasn't that way. He tended to think in elegant, but straight lines: "You want to get to there? You want to get from point A to point B? Draw a straight line and get there. Know what your job is and do it. And don't dilly-dally." Also, you have to be able to do your job—an explanation is no good for the conductor. Work ethic, work ethic. I never, ever, met anybody that worked harder than he did and knew exactly what he needed to do to do the job perfectly, every day. I wrote in an obituary for John de Lancie in the IDRS [International Double Reed Society] that he was a little like Babe Ruth pointing at the wall, that famous story. He was in a slump and he was getting razzed, and he got up to the plate and Babe Ruth just pointed at the outfield wall and hit a home run.

De Lancie was like that. He didn't do it with any bravado; he just said, "That's what I'm going to do. I'm going to do that." And he did it. There was force of will there that was just astounding. He was a fundamentally humble person. He used to say, "I studied with a guy [Tabuteau] who was a mechanical genius. He'd come back to the second rehearsal of a double [service] day and he'd have a new gouge that he did in the hour in between, and it was even better than the one before!" He said, "I wasn't like that. I was mechanically inept; I had to figure all of this out." Maybe you're a natural, maybe you're not a natural at something. What are you going to do? The force of will is one of the most underestimated qualities in a successful player.

He was like this to his dying day. I went to visit Mr. de Lancie towards the end, and he was in bed, talking about this and that, utterly calm, cool, collected. Speaking on interesting historical facts of our tradition. The same man I had always known. Clear-eyed and respectful of the art and profession of music to the end.

I'll never forget the first lesson, going in there and seeing this sort of cool gaze; it was fascinating. "Where's the Book?" he asked. The Barret book, of course. What else? He proceeded to open it up to the very first, elementary articulation and melodic exercises. I knew that music was never going to be the same for me.

I was talking recently to Marilyn Zupnik, a great oboist whose career was largely in Minnesota, who went to Curtis four or five years before I did. She is, interestingly, the daughter of the man who was associate principal oboe with George Szell for some 30 years. Marilyn and I started telling stories about first lessons, last lessons, and everything in between at Curtis. In common were two things: that tremendous force of will and the very, very lucid, simple explanations of what we were going to be doing. And then just hammering that, week in and week out, so that it was forever fixed there.

Auditions

I'm speaking not just to an oboist, but any audition-taker. The first thing will sound very funny: take the audition. We talk ourselves out of too many auditions. I watch students with frustration when they do this. I had so many good reasons. I'd say this is fixed for this person or that person. Sometimes that's true, but just as often as not it isn't true, and you're just looking for excuses. I certainly was.

Realize that at a certain point in your life, you must take *every single audition*. There's a passage in Philippians where he talks—there's a lot of imagery in the Bible about running the good race—and it's "Not looking backward, but looking forward to the prize." Of course, he's talking about the ultimate prize. But I think there's an important, practical, life lesson in there. It's not that you shouldn't be aware of the mistakes that you made in the last audition. You have to say, "This went right; this went wrong." Beating yourself up and saying, "I'm awful. I suck. I'll never get this right": it's an indulgence.

On the other extreme, there are those that, in lessons or in auditions are just extraordinarily pleased with themselves, and I always look at them with total amazement. After an audition what you've simply got to say is, "That went well. I'm happy about that. That didn't go well. Why didn't it go well? Next time, what am I going to do?" That ability to piece yourself back together and make every single one of these a learning experience is, by the way, something I wasn't good at. Obviously I wasn't great at it, because I had to take twenty-two of them before I got my first job!

Know yourself under stress. What sort of things are going to trouble you? What do we become when we're nervous? One thing I learned was, when I get nervous, my endurance goes. My sister was a singer and she found it to be exactly the same way.

Fingers can go, but that goes even more, the ability just to keep that embouchure together.

Know what kind of reeds you need. I knew that if I had nothing else, I needed something that held itself together with no effort in the upper register. When you played Brahms Violin Concerto or whatever, it just held itself together; you didn't have to think about it. That's something that was part of Curtis training and training with John Mack: you don't hold the reed together, it holds itself together. And what weight of reed do you need to play convincingly for twenty minutes?

In terms of preparation, imagining context is everything. Auditions have no context. One of the things we try to teach kids now is how to do that. That's one of the reasons for that Presser book. All the Jeanne Baxstresser books—there's a whole series—[the main feature] is their piano accompaniments. Martha Rearick, may she rest in peace, made these beautiful reductions for piano, because you want the kids to be learning context. Of course, they're supposed to be listening to recordings or, even better, going to live concerts. So when you get there in that chair, all alone, with a screen, on that stage, playing to a largely empty hall, you must imagine the phrase preceding yours being played by the violins, the clarinet, whoever. You must try to capture that in some way.

I'm saying things that I'm sure have occurred to a lot of people, so I don't want to pretend to have invented it. But I will say that the audition world in the sixties was a very different world. If you talk to guys that were older baby boomers, it wasn't that what they did was easy, but the rigor of the screen and the anonymity and the numbers were not there as much. De Lancie had been used to a world in which if you studied with him at Curtis, you were going to get a job. It might not be his job, a job of his stature, but you were going to be well employed. By the time I was a participant in orchestral auditions, de Lancie and other teachers had had to adjust their thinking. I could see this. We got out of Curtis, Marty and Bob and I, and we were in this unbelievably competitive environment and needing to be able [to] execute using a very particular skill.

There's the whole set of things that you need to be able to do. We were trained to do very rigorous metronome work by de Lancie, just in our day-to-day practice. I began setting up my own mock auditions. I didn't play for people much at all; I didn't need one other voice in my head. But I began doing things like running through the lists in the final weeks. If it was a very long list, maybe half a list, but not allowing myself to stop, really doing a per-formance. You have to think the way you have to think in an audition. Then I would play in strange acoustic environments. I would go to a church that I'd never been in and get permission to just go in. I'd be off in the sanctuary somewhere, and I'd give myself ten or fifteen minutes to soak up the reed, and warm up a few notes, and I'd play *Tombeau [de Couperin]*, Brahms [Violin Concerto], [Debussy's] *La Mer*, bam, bam, bam. I didn't necessarily record it; I'd just make myself do it. It is not just a musical exercise; it is, as importantly, a mental exercise.

I didn't gear my playing for one audience or another. I learned that was deadly. I remember one audition saying, "Your playing is too soloistic and strong. This isn't second oboe playing." And the next audition they'd be saying, "Well, it's too controlled; it's a little understated." What sells is how convincing you are. What I said before applies: de Lancie was a musician that conveyed the sense that he was doing what he wanted to do and what he needed to do when he wanted to do it. Some people are natural at conveying that in auditions and some people are not—no matter, you must learn.

As for routines that you do in the practice room beforehand: I needed to be quiet, not socialize. I might have some good friends there but I wouldn't be socializing with them. I wouldn't walk into the building more than thirty . minutes before I needed to play. If I found out I wasn't supposed to play for two or three hours, I would leave the building, go somewhere else. I never did more than ten or fifteen minutes of warming up, and nothing fast. Always very much under tempo. When I was in West Virginia, I had a counselor who taught me, ostensibly, self-hypnosis. He used to coach people like the field goal kickers in football teams. I never was able to induce that state, but I developed deep-relaxation techniques—techniques common to all forms of meditation. I did it both while playing and at other times in the day when I needed to focus or relax. In fact, I probably should still practice it. Particularly in my mid-twenties, I needed something that would quiet my brain down, just keep me on the most fundamental tasks.

Curtis is the kind of place where a lot of kids get jobs when they're, you know, twenty. Rick Ranti is one of my closest friends in the BSO; he's a kid, still, in my mind. Rick was at Curtis a year and a half when he won his job, playing second bassoon in Philly! He's also a very humble person. In a certain sense if you play a double-reed instrument and you're not humble, you're insane! [Laughter] Because they're instruments that are designed to make an idiot out of you. If you pat yourself on the back, you're dead—you're about to miss something.

When that moment arrived and I was offered the job in San Francisco, I was virtually in tears. I'd been thinking for some time, "If ever I actually do this (which seemed doubtful), I've got to find a graceful way to accept the job." I'd seen people do their Rocky imitations—mostly the guys, I must say. A lot of testosterone. But, by gum, when the moment came, it was just shattering. Shattering. I sort of bowed my head, and just mumbled something.

I am a religious person, and I believe profoundly that there is nothing I have that was not gifted to me, graciously and providentially. I am so aware of the vicissitudes of the profession, and of the enormous good fortune I had in being able to accomplish the goal of playing beautiful music in a wonderful orchestra. I have known so many fine people that are so very much more talented than me and are much less happily employed than I am. I am very happy to be doing what I'm doing, and I'm really, really lucky to be doing it. The luck of the good reed, the luck of being in the right place at the right time—if you told me I would be sitting here talking to you this building, I would have said you were crazy. At age twenty-nine, if you would have predicted my career, I would have said, "You're nuts. It's just not going to be." You've got to have a real respect for luck and for persistence.

Here's my advice: you the anonymous audition-taker, take as many as you can until you can't stand doing it. At that moment, see if you can look in the mirror and say to yourself, "I have done everything I could have done." Be sure you can walk away from it saying that, because, for sure, for the rest of your life, you're going to be asking, "what if?" if you don't do it. By the end of it, I can honestly say, there was no aspect of it, no aspect of oboe, reeds, music, psychology, physiology, that I had not examined. Was that a gift? For many years I would say to people that my twenties were a wasteland. My dad said that it took ten years to recognize my old personality. You could argue from age seventeen right to age thirty, it was boot camp. Certainly, you were focused. But clearly there were gifts from that. The gift of having a sense of how much you owe to fortune and God. I don't know if I would have phrased it that way at age thirty, but I certainly realize that now. And the work ethic, the knowing that you had better work as hard as you can every day that you're on that job, and know that the day you have to hang it up. . . .

I'll tell you a story about hanging it up, for John de Lancie. I was there for his last service with the Philadelphia orchestra. A couple days before, he had played [Ibert's] *Escales*. He was such a cool cucumber. Amazing, amazing performance nerves. It sounded fantastic. It was a solo he coached me on, and there he was doing it incredibly well, just as he'd described. He put the oboe down after that show, turned to me, and he said, "I want you to tell them when they ask that when I hung it up, I could still do it." He was, I think, quite obsessed with it. It was a constant concern for him that he do it at the right point. I have the same concern. You owe something to the art and you owe the profession some dignity and the best of your efforts. That's something that those experiences in my twenties cemented. By the way, that first year for me in the profession playing second in San Francisco—that was the year Marc Lifschey was fired as principal oboe—his last season. As I was leaving, they actually tried to demote him, one of the greatest musicians to hold an oboe in the 20th century, into my vacated chair. In a strange way, that departure to the Met was a catalyst in my thinking about the profession; I realized that this is a very fragile thing, a playing career. As much as we love it, the enjoyment, the pats on the back, the camaraderie, it's fragile. Enjoy it while you have it. Know that and work like the devil to maintain it. Then, if you're lucky, you'll be able to leave it gracefully and on your own steam.

Breathing

I work on support and making sure that your wind is ready upon attack and your sound is already in motion as you're trying to make a phrase. You remind me of a funny moment about breathing because people talk about "Breathing, breathing, breathing!" And de Lancie used to get quite disgusted when people talked about breathing. I could tell you, sitting next to him, he blew pretty hard; he took a lot of wind in and there was a lot of force and he could play hard. But it was sitting in wind class, and—I will spare the name, why can I remember the names from then and not from two days ago?— there was a flutist and he was playing. He was trying to get himself loose, sort of flapping his legs back and forth. It was very funny and de Lancie said, "What are you doing over there?" "Oh, Mr. de Lancie, I'm just trying to make sure that my breathing is right." I'd heard him use this line a couple of times, "You know how to breathe! You breathe in (immense, effortful breathing sound) and you breathe out (immense, effortful breathing sound)!" That was part of the deal with him. "Don't make this complicated." Or "Ferrillo . . . you think too much!" I still probably think too much.

When he was retired, he came to visit us at the Met. I remember a conversation over dinner with Elaine Douvas. Elaine was talking about a very specific thing that she does with her embouchure. Right, wrong, whatever—this is something she does. And it was a very nudgy little detail, and I remember saying, "Oh dear, I wish she hadn't confided that in him," because I could see this expression on his face like, "Why are you making this so complicated?" He really was a guy that liked to think in straight lines. He couldn't stand fussing around. I worry about a lot of fussy details, too.

On Teaching and Performing

You don't really separate the two out, although there are moments it can haunt your playing, as in, "How did I teach this the other day? You know, I don't think I really did do that." [Laughter]

Reminiscence

It wasn't a single concert; it was four performances of *Rosenkavalier* with Carlos Kleiber at the Met that were just mind-blowing. They were positively mind-blowing. It is the most inspirational, the most unbelievable combination of shape, line, detail, nuance, emotional depth, interpretive depth of everything that I've ever done, and people were hanging on the chandeliers. In my mind, those are the greatest performances I've ever been a part of, best I've ever played in my life. I've had a couple of other experiences that were pretty darn wonderful and came pretty close to that, but I would say that that absolutely takes the cake.

8

László Hadady

László Hadady graduated from the Franz Liszt Academy of Budapest. From 1976 to 1980, he was soloist of the Hungarian State Concert Orchestra. He also played principal oboe in the Latvian National Symphony Orchestra, Paris Opera Garnier, Paris Chamber, and French Radio Orchestras. From 1980 to 2010, he was solo oboist in Pierre Boulez's Paris chamber orchestra, Ensemble Intercontemporain. He performed as soloist with the London Philharmonia Orchestra, the Chicago Symphony Orchestra, and orchestras in Great Britain, France, Argentina, Germany, Latvia, Russia, the Netherlands, and Hungary. He has conducted orchestras such as the Sinfonietta Rīga, Budapest Symphony, and Debrecen Kodály Philharmonic Orchestra. Since 1995, he is professor at the Conservatoire National Supérieur de Musique de Paris. He has made solo and chamber music recordings for Deutsche Grammophon, Sony/CBS, Erato, and Naxos. This interview was conducted by Michele Fiala, with Alain de Gourdon providing translation, at the 2009 International Double Reed Society Conference in Birmingham, England.

Early Career

My uncle was a great musician. He was a pianist, composer, conductor, professor, and he was a student of Bartók and Kodály. He played with Bartók in concert: two pianos. I began with piano and after two years, the oboe. I was eleven years old. My uncle said, "Ah, the oboe is a beautiful sound and not too many people play it very well. So play oboe." That is the shortest story.

Great Oboists on Music and Musicianship. Michele L. Fiala and Martin Schuring, Oxford University Press (2021).
© Oxford University Press. DOI: 10.1093/oso/9780190915094.001.0001.

Teaching and Fundamentals

Two things are very important. The physiology: breathing, position of the oboe, posture—and to be musical. For breathing, shoulders will be down, everything will be down. The breathing will come from far, you know, from the bottom. Shoulders should not move—very relaxed, shoulders, always. Breathing is never good enough; you can always improve the way you breathe. It's true for normal life. We don't breathe enough or well enough. And very few teachers teach the way to breathe. It is very important. It is the beginning of the playing of the oboe, or of any woodwind instrument. Because if you don't breathe well, you will always have some problems. If you can't run, you can't play football.

A good exercise is to play without the tongue. The staccato etude, or a Bach Partita [sings many notes with air starts]. After singing, sing in the oboe. Play multiphonics to open the sound. Multiphonics are very important. Many exercises. Three things are important when you play oboe. It is respiration, breathing; the throat; and the mouth. The lips and the mouth. Pressure of the lips. Not only the lips I mean, but inside. Maximum of opening for the throat. It's only possible to open the throat if you have good breathing. Absolutely. The mouth and the throat need to be open.

The embouchure should have a minimum of pressure. The wind is very free. Very much like the American school. Americans use an "O" mouth—a vertical shape—and Europeans use a horizontal embouchure. The vertical is much more natural. Transcendence.

Reeds

I play American reeds. American long scrape. Since twenty-seven years, since many years. When I began to play in Hungary, I began with German—you know, East German instruments were very cheap at the time. When I was a little older, I had Buffet and Rigoutat instruments; at that time I was playing like French people. When I won my position with Boulez's orchestra, it was with really French style and French reeds. Like Holliger, like Maurice Bourgue.

Later on I changed when I bought my first Lorée oboe. I met many good American oboists like John Mack, Ralph and Harold Gomberg, Ray Still,

John de Lancie, Joe Robinson, a very good friend from New York. So, I exchanged ideas with them. But I'm not in a French box or German box or American box. I try to do the best of everything and make my own character combined from French technique, American reeds; I like the flexibility of the English.

Expression

The most important thing is the style, After, the most important is the structure, the analysis. After, when you know the style and structure, play it with many characters. Different characters. Try to tell a story with each sound you make—not only to be nice. Each sound has importance inside a structure. No one note is [sings a "straight" note]—never straight, always one tone as something to expand, a musicality. And never two times the same thing.

Direction, intonation, articulation, colors, and if you have all of that, the sound will be beautiful. The sound is the last but very important. People say, "Ah, you have beautiful sound!" And, "Ah, the sound is magnifique!" But the sound is last. If you are a musician, if you play music, structure, interesting, colors, dynamic, the sound is good, right?

If someone tells me, "Ah you have a wonderful sound," it could be like a beautiful car with wonderful wheels but no engine. I think that in America, the sound is sometimes too much. And Europe, not enough.

Vibrato

Vibrato is part of the style. In Baroque, I make no vibrato. In Romantic, lots of vibrato. And in Haydn, Mozart, sometimes different vibrato. And in contemporary music, sometimes it is asked to be very straight, no vibrato. Again, it depends on the music you have to play, but vibrato will be different, for sure.

Versatility

I play contemporary, contemporary solo. Chamber music. Chamber music, solo. I play in chamber music ensemble contemporary twenty-eight years with Pierre Boulez. I play in a symphony orchestra: New York Philharmonic,

Bamberg, Budapest Festival Orchestra, principal oboe. I think I play all possibilities. And what is the difference? In solo you are alone with the composer. In orchestra it is chamber music. If you play in quartet, quintet, or symphony orchestra it is chamber music. The listening and the mix. To mix well with the sound of the harmony of the woodwinds, that's very important. Find the balance of the orchestra.

The very big difference is between contemporary music and classical music. I play contemporary music every day for twenty years. And this is a fantastic opportunity for the oboe. You take a contemporary piece with dynamics from four p to four f. This is ten different dynamics. And you play ten different dynamics. I am obliged with contemporary music to have more, to open the sound and to be able to play from pianissimo to forte. The speed and technique in contemporary music is important, the staccato, or the legato and articulation. Low register, high register. I want it to give more capacity, more possibilities to the instrument. So it's why I wanted to play modern music. I play an instrument that goes to low A because I want to go to high C, because I want to go more than two and a half octaves, maybe three octaves. Or even more? It is extreme, but interesting.

I want to be an oboist from the twenty-first century, not the nineteenth. Or twenty-second even, but not somebody from the past. With the roots from before. I like to put the instrument more to its maximum. I like to explain the music but to be true. Not to be pleasant or to be nice but just to say, "I know the piece, I know the composer." If the music is true, it's good. It's not beautiful, the music. It is true and afterwards, beautiful. Without the truth, music is impossible. It doesn't exist. It is a beautiful sound without music.

Performing

The most important thing is when you play, you have to be well with yourself. To be happy, to enjoy what you do. The most important is not to play well or badly. It is to be happy with what you do. I wouldn't exchange my position with any other oboist.

Being a musician, you are never sure of yourself, you always doubt. I am never truly pleased with what I do. But when you are in front of the public, you cannot duck anymore. You have to do things. At the end, when you are onstage, you have to give. You leave your problems away and you are, and you do.

You have to convince the audience that what we do, we do with our heart and I offer that. It is what it is, but I offer you that. Please, take it. You know, the best you can, but I do my best. Of course, I have some limits because if you break your nerves, it's forever. One time they wanted me to play a piece, so difficult, not interesting, and I said, "No, I don't want to do that." That was more than I was able to do. I don't want to break my nerves.

I try to control things. You can never be sure, but normally if you are that way, you are successful. Always something can happen, but normally it works. If you do sports or if you prepare for the Olympic games, for instance, if at home you can jump two meters, the day of the competition you will be able to make one meter and a half but no more because of all the stress and all the things that can happen in competition. So always you have to try, you have just to know your limits. You will always give a certain percentage of what you are able to do because of the stress of the audience. Many things can happen, so I think you will always give a little less than your potential.

9

Carolyn Hove

Carolyn Hove has been the solo English horn player in the Los Angeles Philharmonic since 1988. She previously held the English horn position with the San Antonio Symphony for two years. She graduated from the Oberlin College Conservatory of Music. Hove has appeared as a soloist in many venues, including the Dame Myra Hess Concert Series in Chicago, Alice Tully Hall in Lincoln Center in New York, and in appearances with the La Jolla Chamber Music Society, the Los Angeles Philharmonic, and many other ensembles. Her three solo CDs are on Crystal Records and feature premiered works. Hove maintains a busy schedule as a teacher whose activities have included guest lectureship at leading music schools throughout the United States, Europe, Asia, and Canada including the Royal Academy of Music and the Guildhall School (London), the Royal Northern College of Music (UK), Baptist University (Hong Kong), Japan Double Reed (Tokyo), the Banff Centre (Canada), the University of Southern California, the University of Texas, Ithaca College, and the Music Academy of the West. Hove has served on the Executive Committee of the International Double Reed Society. This interview was conducted in Los Angeles with Michele Fiala in 2011 and updated in 2018.

Early Life and Career

My parents were musicians, so I'm from a musical family. My mother was a violinist and my father was a very good singer but he made his living as a band director and also as a music administrator. I grew up listening to violin lessons on Saturday mornings and I started taking piano lessons when I was five. My older sister had decided to play the flute. I had tried the violin when I was in the second grade and had failed miserably, so I wanted to play a wind instrument. I decided that I wanted to play the oboe. We had a lot of

Great Oboists on Music and Musicianship. Michele L. Fiala and Martin Schuring, Oxford University Press (2021).
© Oxford University Press. DOI: 10.1093/oso/9780190915094.001.0001.

Philadelphia Orchestra recordings and we used to listen to them—all kinds of orchestral recordings. I've never been without classical music in my life. I think I was nine years old when I announced to my parents that I was going to play the oboe, and my parents said, "Oh no! Not the oboe!"

My father said to me, "You're going to have to make reeds, and you're not going to want to do that." And I pulled myself up to my entire height, however tall I was then, and I looked at my parents, and I said, "I can make reeds." Of course, I had no idea!

The first reeds I made, my dad and I made together, but then I worked on my own. About a year before my father passed away in 2005, he was in the hospital and I was sitting with him. I said, "Hey, Dad, do you remember what you said to me when I told you I was going to play the oboe?" And he said, "No." So I said, "Well, dad, let me tell you the story." I told him and he kind of laughed. And I said, "I sit at the reed desk now for hours on end and I think to myself, 'You know, Carolyn, you couldn't make reeds when you were nine years old and you still can't make them now!'" And my dad just howled. I had no idea what I was getting into. I know there are a lot of players that really enjoy making reeds, but honestly, I'm not one of them. I do it because I have to do it. But that was my parents' response when I told them I wanted to play the oboe: "Why the oboe?!" I recall that a large part of my decision was because my mother had told me that it was a solo instrument and difficult to play. That got my attention!

My first oboe teacher was Bob Mayer [Robert M. Mayer]. He had been the English horn player in the Chicago Symphony, but had retired from the orchestra by the time. He started me on the oboe when I was nine. I still remember my first oboe lesson with Bob Mayer. I have a photograph of me standing with him wearing my little dress, my little teeny-weeny white ankle socks, and my little black shoes. I was a little girl who couldn't wait to start to play the oboe.

My mother drove me an hour each way, every other week on a Sunday morning to take my lessons, which were half an hour long. Bob expected all of his students to stand up to play their scales. And if you played your scales well, you got to sit down and play the rest of your lesson. So, I learned to play scales, and they had to be memorized—both major and relative minor. After a while, I had to play scales in thirds. Bob was really great for teaching fundamentals. Really good technique, that was his forte—absolutely getting you to be a solid player. He could get anybody to play the oboe because he was really great at the basics. As a beginner, within fifteen minutes, you were playing notes on the oboe. He was incredible that way and he was fun with a great sense of humor. He used to call me Snookie. Judy Zunamon Lewis, who plays second oboe at the Lyric Opera in Chicago, and I met because she also studied with Bob during the same time period. We became friends, and then worked together quite a bit when we both lived in Chicago. He used to call her Snookie, too, so I think he called a lot of his students by the same nickname.

When I was a junior in high school, he and his wife decided to move to Florida, so I needed a new oboe teacher. At the time, my mother was the concertmaster of the Elgin Symphony and Margaret Hillis was the music director. She was [also] the director of the Chicago Symphony Chorus. So my mother talked to Miss Hillis and said, "Bob will be leaving soon, so Carolyn needs a new oboe teacher and she's having a lot of trouble with reeds. Do you have any suggestions?" Miss Hillis said, "Yes. Talk to Bev Schiltz." At the time, Bev was playing bass in the Elgin Symphony as well. So my mother went to Bev and she said, "Let me talk to Grover."

Ostensibly, my first lesson with him was only going to be about reed making. So we worked for an hour on reed making. And then for half an hour he worked on my playing. I was a senior in high school, I think, and my mother said, "We've learned an awful lot. This has been great. I know you're very busy with the symphony but is there any way that you might have some time in the future to help us again with reeds?" And he said, "Yes, come back in two weeks. And I want you to bring such and such to play." Suddenly I was his student, which was astonishing, because he had recently quit teaching at Northwestern. But, he took me. So, I started studying with him as a senior in high school, and he opened up all kinds of amazing horizons to me. He was incredible. Over the years, he and I became very close and he was a very special man in my life, like a second father. He's the one who told me that I needed to go to Oberlin to study with James Caldwell. I wasn't able to go as a freshman, but I transferred in as a sophomore.

Becoming an English Horn Player

I didn't play a note of English horn the entire time I was a student at Oberlin since I wasn't an English horn player. I didn't become an English horn player until I graduated from Oberlin and was living in Chicago. I was there for six years, freelancing, taking auditions, and that kind of thing. I asked Grover,

"Do you think I should buy another oboe so that I have two oboes?" And he said, "No, you need to buy an English horn. I've got an English horn that I can sell you." So he sold me my first English horn, and that's the horn I won both the San Antonio Symphony and the Los Angeles Philharmonic auditions on. It's a very special horn. I no longer own it; that's another story.

I liked playing the English horn, but I was still doing a lot of principal oboe work, freelancing in Chicago. I was principal oboe of the Elgin Symphony. I was playing in a chamber orchestra and doing studio work. I started playing new music when I lived in Chicago. That's where I got bitten by the new music bug. I did opera; I did ballet, Baroque music, and chamber music. It was during a run of the Prokofiev *Cinderella* ballet, when I played English horn, that changed my direction. In the third act there's this lovely little Orientale that has a beautiful English horn solo. It's very haunting, typical of Prokofiev's amazing writing. The English horn solo starts it out. The piece develops, the oboe has a lovely solo, and then the English horn comes back and plays the solo again. I thought, "Oh my God, this is just way too much fun." Grover and Bev came to one of the performances and he called me afterwards. He was very sweet. He said, "Bev and I were there today and I just want you to know that your English horn playing was absolutely it; it was right on the money. It was very nice." Grover was not the kind of teacher to give a lot of compliments. He's not nasty like some teachers, but he wants to keep you working, so he doesn't shower you with praise and pat you on the back and tell you that everything is great. If it's good, it's good. Fine. If it's not good, this is what you need to work on. He's very matter-of-fact that way. So I was honored. That's when I got the idea that maybe I should become an English horn player.

In 1986, there was an opening in the San Antonio Symphony for English horn and assistant principal oboe. I called Grover and I said, "That's my job. That's the one I want, so I want to spend the summer working on English horn with you because I really feel like I don't know enough about what I'm doing on English horn." He said, "Okay, great. Come next week." We spent the entire summer working on English horn and getting me ready for that audition. So that's what did it.

In April of 1988, I auditioned for my current position with the Los Angeles Philharmonic. And when I won the audition, it was the most exciting day of my life—the day that changed my life completely. April 13, 1988, in case anybody was wondering. I called Grover's house to tell him that I got the job and Bev picked up the phone. I'm very close with Bev as well; she's a great lady.

She said, "How did it go?" I said, "I got the job." And she said, "Oh! Grover's going to be so pleased! I can't wait to tell him when he gets home." Of course, he was thrilled.

If you're going to be a serious English horn player, it's really important to study with an English horn player who knows what they're doing. When you're an oboist, you spend your time working on the oboe because the oboe is an overwhelming project. Most oboists don't spend an enormous amount of time on the English horn. They can pick it up and play it and sound reasonably good on it, but if you really want to be an English horn player, you need to work with somebody who's been there, done that, and has solved these issues and can say, "Try making your reeds this way. You need to think about this in this excerpt. You need to think about blowing this particular way; it's different from the oboe." It's important.

If you're an oboist and you're interested in playing the English horn and getting familiar with the instrument, what should you play? I tell people to pick up the Barret and play the Forty Progressive Melodies on the English horn, because they're completely different on the English horn than they are on the oboe—especially when you're starting at the beginning and they're not technically demanding. You don't have a lot to think about. You can focus on, "What are the issues on the English horn?" You already know the tunes. Your fingers already know where they're supposed to go. It's going to feel different on the English horn, but I find it's a really good way of approaching the English horn and getting the feel.

I didn't know right away that I was an English horn player, but then it kind of just hit me. I felt like I loved the oboe, but English horn is so much more fun. This is much more like me, plus I love the alto color and range. I often say that the English horn feels like my favorite pair of jeans, and the oboe feels like I'm wearing a pair of jeans that's at least one or two sizes too small. And people understand that comparison.

On Teaching

I've been lucky. I've had good instruments and I've had lots of help. Now I feel like I'm in a position where I'm able to help other people, which is nice. When you see the light bulb go off and all of a sudden a beautiful sound comes out and they start really getting it, that's really fun. That's one of the things that's so fun about the master classes that I do. We work our tails off for four and a half days and I've had students come to me that say, "Ms. Hove, you changed my life," which is really sweet. It gives people the tools they need to feel better about their English horn playing. Answering questions about their reed making and getting the right bocal on their horn is so gratifying, to send people away feeling like, "Okay, I can do this." That's part of the reason I do it. It's been my goal for a long time to bring the English horn up out of the dark corners and make people realize, "This is accessible. It can be done. It's not impossible. It's not a big, deep, dark secret."

I often get people who come back from year to year, but nine times out of ten I get a completely different group. So I'm constantly meeting and working with new people, which is great, because it gives me the chance to spread it around. It's nice to see people over and over, but it's also nice to have so much interest from other people in different parts of the country.

On Vibrato

I was young when I started playing and I was so desperate to sound like a big kid that I started with a lip vibrato—really scary. And then I was told that I had to do a diaphragm vibrato, which is really a stomach vibrato, and you can't control that very easily. So when I started studying with Grover, he said, "You know, this isn't working. You need to get it up in your throat." He started with the whistling and all his little exercises to get the vibrato up in my throat. That's what I have done with students that have problems with vibrato. I try to have them work with a metronome and I think, "Ho" or "Oh" or whistling. I think whistling works a lot better than "Ha-ha-ha-ha" because when you're saying "Ha-ha-ha-ha" or "Ho-ho-ho-ho" it's still coming from the stomach. Whereas if you're whistling, it's coming from your throat.

When I used to teach younger kids, I would tell the girls to get a light-weight scarf and tie it around their neck and I would tell the boys to put on a necktie. If they could feel the scarf or tie tightening and loosening, then their vibrato was going to be in the right place. I think that having the least amount of distance between your tongue, your teeth, the reed, and where you're producing your vibrato is ultimately going to be the most efficient.

I've always taught it with the whole group of eighth notes, triplets, sixteenth notes, quintuplets, sextuplets, you know, working that way. And not moving on to the triplets until you really have it well with the eighth notes. And not moving onto the sixteenth notes until you can do it correctly with the triplets, etc. You may never get to sextuplets and that might be okay.

Wellness

I run four miles, three days a week. I started running because that seemed like a really good way of burning off stress. And good for my heart, and good for everything. I got addicted and I love it but I can't run every day. Even four days a week sometimes is a bit much. Ten or eleven years ago, I started also doing yoga because I wanted to go about relaxation and strength training in a different way.

Michele Forrest, an oboist friend, is the one who pushed me into doing yoga because she said to me, "You really ought to come to yoga with me sometime; I think it would be really good for you." She gave me a schedule for the place where I now practice yoga and it took me about another year before I finally got around to getting there. I became addicted immediately. I'm trying to do either running or yoga six days a week and then I walk my dog about a total of four miles a day. He needs the exercise and it's not bad for me to walk, either!

All of these things give me the opportunity to have my head in a different place. As performers, we can really focus on the minutiae and we can make ourselves stark, raving mad. The physical activity, for me, has helped enormously and I think that by doing the running and the yoga and the walking, it's going to prolong my career because I'm healthier and I'm stronger. There are many of us in the Philharmonic who are all the same age and it's very interesting to see, those of us that are more physically active seem to be successfully avoiding injury. It doesn't mean that we're completely injury-free and it doesn't mean that we're pain-free, but with those of us that are really making the effort to stay in shape, there seems to be a difference. This kind of exercise is really beneficial for a musician. We do so much sitting! And with reed making, you sit in there hunched over a desk for how many hours? It's not particularly good for your spine, your shoulders, your neck, and your back. That's one of the reasons I do what I do. Plus, I enjoy it. I absolutely love it and I meet interesting people and I like that. I don't want to only be around musicians all the time.

Exercise and Performance

One of the most important things that yoga has taught me is to be in the moment, and that nothing is so unbelievably important that the sun won't rise tomorrow morning. And the breathing and the centering. I have found myself using some yoga breathing onstage on a number of occasions. Especially if I'm doing something that's stressful, I revert back to what I've learned, which is fantastic. I think that a yoga practice, awareness of yoga, would be really beneficial to all music students because it teaches you how to use your body and teaches you what you can do and what tools are available to you, rather than just dropping a pill when you get stressed out.

Fundamentals

Long tones. [Sighing] For tone production, vibrato, evenness, keeping your tone color even from one pitch to the next. Being an English horn player, that's what we do—we play low and slow. I work really, really hard to make sure that my color is coming as close as it possibly can to match from one pitch to the next, and you can't really do that if you're only focusing on technique. So that's something that I work on. Scales are always a really good idea. And I'm always looking for new music, so it's fun to read through things. Not that it's possible to always do that—it depends what we're doing in the orchestra. If we're doing things that are new or take a lot of work, that's one thing, although I've been there for so long that there's very little repertoire now that I haven't played at least once. But fundamentals are really, really important and when I was a student, my first hour of practice every day was only scales. Regular scales, scales in thirds, scales in trills. . . . That's all I did for my first hour, because I felt like I really needed to have a solid technique.

I do a little exercise. I think I've demonstrated it before at some master classes at IDRS [International Double Reed Society] conferences and other places. I'll start on the half-hole D and I'll do four beats, metronome 60–66. Then go a half-step lower to C♯ for four beats, come back to D, then start going down chromatically. So, D, C♯, D, C♯, D, B, you know, down the octave. Then I come back to the top, three beats, same exercise. Then two beats on each note, the same exercise. Then one beat on that same exercise. And then I start over again going up, in half steps. And that I have found to be very helpful for a lot of people who've worked with me, just to get that sense of evenness. Because you're not thinking about anything. You're not thinking about fingers in terms of technical things; you're thinking of your fingers in the sense of how light your finger-pressure can be.

On English horn, because so much of what we do is long, slow solos, if you're slamming your fingers down, you can't do a nice, smooth legato. I have demonstrated this and I've taught this to so many students where they're not even aware that they're using too much finger pressure, and then as soon as they lighten up, they can make beautiful long lines; they can play the New World Symphony beautifully. They can play *Roman Carnival*. It's all of these things. As an English horn player I'm very aware of this, because it's what I do. I demonstrate it in my master classes, too, when a student will be up there and the finger-pressure is too heavy and I'll have them play the same thing with lighter finger-pressure and I'll ask the group, "Do you hear a difference?" Nine times out of ten they're all saying, "Oh my gosh, completely different." So that's something that you need to be aware of as an English horn player. On oboe, too, but the jobs are so different.

The reason I picked D is that D is a particularly ringy note on the English horn, so I figured, let's have you start on a ringy note and have you try to match that color, rather than some of the other ones that aren't as pretty. But you could start at any pitch you wanted to, really. That's just what made sense to me. And if you can't play downward slurs, then that's a problem. It really keeps you honest in having to play those downward slurs. You have to play downward slurs on the oboe, too, but on the English horn, maybe it's a little bit different. It's a good thing for oboists to play the English horn, because you breathe differently, you blow differently, everything about it is different. I think it can help your oboe playing. It's very easy to be tight on the oboe, but you can't be tight and play the English horn beautifully. It can't be done. The fact that you have to loosen up and blow differently on the English horn can be very beneficial.

English Horn

It's a big instrument and there are some people with really small hands who have a tough time making the reaches. If you have a really tiny hand it's going to be pretty tough to play the English horn comfortably. But the weight and the support mechanism, that's something I harp on all the time. Every time I see someone come in and they're not using any kind of support mechanism, I cringe because the instrument is heavy. It's very easy to get tendonitis playing the English horn. I did, when I was playing in the San Antonio Symphony. The first time I ever got tendonitis was playing English horn without a neckstrap or any kind of support. We were doing a week of children's concerts, playing *Petroushka* twice in a morning, and there's a lot of English horn in that. By the end of the week, I was in pain and it was bad. It took a long time, and I still have to be very careful. People really need to explore the options of support mechanisms and take them seriously. Not everyone wants to use a neckstrap and that's fine; you don't have to. But you need to find something unless you're a man who's 6′6″ and lifts weights. Then, probably, you're not going to have a problem. But let's face it: the majority of English horn players aren't athletes in that way, aren't built that way, and so I think you need to do something, otherwise you're really asking for an injury. Without the support mechanism, the reed vibrates differently because the weight of the English horn pulls itself down and the reed gets buried in your lower lip, and it changes the way the instrument vibrates. All anybody ever has to do is try it and really listen and they'll see that a support mechanism makes a huge difference.

You're not going to be as agile on the English horn as you're going to be on the oboe. The springs are generally a little bit tighter and everything about it is bigger. It's a little bit slower. Psychologically it's a very different—at least playing in orchestra—it's a very different chair, which I love. I love the independence. I love the fact that I'm down there on the end and I'm kind of part of the woodwind section but I'm also kind of part of the viola section, which is really great because I love the viola. It's a different way of going. It's a solo chair but it's so much more independent and so much of the time I feel like I'm pretty immune from a lot of what goes on with the issues in the wind sections. They have to be really careful to work so well together and match everything, and when you're playing English horn, you kind of get to do your own thing, which for me works really well. Yet you're still a team player because you're still part of the woodwind section; you're still part of the orchestra. I'm convinced that English horn is the best job.

One of the hardest things about the job is sitting and sitting, waiting to play a big solo, then coming in and having to sound like God. I remember Ariana [Ghez] saying something to me. She said, "I don't know how you do that. You have to sit there and sit there. I would go crazy if I had to do that. It's just so much easier to keep playing." But you get used to it, and I think it's also where some of the yoga and the running Zen qualities come in. You have to be secure enough in yourself as a musician and as a player and trust yourself that if your reeds are good and if you're focused and you're centered, you're going to make it work. Certainly when I first joined the San Antonio Symphony, a lot of that was very new to me. Now I'm used to it. A perfect example is the New World Symphony. That part is actually second oboe/ English horn. Well, most of us English horn players don't play oboe on that. Most of us get used to planning it in such a way that you can play a couple of notes at the end of the first movement. You can double some things, do the transposition and then you at least have a sense that your reed is going to work, and then you just have to trust that it's going to work. But it takes a lot of discipline to keep from freaking out when you're a young player. After a while you realize, "Oh yeah, I can do this." But when you're new at the job, you have a lot of questions. "Well, can I do this?" I actually find it harder to make fast switches between third oboe and English horn (like in Bartók pieces) than to sit and wait to play an English horn solo.

A Memorable Performance

There are many memorable experiences because I've been really fortunate. I have a really great job and I get to play good music all the time. Esa-Pekka [Salonen] came back to conduct to orchestra for the first time since he had stepped down as music director. He came back, and it was great to see him. We did Bartók's *Bluebeard's Castle*, which is an amazingly powerful piece. Willard White was singing the part of Bluebeard, and Anne Sofie von Otter was the mezzo singing the part of Judith. In Disney Hall we have the ability to do incredible things with lighting because it's a very modern hall, so we were playing the piece and Willard and Sofie were out there in the front, just singing. There was no stage acting at all. But they had done incredible things with lighting, so they had the entire stage lit with these kinds of eerie purples and blues and it was really creepy. And at the moment that she opens the door to the room that is filled with gold, piles and piles of gold, and it's very bright, all of the lights in the house went on, so it was unbelievably bright. And at the time in the score it's really loud and there are these incredible chords. I got goosebumps and I had tears in my eyes because it was just so powerful a musical experience. I talked to Esa-Pekka while he was here. He and I have always been really close and we've done a lot of really fun work together. I said to him, "You know, that was just goosebump time for me. It reminded me of why it is I do what it is that I do." It's for moments like that, where it's just the chill factor. The music is so overpowering that you can't imagine doing anything else with your life.

Artists Who Inspire

Fima [Yefim] Bronfman is absolutely one of my favorite pianists on the planet. We recently did the Brahms Second Piano Concerto with him. Divine. We've had many amazing singers onstage. Thomas Quasthoff, oh my God, what a voice. [Dietrich] Fischer-Dieskau was someone I liked to listen to. Gil Shaham. I could listen to him play the violin all day. Martha Argerich. The late Lorraine Hunt Lieberson. How many times did she give me chills? Dawn Upshaw. We did a lot of work with her. Willard White, oh my God, that incredible voice. Those are the people who really inspire me. It's fun to listen to them, to hear their artistry and what they can do.

Making Music

We can get really hung up with the mechanics of playing the oboe and English horn, and worry too much about what the instrument is that's in your hand, rather than thinking about the line. The solo that seems to hang more people up than not is the New World Symphony. It seems simple, but it's not so simple. I have a wonderful story about a former student of mine who has a magnificent orchestra job now. She was studying with me at the time and she said, "I can't play this piece at all. I really can't play it." I felt the same way when I first started playing English horn. She played it and it was okay, and I said, "I want you to sing this to me." She looked at me like I had three heads and I said, "Look, I don't care what your voice sounds like; that's not what I'm after. I want you to sing this to me." So she sang it to me. I said, "Okay, great. Now pick up the English horn and play it the way you just sang it to me." She picked it up, played it on the English horn and it sounded beautiful. I said, "Okay, now do you get it?" And she replied, "Okay, now I get it." It is really important to put the instrument aside and get back to the essence of the music. No, I don't care that the third space C in the English horn tends to be flat. I don't care about that. Make music. What's the line? Where are you going? What are you thinking about? How are you going to sell this line?

How are you going to make the person who is sitting at the back of the hall be thrilled that they were fortunate enough to be able to get a ticket to come hear the orchestra tonight? That is the bottom line. Are you going to make music, or are you going to act like an oboe player or an English horn player? There's more than one way of going about it. My mother said to me, "You can learn something from everyone, even if it's how not to do something." That's why I think it's so important for us as musicians to keep listening to everyone and to keep our ears open.

Playing in Orchestra

Playing in orchestra is just giant chamber music. You must have the ability to listen to the people around you and if someone is passing a phrase from one instrument to the next instrument, you have to be willing to get your ego out of the way and play it the way that somebody passed it to you. Move your ego out of the way so that you can be a good team player. That's important. Playing in an orchestra, it's the sum of many parts. It's not only about the particular solo that you're playing. Being a good, supportive colleague is incredibly important when you're playing in an orchestra because someday you may need the support of your colleagues. The more supportive you can be to your colleagues in every manner can bring only good things. You're part of a team. When we walk out onstage at 8 o'clock at night, we put any personal differences aside. I'm really fortunate to play in such a wonderful orchestra as the Los Angeles Philharmonic.

10

Nathan Hughes

Nathan Hughes is principal oboe of the Metropolitan Opera and serves on the faculties of the Juilliard School, Rutgers University, and the Verbier Festival in Switzerland. He previously served as principal oboe of the Seattle Symphony, which showcased him in more than two dozen performances of eight different concertos during a three-year period. An avid chamber musician, Hughes regularly performs with the Met Chamber Ensemble at Carnegie Hall. Born in St. Paul, Minnesota, Hughes had early training in voice and piano. He earned degrees from the Juilliard School and the Cleveland Institute of Music, from which he was awarded the Alumni Achievement Award. His teachers included John Mack, Elaine Douvas, and John de Lancie. This interview took place with Michele Fiala at Nathan Hughes's apartment in Manhattan in May 2009.

Early Life and Career

My family is somewhat musical. My father is a professional bagpiper, believe it or not, and I wanted to stay far away from anything that had anything to do with the bagpipe, double reeds, or anything. But they encouraged the children in our family to be involved in music. So my earliest involvement was singing in the Minnesota Boychoir, and I did that for seven years. That's really what sparked in me the interest in music, finding the beauty in music. I have so many fond memories of that time, and remembering beautiful sounds, and really enjoying that. There was also a social element, and we toured. That was what got me excited about music, and from there I started piano. I studied piano for about a dozen years, which I think was a very helpful tool. Singing and the piano, early on, were critical in helping me be the person I am today with music, in a lot of ways. When my voice started to change—this was a boys' choir—I started thinking, "Well, I have to do

Great Oboists on Music and Musicianship. Michele L. Fiala and Martin Schuring, Oxford University Press (2021).
© Oxford University Press. DOI: 10.1093/oso/9780190915094.001.0001.

something else." So I started looking, and we were listening to instruments and trying to pick something and for some reason the oboe was kind of striking to me. From there things went very quickly. Youth orchestras, then I went to a school which was new at the time. It was called the Harid Conservatory. I think now it's still called the Harid Conservatory but it's at Lynn University. This was a brand-new school at the time. They had a lot of money for scholarships. It was a full-tuition, room-and-board situation, down in Boca Raton, Florida. It was a college-aged school but they let me in a couple years early. That was how I started my study, which was a great way to test the waters, see if this was something that I really wanted to continue. Had a very nice experience there.

From then on I went up to Cleveland Institute of Music, studied with John Mack, and in the summers during this whole time I was spending time with John de Lancie. These were my earlier influences. I did a Master's at Juilliard with Elaine Douvas. Then, I played principal oboe in the Savannah Symphony for a year out of school, and then I came back to New York for a one-year position, principal oboe with the Met. Then I went out to the San Francisco Symphony as associate principal for another temporary position there, for just half a season. Then I was in the Seattle Symphony for about three and a half seasons—as principal oboe there—before I came back here. Now I'm in my third season at the Met.

Teaching wise, I've been always interested in it. I started teaching when I was down in Savannah, at Georgia Southern University, and when I was in Washington, at the University of Washington, and now Juilliard. I've always been interested by it, fascinated by it, and see it as a great way to improve myself as well, so it's something that I've always tried to do as much as possible.

Operatic Influence

It has influenced my playing quite a bit. It's a completely different environment than the symphony orchestra. Flexibility is a major component of it. I've had to develop what I'd call good radar. Singers are very free. They're not as locked into things as instrumentalists. They're very flexible with timing and dynamics and rhythm and things like that. If you're playing with them, you have to be super flexible and be predicting what's going to happen next. You have to develop some kind of radar to sense what's going on and what's going to happen.

Operas are much longer than most symphonies. I consider an opera like running a marathon and playing a symphony like doing a sprint, because you have to pace yourself in a totally different way to last the five and half hours through *Die Walküre*. I'm amazed at how flexible we all are as humans, but just coming into the job, you feel it, that first season. You really feel the aches and pains of sitting there for that long, as well as trying to keep your attention through really long stretches where you're not always playing. And then you have to come in after sitting for a while and sound as though you've been a part of everything, you've been playing that whole time, and your sound is hot, everything you're playing is warmed up.

Because the voice is such a natural instrument, I find myself, whenever I get focused on instrumental, mechanical elements of the oboe, trying to fight that as much as possible. I mean attention on the reed, noises, mechanical noises of the instruments or fingers slapping on the instrument, all sort of things that take away from the music and aren't really natural—they're just a mechanical thing that goes along with playing the oboe. I've been striving more and more to get rid of as much of that as I can in my playing so that it's a little more natural, like the singers do.

Singers have this larger-than-life quality when they're up there onstage. It's not just a dynamic thing, although most of them have a huge dynamic range; it's everything about it. They're wrapped up into what they're doing. The role is not just music. They have text involved, they have costumes, they have makeup, they have this whole thing, so they're just engrossed in what they're doing. There's something about that intensity that is inspirational. As instrumentalists, when you're playing in an orchestra, we go through lots of repertoire, fast. Sometimes you don't have time to sink your teeth into something the way a singer has done, so I'm always reminded to dig deeper.

I'm also blown away at their ability to expand and not get ugly. Some of them seem like they have this endless dynamic range, endless color range. They can do anything they want. There's something about the voice that if you're really good at controlling it, it has very few limitations. To strive for that on the oboe is a nice thing to look for. I am truly amazed at some of the sounds that come off that stage, where there are no words to describe, I'm just . . . wow. I sit there and am just amazed at what I hear. It's very enjoyable.

Mental Practice

Running has been such a helpful tool. This is how I memorize everything—any concerto I have to play or whatever. As soon as I know the piece well enough to be able to solfège the whole piece, when I go running I solfège the whole piece as I go out, one direction. I turn around and I solfège the whole thing when I'm coming back. This way you aren't slamming away hour after hour on the instrument hurting your hands and your everything else and yet you're practicing the piece. You're figuring out how you want it to go in your mind. This is something I apply in my playing a lot—trying to hear something before playing it, trying to visualize it. We can get so tied up into what we're doing. To get away from it, to visualize what you want it to actually be, is critical to help us raise the level of what we want to do with something. I'm a firm believer of mind over matter. If you have a concept of how you want it to sound, if it's strong enough, when you finally get the instrument in front of your face and you're playing, you naturally will adjust to make that come out.

I do that with teaching a lot. I try to make sure that the student is hearing what I'm talking about, so I'll do a lot of demonstration, and then a lot of experimentation. You can give hints with somebody about physical things to try: "You can hold the oboe this way, you can hold it that way. You can put your embouchure this way. You can blow like this. You can think about it like this." But if you just have the concept in your head, if you have it visualized, our bodies will adapt. All the physical things will find a way to make what you're hearing in your mind come out of the instrument. It's simplified to think of it in that way but ultimately, that's what it's all about: having the concept in your mind of what you want it to sound like.

Interpretation

This is where I feel that my background with piano has helped a lot. As a single-line player, there's a lot of danger in not studying a piece in its entirety. It's very easy, when we're just playing our one line, to forget about all the other components that go into a work. Usually there's accompaniment of some kind, or you're only a part of what's going on.

It's important to know why you're playing something the way you're playing it, and have it based on facts about the piece. I'm looking for the intentions of the composer. To study a piece is to look for all the elements that go into that. Harmony, for me, is a major, major, major component. Melody, of course: how it goes up and down. Rhythm. How it's orchestrated. I'll look at all these elements and see how they're combined to try to piece together the puzzle of how to play something. Where the phrase begins, where it ends, what the height is, what the mood is of a particular phrase. If there's text involved, that's also a huge clue of how to play something. I try to look at as many elements as I can, outside of the oboe part. The oboe part, everybody's going to get into that enough, because we're playing it and we're thinking about it all the time, but I remind myself to look at the whole picture and to get an overview of what's going on. I try to get a general mood. I look at it on several levels of detail. I actually think this is an art form unto itself.

Any phrase, any piece, can be looked at like Schenkerian analysis. You can look at one note, the entire phrase, or the whole piece. You can break it down to the next level: there's a beginning and an end and a high point in the middle. That's the whole piece. Every phrase can be broken down in this way, too. What is the general arc? What is the general shape of a phrase, the long line? I will also look down to smaller levels, details. Why is this interval special? Why is this note highlighted? Interesting elements within the phrase. I'm looking big and small, and I'm trying to find the right balance between the detail and the bigger picture. It's the balance of those two elements that I'm always looking for, to find how to play a phrase the way that seems like it's bringing the composer's intentions to life.

On Reeds

Ultimately, I'm looking for something that doesn't get in my way. I want to play music. It's the same thing that I'm looking for in an oboe—I'm looking for something that allows me the color range that I need, the dynamic range that I need, and with a minimal amount of effort. That's ultimately what I head for.

On a more detailed level, there are a few things I look for with reeds. Predictable response is critical, and I say it that way because it doesn't just mean easy response, it means predictable response. I'm comfortable with different resistances on a reed, but it has to be predictable. It can't come out when it wants to speak, because we're always playing when somebody else instructs us to, whether it's the conductor or the accompaniment right before we start. We're always playing when something else dictates it.

I need something that has a huge dynamic and color range. A lot of that comes from the integrity of the opening of the reed. If the opening collapses when you get soft or isn't large enough, those two elements will constrict my range of color and dynamic. Obviously there are extremes of everything, and if it's too open that'll be a whole other set of problems that get in your way more, but the integrity of the opening has to be there to get that range. So I do aim for that.

Pitch stability is pretty important to me. I think of it as a flexibility within stability. I get my flexibility by having a stable setup. If you aim at it from a flexibility standpoint as your main thing, you'll end up being more constricted, because you will be manipulating the reed too much. Going at it from the direction of stability and getting your flexibility from that has a lot to do with tight sides of the reed. This also gets me a lot of resonance and ring in the sound. To have enough resonance and ring in the upper register, there does have to be some pitch stability. If we're holding it up it'll cut out color range.

Many different formulas work. It's a combination of so many elements that when looking to make a reed work, everything plays off another. The gouge plays off your shape, and your shape with how you scrape, and the diameter of the cane, and the hardness of the cane, and the staples you use, and all those things play off one another, so nothing is isolated. When I'm experimenting with reeds, I always take the golden rule of "Only change one thing at a time." There are enough variables already. But trying to find a combination of parts of the reed that give you a successful product, there are a lot of formulas that work. Find one thing that kind of works for you a little, somewhat, and then try to go with it.

I tell students, especially earlier on, to start with a formula that somebody suggests to you, a combination of elements in the reed, so that you have a home base to experiment from. If you don't have some sort of groundwork set there, you won't know what's making the effects when you change one variable. I encourage them to start that way. Usually their teacher will give them a formula that they use, and then experiment, changing one thing at a time and seeing if you like the results. A lot of experimentation is key. And, cane, cane trumps all. A good piece of cane is worth a lot.

On Breathing

Breathing is a very natural thing. It's very human and listening to singers reminds me of how useful breathing is. You can breathe almost anywhere in a phrase if it's done well. It can be used as a tool to enhance what you're trying to do. Singers run out of air a lot sooner than oboe players do, and so they have to breathe a lot more often. They can breathe in a way that brings passion to a phrase and I find that inspiring.

There are basic elements of breathing. With a beginner, you're trying to make sure they're breathing deeply, not getting a lot of tension in their shoulders or chest. I usually don't have to work on that too much with my students. Most of them are breathing naturally. Where to breathe in a phrase is more of the critical element, and that is something that ties into how to decide where a phrase begins and ends and where some key elements are. I try not to break up an idea too much. I think it's good to work on the way you end notes before breathing—being able to taper off a note nicely at the end of a phrase or, if it's a breath in the middle of a phrase, to be able to leave a note with an upward inflection and take your breath quickly and then take the next note. That's a technique that is critical and needs to be learned. And it's not so easy.

Certainly if you can get students to sing something, most things come out pretty darn naturally when we sing. The release that's at an end of a phrase, most people don't have a problem with. It's hard to do, but they have no problem visualizing it. It's the one that's in the middle of the phrase. If you just take any phrase that is obviously building up energy, and if you can get them to sing that phrase and have them breathe at different points but not lose the energy, that'll get the concept there. Then, when they get the oboe in their mouth, try to have the last note to have some energy, to have some vitality in the sound. Vibrato can help a lot, if the vibrato is energized toward the end of that note. Making sure that the end of the note has some follow-through to it. That the note right before you breathe has some ring, has some resonance, so it's not cut off like a sliced-off note, and it's not tapered, necessarily. It's like you're sending something out into space. And then you try to pick up the note afterwards as catching where that left off, dynamically, color-wise, everything. It's not something easy to get, not something easy to teach.

Support

Support is a very interesting word that everybody has different definitions for and interpretations for. Support for me mostly comes into play when you're talking about legato and you're talking about evenness of tone. The oboe's such an odd instrument, the notes having so many different colors, naturally themselves, and having so many different resistances themselves, that to even that out somewhat has a lot to do with support. There's the saying that, "Make sure that you're playing the instrument instead of the instrument playing you," and I think that support has a heck of a lot to do with that. It's something very difficult to work on. I go back to my concept of visualization here. I demonstrate a lot in lessons with students, and try to play the most beautiful legato I possibly can, with the most even tone I can. I have a rather lengthy exercise routine which covers a lot of fundamental elements of playing the oboe, and one aspect of that is very slow scales. This, I believe, will develop support eventually, because if they're trying to go for this seamless line that's very even, I don't think you can get that unless you're supporting well.

I'll tell them to experiment with different positions in their mouth, of forming their mouth different ways, maybe a different vowel sound, perhaps, possibly different orientation with the embouchure, things that eventually get them in position to get that result. I always try to start from the result standpoint and then see if they can get there somehow. The result being the seamless legato and the evenness of tone, and then just go for as many angles as we can until something clicks. A sostenuto quality is something that supporting helps a lot.

Fundamentals

I believe a lot in these. I don't think I would be anywhere near where I am with the oboe if I didn't spend many, many, many hours with this one. Ultimately, we are trying to eliminate mechanical problems of the oboe and we're trying to just have music. And what that means to me is having command over the instrument. I've tried to come up with a routine that covers all the technical aspects of getting command over the instrument. It's a series of long tones, scale patterns, articulation exercises, and some tuning exercises. There are many exercises that go into each compartment.

In the long tones, you can work on so many different elements: the dynamic range, the color range, the control of pitch/color in coordination with dynamics, so that you're not just playing one color when you're playing a specific dynamic. We want, ultimately, to play a certain color or a certain way, a mood that we're going for, out of choice, not out of a necessity for the instrument. On the oboe, when you get to your loudest dynamic, it's one of the most difficult things to play with a tone that you might play with when you're playing mezzo piano. When it gets loud, it can have an edge on it, or something a little raw on the oboe. Some pieces demand that. In some pieces it's totally necessary, so when it's a choice, you use that. But if that's not demanded, I want to be able to use a different sound and practicing long tones with a huge dynamic range is a good way to develop that. Also, do some larger intervals to develop control over air speed, because different registers in the oboe require a different speed of air, different voicing of the notes. Connect up and down large intervals.

Then scales. I use several different patterns. Play them slowly to work on that support aspect, get the evenness of tone, the legato. A lot is gained by playing slow scales. It's pretty amazing. And then, ultimately, faster to get facility and fluidity and be comfortable in all registers of the oboe, especially the extreme high range, with a lot of pieces being composed higher and higher.

I do a lot of the same scale patterns with different articulations, some all articulated, some mixed articulations, as well as different lengths of notes. This is to have a huge palette of colors that you can use when you're articulating, and never be caught not being able to do what's necessary for a piece. If a piece needs something much shorter, much longer, more legato, more percussive—you have a bunch of colors there to use. I usually simplify things for my students and I ask them to play three different lengths when they're doing their articulation things: very short, a middle one, and a very long one. I actually do that in the long tones as well when they're playing even one note, to very, very subtly have a legato tongue for each beat, just to have control of a very smooth articulation. This develops a lot of different things. One of the biggest challenges is articulation, for an oboist, and these exercises help you develop different ways of doing it. To be able to play a phrase and to articulate any length of note and still have the integrity of the line is not easy to do. Articulation can sound very mechanical on the oboe, so I'm striving to make it sound not-mechanical, almost all the time. There's a small percentage of pieces that demand a percussive, more mechanical-like articulation, so you need that tool there.

Intonation exercises. Most of these I do with a tone generator on, and they're to remind you that you can't just play anywhere. You have to play in tune with yourself. I think of playing in tune with my own low notes, or put on a tone generator and play with it. Any instrumentalist who plans on playing in any group knows that this is a very critical element, so just work on it all the time and be diligent about it.

All these exercises are a great tool to help you get on track when you're lost with reeds, sound, control over the instrument, all those things. When I have trouble, I can go back to the basics and say, "Well, can I do all of my exercises still?" They're a checkpoint. They're a help to get back on track when things are off, because that happens with everybody and you need tools to help you get back.

On Vibrato

This is another element that I work on a lot. My motto is "versatility" and "Do whatever is asked of you." I've been playing in orchestras my whole professional career, so I know that you are asked to do many different things. You have to be ready to make the conductor's idea sound good. Or to make the composer's idea sound good. That requires a variety of controls and tools and vibrato is another tool. I'll practice with different speeds, starting with none, increasing to the fastest, widest vibrato I can, back to none. Switching it around so I can start with one that's very active but it's very soft.

Vibrato should enhance what you're doing already with the line of the music and not distract from that in any way. Mostly that applies to pitch. I don't want the vibrato to confuse the pitch. I want it to confirm it and I want it to make it sound beautiful, make it sound more rich, more resonant, and not bring all the attention to it. I would like to be able to use a vibrato that is continuous from note to note. Sometimes, maybe, it's used to highlight just one note. But mostly it's incorporated into my sound. I often play something without vibrato first and make sure I have things sounding good without it, and then hopefully it sounds better with vibrato. A lot of people change notes and when they change notes they start their vibrato new again, or they start after the note starts, and I don't think it's something that they intended to do. If they intended to do it, if it serves the musical purpose, great. But if it's just the way it happens to come out, that's not a good enough reason. I want the vibrato to do what I'm intending it to do and not just what I'm programmed to do.

On Auditions

I enjoy seeing both sides of it in close proximity. We just got finished doing our bassoon auditions at the Met this last week, so it's been fresh in my mind from the standpoint of sitting on the panel. Auditions are a really tricky business. From the jury's perspective, everybody's listening for something different. That's something to remember when you're on the other side. Everybody on the other side of that jury, even within one orchestra, are all unique individuals that have their own opinions. I have never been in an orchestra that is filled with clones of each other, all thinking exactly the same about what they're looking for. These are human beings with lots of opinions. As far as what I'm looking for when I'm on the other side, the biggest thing I'm looking for is inspiration. I want to have a colleague showing up to work, knowing that I'm going to be inspired by what they're doing. On every level: musically, technically, tone-wise. I want to be inspired.

I also listen for versatility, no matter what position they're on. Versatility. Whether it be a section violin job or a principal flute job or a second bassoon job, they all have slightly different roles, so I might lean slightly in one direction with the versatility in terms of how I want them to be able to fit in the group. But most people in the orchestra, no matter what position, have to put on another hat at some time or another. I want somebody who plays soloistic at times; I want somebody who plays very introvertedly at times. Not only does their role vary within the orchestra, depending on what we're playing— the repertoire that we play is a huge range. We play so many different kinds of composers and pieces that you have to be a player that can do everything. So I'm looking for versatility.

Some things are a given. Technically, very secure and no major problems there. One other very critical one is intonation. I listen very carefully for that, especially if it's someone in the woodwind section who I'm going to be playing with. It's such a critical element that affects all of us, more than just about anything else. Rhythm can usually be beaten into somebody by a conductor, to play at the right time and the right place.

To be able to play an audition successfully, you have to show a lot of different things. For a committee that has these different personalities, you have to be extroverted at times, you have to be introverted at times, you have to have no glaring problems, especially in early rounds. First rounds are "elimination rounds" and people are listening to tons of players all day long. You have to make sure that everybody who has a different opinion on that other side gets a little taste of something they like. You have to give a little something to everybody. Otherwise you won't get a vote from them. You do have to play the different characters of the pieces; you have to show them. You have to switch gears fast, and play something that is high energy and exuberant and then play something that is tranquil and serene. In every round you need that variety. You can't just do your first round being all soloistic and extroverted and then show your other side in another round. That won't work. You have to show this palette of different ways of playing something so that you get votes from people who like things all different ways. A different character for every different excerpt, every round is important.

You can't please everybody and you have to do what you believe in. The only way you'll play well enough, you'll play convincingly enough, is to truly believe in what you're doing. You can't cater what you're doing to what you think people want on the other side. It's impossible to know what anybody's thinking, and I think people go wrong in that direction.

I don't think there are as many secrets to auditions as people think. They think, "If I can just get the audition-taking secrets, I can get the job." I don't think that's it. I think you have to have the fundamentals of your playing down and you have to have the ideas about the music in your brain and be very convincing about those things. Those things can't be stressed enough. Those are the most important things.

Then there is this element that an audition is this foreign, unreal environment. We don't perform like this. You're all alone, which means you're under the microscope. And when you look at something under the microscope, it's different than when you look at it in regular daylight. If you can remember that all the time, that'll help a lot. Because refinement usually goes very far in auditions. Refinement is big, because it is under the microscope.

You have to know the pieces inside and out. It's unreal that we're working on a very small excerpt out of an entire piece. It's very important to have the context of the whole piece in your mind, so that you're making intelligent decisions about how you want to play a piece of music based on its broader spectrum.

Sometimes we play the same excerpt over and over and over. It's hard to keep it fresh, so I try to look at it from a different angle. Study the score and analyze some harmonies so that you're looking at it from a different person's perspective, maybe the conductor's perspective. If you can look at it from another angle, that helps it stay fresh. You don't want it to sound dull when you get to an audition. You want it to sound alive.

Technical things have to be where someone could wake you up in the middle of the night and smack you in the face and it'll come out. Because when you get nerves and foreign environment involved, it can go haywire. I usually start very slow. I mix up the rhythms and do turned around, backwards, forwards, anyway I can possibly think of until it's not going to go wrong.

The slower excerpts are the ones that need to be digested. You need to have a concept that is very convincing, something that you believe in. Those I don't necessarily slug away at every day. I'll alternate and mix it up in my preparation so that it stays fresh and so that I'm coming back to it at different times.

Another thing that is very important is to practice the mental routine that is necessary to switch gears fast at an audition. You play one excerpt, it's thirty seconds long, and you turn the page and you have to play something that's totally different. You have a couple of breaths in between, not even a minute, and you have to switch gears. For me, it's a series of cue words that I use in my brain, and it's some breaths I take, and something that allows me to switch gears. It's a mental routine that needs to be practiced, so that you're not thrown off when you get into the audition situation. The keywords are something about the music, just to get me in the zone for the next excerpt, because they're so different from one another and auditions are so short. Excerpts are so short that you can't wait a minute until you get into something. You have to be, from the first note, in character.

Prepare in a lot of different acoustics, because every different acoustic will favor a certain kind of sound, a certain dynamic, a certain kind of player. And where an audition is held varies greatly. At the Met we listen in two different rooms, and they're so different from each other you can't believe. One type of player sounds good in one and one type of player sounds good in another. An audition can be skewed that way. So as a person getting ready for one it's critical that you're practicing in kinds of acoustics so that your setup, your reeds and your oboe and everything, play in a way that will sound good in many different environments, not just in a really live one or a really dead one.

Career Reflections

I feel very fortunate to be where I am career-wise, and thrilled with everything that's going on. I'm always looking forward to the next great performance or the next great piece of music that I haven't studied, or the next way to try to teach something to a student. I feel very fortunate to be already where I am, so I'm definitely focusing more on these musical aspects.

11

Gordon Hunt

Gordon Hunt was born in London and studied with Terence MacDonagh. He is currently principal oboe of the London Chamber Orchestra, and formerly the Philharmonia and London Philharmonic Orchestras. He is also principal oboe of the World Orchestra for Peace. He has appeared as soloist with conductors such as Ashkenazy, Sir Andrew Davis, Giulini, Kondrashin, Muti, Sir John Pritchard, Sir Simon Rattle, Sinopoli, and Welser-Möst. Hunt has recorded a wide range of music for BMG, EMI, Bis, Decca, and Virgin. He is the original "Gabriel's Oboe" in the Morricone score for the 1986 film "The Mission." He has been music director of the Danish Chamber Players and the Swedish Chamber Winds and has conducted orchestras around the world. Gordon Hunt is professor at the Guildhall School of Music and Drama and honorary associate of the Royal Academy of Music. In 2010 he was designated a UNESCO Artist for Peace. This interview was conducted by Martin Schuring and Michele Fiala at the 2009 International Double Reed Society Conference in Birmingham, England.

Early Career

The biggest influence on me was, and in some ways still is, my main teacher at Royal College of Music, Terence MacDonagh, who was Beecham's first oboe in the Royal Philharmonic. He trained in France with Myrtil Morel. His whole approach to playing has always influenced me very much—the vibrancy of his sound and flexibility, and a singing quality.

After college I went to an orchestra in Wales, the BBC Welsh Orchestra. That was great because we had repertoire flying past our eyes—everything either recorded or live or broadcast. That was a great training for me, so after three years, when the job came free in the Philharmonia Orchestra, I was ready. I've been in the Philharmonia twice—from 1975 to 1985, and

Great Oboists on Music and Musicianship. Michele L. Fiala and Martin Schuring, Oxford University Press (2021).
© Oxford University Press. DOI: 10.1093/oso/9780190915094.001.0001.

then the London Philharmonic until 1990. Then, in 1993, I went back to the Philharmonia and I've stayed there. I suspect I'll be there until I fall off my perch.

On Orchestral vs. Solo Performance

What I've discovered over the years, as far as oboe playing is concerned, is that if things are in place there isn't so much difference. I could put it as simply as saying, "A good reed is a good reed," and if it's good enough, you could play a Mahler symphony on it, or, for that matter, the Strauss Oboe Concerto or the Mozart Oboe Quartet. In practice, there are different facets and you choose reeds to suit certain circumstances. But I try to make things as simple as possible. That's the idea, both with the playing, musically and with the reeds. I just try to keep it simple.

On Tone

It's the sound that I regard as essential. Going back to the way my teacher played and the way he taught—to me, sound is not just a sound, it's a voice. And, like any singer, that voice must be personal. It's got to come from somewhere inside, not imposed so much by technical ideas, but it's got to be something that's felt. Something that says something about you when you play, in the way that the singer naturally does. So, for me, it's not enough just to make a nice sound. I hear far too many people these days doing just that: making a "nice" sound. It's always pretty; it always sounds beautiful. And after a while you think, "So what?" Life isn't beautiful all the time. Music isn't beautiful all the time. You have to be able to express all these things. The reed is that instrument that enables you to do that, in a way. But before that, it has to come from you.

I don't advocate playing sharp. I hear too much of that. I'm very insistent with my students that they check their pitch and learn to play at the right pitch because, left alone, they'll all play sharp. Most of us do, if left alone. We have to make sure we don't. Sometimes, if a student has been playing alone for half an hour in a lesson, and I check the pitch, it's so wildly sharp and they have no idea. There's no use going into an orchestra that plays nominally, let's say, once settled down, 441 [Hertz], and playing at 443. They're not employable.

Within the flexible, singing sound, you have to be able to play very quietly. To a lesser extent, you have to be able to play very loudly, and everything in between. But the "very quietly" is what most oboists struggle with, especially in the low register. My teacher had a great expression when I asked him a question, which I might have been thinking about for the whole week before my lesson, or even over the holidays, and I thought he'd have the answer. And his answer often was, "You'll find your own salvation." That sometimes seemed to me very frustrating. He was absolutely right. Students need guidance, obviously, and sometimes a lot of guidance. Ultimately, though, for me, playing the oboe is all about sensation. It's all about how it feels to achieve a certain result. I can't tell how any student feels. I can give them ideas; I can tell them what I've learned, how I go about things, but ultimately what's going on in their mouths, their lungs, with their embouchures, in their brains, whatever—I'm not there and so they have to do it. If you want to play quietly at the bottom of the instrument, damn well go and try to find out how to do it. Ask questions, sure, but then figure it out.

On Reeds

I'm always learning and I'm always open to new ideas. I changed my scrape a few years ago, in response to playing with Dick Woodhams, always having admired, amongst other things, the way American reeds have a very easy speaking quality. They always feel very safe to me. So I altered my scrape to mirror some of the things that an American reed has. I might say an "expanded" American reed, but without altering my voice. And I think it's helped; I think it worked.

Europeans do many things differently from Americans, of course. There's a different gouge, different length, different shape, all the rest of it. And that's having to do with the balance of the scrape. We need security, don't we? In order to effectively produce what I've been talking about, our voice, and to communicate effectively, musically, first of all we need security. We need to know that the notes are likely to come out and that we can make a diminuendo, etc.

I have always believed that half the battle in playing the oboe is learning to make good reeds. But the other 50 percent is learning to play on bad ones and making it work. And that's part of technique. It comes back to "how does it feel?" We've all had reeds which are a bit too hard, which we daren't scrape because it might ruin the sound, so we play the concert on them. That goes in your memory bank. "It felt like that last time, yes, this reed's a bit like the one I had in 1984. I better play the way I played then. It feels like that." On those rare occasions when we have that perfect reed, somehow we don't need to think about anything. Pity it doesn't happen more often.

The center of the sound is most important. And that comes from several factors, gouge and shape, and we all spend our lives fiddling around with that. I'm not sure how advantageous it is to fiddle around with it too much. If you have something that basically works for you, best to stick with it. Both with the gouge and the shape. But the cane that we use has a huge bearing on that, and what I look for is cane that has a center to the sound. If it has that, and only that, it's going to be a very brittle kind of sound. But if it has that to begin with, you can usually scrape the rest of your sound into the reed and make the thing blossom. If you don't have the center of the sound, you've got nothing to go from. That's largely where projection comes from. If you have the right center in the sound, you can play very quietly and still be heard right to the back of the hall. Musically, to play quietly is sometimes the most touching thing to do. But if you have a sound which is quiet with no center, then ten rows back, people aren't going to hear any detail. If that sound has projection and a little center, it will carry to the back of the hall. You have to aim for that.

Louré

There is one word which my teacher, Terry, wrote in the slow movement of the Mozart concerto, a copy I still have. And it's a French word—*louré*. It's all to do with how notes are connected, one to the other. Smooth is one definition. Connected is another. But Philippe [Rigoutat] said kind of "enveloped," and I think that's probably the best way of describing that particular way of making one note go to the next. I would say that perhaps 80 or 90 percent of oboists that I listen to don't understand that concept. The wonderful legato that an oboe can get, which is all part of "the voice," which singers do naturally, is something that oboe players don't have very often. They're playing "legato" but they're not playing *legato*.

All instrumentalists should be trying to emulate the voice. That's not the end of it, because we can do a lot of things that vocalists can't, and they envy us our ability to do these things with an instrument. But for me, it's about being vocal. Of course, it's very impressive, listening to a million notes on any instrument. And one can wonder—I certainly wonder—how some people manage it. But much more impressive, and much more touching musically, is to hear someone play a very simple line which actually goes into you and does something to you. For me, that's the heart of oboe playing. The heart of making music. You have to think about it and nurture it, both in terms of the quality of your sound, the flexibility of it, the ability to make different sounds, to change it. Vibrato comes into that as well. Vibrato comes into this concept of *louré*, because if vibrato is used correctly and not overdone, and it's used flexibly, then it doesn't just color a note (which is the obvious thing) but it leads a note to the next. If it's used in the right way, the listener is drawn along that line so that what happens next is always known; there's a kind of structure to what's being played. I try to think about that and I try to pass that on when I'm teaching.

On Vibrato

Musically, I would always pick, for instance, something like the slow movement of the Strauss Concerto. That is an absolute perfect example of finding a line and using the vibrato in a musical way that's not obtrusive. Vibrato, for me, should be in the sound, not on the sound. As an oboe player, if you like my vibrato, you might say that because you're an oboe player. But I'd hope that before you noticed that, you almost hadn't noticed it. And then afterwards, you thought, "Ah yes, that's the way he's doing it."

On Professional and Personal Characteristics

Dick Killmer says that some people take up more space than they actually should. I think that's a brilliant way of putting it, because you can do it personally or musically. And that, ultimately, makes you unemployable and not nice to be around. You have to learn how to fit in, and it doesn't mean you have to be Mr. Nice Guy all the time or Ms. Perfect, but you have to be able to deal with other people and all their problems, too. Learn to back off when necessary and not take up more than your allotted space. Do that with your playing, too. We need a certain amount of generosity and, on the other hand, a certain amount of self-assurance—knowing when to stand out and stand up for the way you want to play or the way you think something should be played. But always open-minded and always open-eared, of course. That's the secret, both to your own playing and to everyone else's.

On Breathing

Very often I'm faced with students who get out of breath or even dizzy. But if you're playing on a reed that is free enough to express yourself, it's much easier to take a breath effectively when you need to. The word is "effectively," and playing something like the opening of the Strauss, or the slow movement of the Strauss, you shouldn't be out of breath. Every breath you do take, if it's organized properly and you're relaxed about it, in your throat particularly, should put you back where you started. You shouldn't ever be compromised. Obviously, if you're going to play a huge long phrase, you are going to be at your limit. But, that's a different thing. If you're choosing places to breathe, and you're breathing in a relaxed manner, there shouldn't be any "out of breath."

First of all, you have to plan where to breathe and work out what you can do. Students are often surprised when they breathe four times in a phrase, and I tell them they don't need to, and that it might be musically better not to. There's an argument for breathing as a musical device anyway, because music does breathe. But if it doesn't have to and they don't need to, they're often astounded just by being told that they can do it. And, "Oh yes, I can!" suddenly.

I don't always breathe in the same places because I like to make things different. I don't always have a set plan. In the slow movement of the Strauss you do need to have a plan, for instance, but in less-challenging long phrases, perhaps you can alter it and therefore make the music slightly different from performance to performance. And why not? Music being a living art; it should never stand still. Students will always breathe in the obvious places, and sometimes it's right and you could say it's never wrong. But there might a great musical advantage in making a nuance at that point, and spinning the phrase a bit longer. Again they'll say, "But I can't do that. I need a breath." I try to convince them that if they don't practice it, then they'll never learn to do it. After practicing it, and finding that they can, they have a lot more confidence. Then, in a performance when they're taking more oxygen out of their blood than they would in their front room because they're keyed up, they still have the experience of having played that phrase and knowing they can do it. It's the knowing that they can do it that makes it okay.

Technically speaking, you need to be relaxed in the throat. Breathing out is something that I'm doing right now while I'm talking to you. It's something we all do naturally when we're conversing with one another. We don't think about breathing out. We also don't think about breathing in because very quickly, while we're talking, we breathe in. Likewise when we're at rest, we just breathe. It's slightly different when you're playing the oboe; it does need a bit more thought. The breathing out, obviously, is what makes the sound. However, we all know that we've got to breathe out the stale air before we breathe in, and that's the hard bit. If you're not relaxed enough to breathe out, you end up topping up until there isn't any room to top up and you've got no options and you fall over.

The breathing in is the easy bit because when we need oxygen, we breathe in, and it's a very relaxed motion. Breathing out, when playing the oboe, isn't and you have to work on it, especially keeping the throat open. The way I try to persuade students and myself, when I need to think about it, is to create the feeling of yawning in the throat. If you think about it, when you yawn, your throat is completely relaxed. I try and play like that. I try and blow like that and that makes the whole business of breathing out and then taking a breath in much easier.

On Making a Musical Plan

I find it helpful to be natural. To look for lines, to look for breathing places, to find how a phrase can be spun. But I wouldn't say that is always the way to do it. I like to leave a little bit to the imagination at the point of playing. Sometimes you can surprise yourself. And if you remember what you've done, maybe you can use it again! We have to be organized in our playing—from reeds to breathing to scales. But I like to feel free, and I like to hear people who sound free and not playing to a formula, either with their sound or with their phrasing.

I'm learning all the time. Technically, little ideas come along and I try them and usually reject them again. But sometimes they work. I'm convinced that most blemishes in oboe playing, not just in quick music, but in slow music, are due to fingers and not the reed. Ninety percent of the time. It's an awkward instrument, as we all know. It's not perfectly designed, and if the fingers don't work just right, you might have a key that's opening and another one that's closing at the same time and that's a nightmare. It's a nightmare and if it's not absolutely right, you've got a blemish. I work on that a lot myself, and with students, too. They normally think it's the reed. In two minutes I can convince them that it's their fingers, ninety percent of the time.

Students should listen to singers and just simply learn. Let's say we're playing the slow movement of the Mozart concerto and it's a bit lumpy. I might get them to breathe through the phrase a bit more. When they get it, the whole point then is to say to them, "Now what did that feel like to do? How did you do that? Do it again. Make it feel like that again." What you'll get is the end result that you're looking for. When they learn to practice like that, that everything starts with how it feels, then that goes into this wonderful computer we call the brain, which is still the best computer in the world, and it gets stored. If they've done it enough, when they need to do F-C-A-C as in the first phrase of the [second movement of the] Mozart concerto and play it legato and make it sound singing and easy, they know how it feels to do it. So it will work.

On Air Support

Like everything else about playing, the support should be a very flexible thing and not a hard wall of pushing. I try to persuade students to take a full breath but not blow themselves up like a balloon. We all know that we've got far more air than we'll ever use for the longest phrase we can manage. So you don't need to be absolutely full. I try and teach students to be relaxed. I teach them to think downwards, both with their breathing and with their whole body, so that they're kind of grounded.

It should feel really not a big deal taking a breath and then blowing. It should be as natural as possible. I see people going red in the face. We all go red in the face, but I see them struggling to blow down their reed and make a sound. I just want to take out my knife and scrape it for them. And I often do, with my students.

I've often wondered—I've not put it into practice yet—if a good teaching ploy would be to take away their reeds at the first lesson and give them a box of extremely free reeds and say, "Now go away and learn how to make a nice sound on those reeds." They'd find that they'd have to relax their embouchures or blow less hard, rather than watch them struggle away on these planks all of them seem to play on.

I used to make reeds for my teacher at one point and I'd heard stories that in the days before that he'd get his students to play some complicated study facing one way and make sure that they had their back to their reed box and he would then go through it and take the ones he thought looked good. They never dared say anything. Ha! I don't know how true that is. I think there is some truth.

Reminiscences

I watched Cho-Liang Lin, Jimmy Lin, violinist, once break a string in the Mendelssohn, where the violin solo plays almost all the time. He managed to turn to the concertmaster and swap violins and not miss a single note in the piece. He had about a bar to do it. And then, having had his string changed by the concertmaster, found another bar to swap back. That was pretty cool actually.

I also recall a live broadcast of Mahler second symphony, in Royal Albert Hall with the BBC Symphony Orchestra and Maazel conducting. This was a long time ago and the world of closed-circuit television hadn't yet arrived. So the offstage horns were to be sitting behind the curtain where the conductor came on. In this case, the curtain was drawn back and there were the seats for the horn players and that was all fine, they could see him and everything would be all right. We reached this point and he very casually gestured in that direction, in a typical way that he had because, actually, they were to play this on their own—they knew exactly what to do. And there was no sound. So he made the same gesture again, without looking, and there was no sound. Then he looked and what he saw was the chairs and the horns, but no one to play them. They were in the bathroom. The orchestral manager hadn't got his timings quite right. The look of panic on Loren Maazel's face was something I shall never forget. It was saved by someone onstage who played it, actually. It was a wonderful moment. There was a very, very long pause, silence where there should have been offstage horns playing and then, suddenly, it started from onstage. But it was the look on Maazel's face. And the way he first started to make them play, without sort of bothering to. He was bothered eventually.

Conclusion

Playing the oboe, the sensation of playing the oboe—back to sensation again—should be largely pleasurable. And the whole setup from the reeds to the breathing and so on, should lead to it being a not-too-painful experience. That's what I would try to talk about to young players. At its best it should feel good. At its worst, yes, maybe you have to work a little harder for it, but we all know you can't have the perfect reed everyday, much as we try. The aim should be that it should feel quite easy. It's quite an unnatural thing to do, so we try to make it as natural as possible. That's what I would say. And sing. Sing.

You've got to have something else in your life besides the oboe. Having a family helps, having people you love puts the oboe in perspective. Because it's an essential thing in all our lives, but it's not the most important thing in life. And when it finds its place, perhaps that's when it becomes a little bit easier.

12

Thomas Indermühle

Thomas Indermühle studied at the Staatliche Hochschule für Musik, Freiburg, where his most important teacher was Heinz Holliger. Indermühle had further study in Paris with Maurice Bourgue. He began his professional career as an orchestral oboist, serving first with the Netherlands Chamber Orchestra and then with the Rotterdam Philharmonic. In the mid-1970s he won prizes at the Prague International Competition (1974) and the ARD International Competition in Munich (1976). He has made more than 30 recordings and has appeared as a soloist across Europe, the United States, and parts of Asia. Indermühle also conducts, regularly appearing with the Ensemble Couperin, as well as other groups like the English Chamber Orchestra. He teaches oboe at the Staatliche Hochschule für Musik in Karlsruhe and the Zurich Conservatory. This series of interviews was conducted by Michele Fiala over several days at his master class in Javea, Spain, in July 2011.

On Early Career

I came from a family of seven children and both of my parents were pianists (my father was also a conductor). Three of my siblings already played piano and my parents assigned one sister to give me piano lessons. They thought I had talent but I never practiced. I didn't like it and I felt too much pressure. One day, at eight years old, I overheard my parents reprimanding the sister who was teaching me. They said it was her fault that I was not progressing. I felt so bad that the next day I asked to switch to the oboe. I figured it would be less pressure because no one else in the family played it.

The first year I had a good teacher, with whom Holliger was still studying. Then I had a teacher in the second year who said that everything was good and did not teach me. I did not learn from him, so I became my own teacher.

Great Oboists on Music and Musicianship. Michele L. Fiala and Martin Schuring, Oxford University Press (2021). © Oxford University Press. DOI: 10.1093/oso/9780190915094.001.0001.

I sat down and gave myself an hour lesson each day. That is how I prepared to apply to study with Holliger.

On Competitions

The boost you get for your career in the sense of getting better doesn't have directly to do with prizes but with your preparing and with your being in the competition, listening to other people and comparing yourself. What the jury then decides is in a way not so important. It's important for the outside and it is of course important for you, for your future. If you win something it's always good. But everybody who goes through competitions should really prepare the program from the first to the last round. Some people come to the second round or third round and they haven't really prepared the final concerto, which is often required by memory. They think, "Well I probably won't go on." Then don't go, because if you think you won't go on to the final, why should you turn up and have 100 or 150 people applying for this and then they have to make the selection? There are other people that really want to go to the end and really can go to the end. Then there may be not 120; there may be only thirty or forty and that would make life much easier. To go just for trying to see what happens makes no sense because then you don't advance and you just disturb the proceedings.

On the other hand, if you really prepare the program up to the last round really well, even if you're kicked out in the first round, which might happen because there might be other people who are the same as you or better or it may be a question of coincidence—even if you play really well in the first round and there are fifty people, how can the jury still remember everybody? It's really difficult. Even then, don't go home. Stay there and look at how the oboe level is now worldwide because that's what's going on. What is the thing that you missed? Maybe you think, "I'm better than all those," but I don't think it's easy to feel that way because those people went on in anonymity with different people saying that these are the ten best or the twenty best of the fifty. So they have something more than you and you should listen to them because it is the other side of what you prepared. The other side is what you missed and both sides are important for you.

You must really prepare everything on time so that you can try it out, play it for your friends, play the program through with pianists, all the rounds. You're prepared like a soccer player that goes to World Cup. He prepares and he's in his best shape. You have the pieces prepared and you don't go home when you're out. You should listen and be learning. Of course it's hard and you're disappointed but you want to know why. Don't be angry at the people who judged you, but ask yourself what the other people have more of than you. This is what it's about.

On the other side, I'm a juror in competitions so people come to talk to me after the day they're eliminated. I always write notes about everybody. I mostly I tell them, "I can tell you something about characteristics about your playing. Some things I liked, some things I didn't like, but don't make a conclusion that those things were kicking you out because what was kicking you out were ten people going to the second round and you were number twelve and eleven people were better than you. Maybe not only on the things on which I commented; maybe on other things: personality or being more convincing. You're out not because of yourself or me but because of the ones that passed. This is a reality. Then we can talk about how I felt, if I liked your playing, what I liked, what I didn't like."

On Tone

I have a choice of sound for myself but my students play all really differently. They have another taste and this is not the primary thing. It must be a beautiful sound but there are so many ways of having a beautiful sound that it would be poor to say the sound must be twenty-seven and if it is twenty-eight, even if it's beautiful we don't accept it. I'm very wide with that on competitions, even when I'm working a lot on Baroque music. I'm quite severe with my students on Baroque style and different Baroque styles: Italian, French, and German. Then you come to a competition and there's a very good oboe player who's a good musician and they have no knowledge of Baroque style but I wouldn't punish him for that because it's a pity. You want the best players to go on and I don't feel angry when someone plays Romantically like Brahms or Schumann when it's Telemann. It's not about only that; it's about the oboe—the totality of oboe playing. The style is one aspect but another aspect is the personality. There are oboists who are playing very convincingly but maybe in the wrong style, maybe in a sound that I don't particularly like but it's convincing. A juror has to be stepping a little bit out of his jacket, from what he wants for himself because only people would pass who play like him, which makes no sense.

On Teaching

At least two or three times a month, my students play a concert in front of the class. My teaching is divided in three sections: individual lessons, group lessons with exercises that are the same for everybody, and playing in front of the class. The individual lessons are very different for everybody because they are different people, but the anatomy about breathing and about embouchure, it's the same for everybody. Anatomy is more comparable. The exercises are more fun to do in a group than to do it alone, with the reed and with your teacher who says, "No, blow this way." If you hear and see all the others, you have much more information. How does it sound if somebody is squeezing and how does it sound when someone is really good? Sometimes the young ones and the not-so-technical ones that seem to be behind, they are very good in the blowing and that gives them a good feeling.

When I first played one piece in a concert, it was a concert with students with piano and oboe, and I was really nervous. I had played other things quite often because I played all the Bach cantatas and my father was a conductor of that kind of music. I had played in front of people but when you stand there and play with piano in a recital situation—I was really nervous. I was studying with Heinz Holliger and once a year there was an evening of the oboe class and I played ten minutes or so. In a total of six years' professional study I had maybe played five times in this kind of situation for ten minutes, and then comes the final exam and you play one hour. So my students play ten minutes four times a month with piano, with cembalo, solo, or orchestra studies. The audience is the rest of the class and the classes are almost always around fifteen people. The rest of the class listens and it's a good audience—critical, but not against you. They know the pieces; they know how you are playing; they know it's not your best day, it's not easy. The others listen, so it's useful for everybody and you hear pieces that you don't know. Sometimes the two-hour concert transports qualities from one to another and sometimes it's like everything goes wrong for everybody. It's like there's a virus. But it's mostly stimulating that people in the group are supportive to their colleagues; they hope it's going well. Getting comfortable playing onstage, part of it is technical—just doing it really regularly as part of the teaching.

I'm there in the last row of the hall, the small chamber music hall, apparently asleep a little bit because I'm in a passive role, but I hear everything and I never say anything if somebody struggles. I don't call, "Do this." No, he has to solve his own problems. Music falls off the stage or music stand or a pad on his oboe sticks. I don't want to help because this is a concert. You have to help yourself. If you say to the audience, "Sorry, I have to interrupt because my instrument is not working," and then come and find me to get help, OK. But I want to be there passively. Because in the lesson I'm very active and I might stop this student many times, I really need to hear him once in totality without my stopping. Sometimes they are much better in those situations than in the lessons. In doing that, one learns how to go onstage. You can only learn it by doing. We cannot learn to swim out of the water, just by learning in books. The feeling of being in the water for the first time, being afraid of going down—you have to get over it for a while. A few times and then it's okay. You jump in and it's carrying you, no problem.

Apart from that, of course there are people who have more talent than others for the stage. They are attractive in the way they do things convincingly. Their movement goes together with how the musical idea is and they have a sound that carries. People, even if they are shy, can be professionally not shy onstage because they are playing well. This thing that is in front of them [the oboe], with their feeling in mind for those people [the audience]: this is professional. You could be very shy but it's like somebody who sells tickets for the train or sells vegetables in the market. He might be very shy but he still sells vegetables. This is a job. A musician privately can be very shy but the moment that he stands there, the trophy comes when his message arrives. If there's no message then he didn't do his job and if it doesn't arrive then he didn't do his job well. The students can learn that because there's obviously a strong message from the composer and they're good pieces. You don't have to be an inventor of things, just an interpreter; through you it comes in the hall. If your instrumental knowledge is strong enough that you can use any structure of your character, you can do it well even if you're shy. To get through this first stage of being afraid of the water, it takes a lot of quantity. If somebody studies with me two years he would have at least thirty-two times to play in front of people. So, the fear of the water should be gone.

On Conducting and Performing

I like to be busy with music and I like to be busy with people. I studied conducting but I'm not chasing after a career in it. I'm sometimes asked to do something and I enjoy very much the combination along with playing as a soloist. It's easy to conduct a solo work but then to do a symphony—it's a nice combination to do with chamber orchestra. Sometimes it just happens that a symphony orchestra asks for me as a conductor. I have no agent, not for oboe either. I go on request, which makes it easier because when you come you are welcome because people have asked for you. And the interest is just to make it work the best possible.

I have ten years' experience in orchestra. And the man standing in front is responsible for many things but all the people might play very well without him as well. He can also disturb them a lot and he can make a bad atmosphere; he can make them nervous. He can make the bad players more nervous and be picking out the good players, which is [a] bad thing. It's the psychological aspect of making a group of those people. You can also divide them: the good ones, the bad ones, and then you really have no group anymore. Then you go for the concert but it might not be good.

I consider also the musical aspect because we don't have so many really fantastic pieces for oboe. We have much good literature and we can be happy with a range of periods that we are in from Baroque to a lot of new music, but whereas a symphony orchestra is very strong in the [Romantic] period, we have not much.

What is interesting with the conducting is that first intellectually you have to learn a piece that is many notes, many things—rhythms, instruments. I don't say the oboe is too small for me, not at all, because every day I have to practice and to get better. It never ends. When you don't play for four or five days because of traveling or exams and you change to a strange climate— very humid and your reeds don't work so well—you always get worse and you have to get good again. I could really live without conducting, but when asked why I like it—I can learn new pieces, pieces that I know from playing in the orchestra. Recently I did the Bartók Concerto for Orchestra and it's not so demanding for the conductor but it's quite tricky at times. But it's the kind of music that's very different than the oboe repertoire. I like this aspect of putting people together so that they play with each other and they play the piece with you together as one group. Many people have all their qualities and you put them together into one thing. One piece, one sound, one feeling, and one common work. On the technical side, you should do it in a way that people can understand your beat and your rehearsing technique. Many things are already done: the music is there, the composer has written something, you have the score, everybody has studied for many years to sit there in this orchestra and won't waste time making something of that. To put together what is there is interesting for me. But I'm happy with the oboe—many things to learn and many things to do. For me it's ideal if a few times a year there are some opportunities to conduct. It should not be too often because otherwise I would not practice anymore. [Laughter]

On Teaching Tools

There is this little plastic device meant to help students who take too much reed in the mouth. It comes from Japan but I think it has to do with me because when I was doing my first summer course in Japan twenty-one years ago, I had to say to all the students, "Don't take the reed in so much." They were all on the staple, especially with the upper lip, which makes a big fat sound but you cannot articulate. The tuning of the middle C will always be very high and you cannot do many musical things. You cannot play piano and registers don't work, low notes don't work, many things. The second year I came there they had those things. I am not sure it has to do with my appearance there or if it was coincidence but the second year that I came they all had these things.

It's not my invention but I use it sometimes. You put it over the reed before you put it in the oboe and it covers—a fair enough part of the reed is free, but when people take it in their mouth they start biting on those things and realizing how far they are on. It doesn't let them go that far and when they have it two or three weeks suddenly they have a more beautiful sound. The notes speak because they cannot go in anymore. So it's good; it's a hard plastic that doesn't get soft when it's wet and it's also not so hard that it hurts you.

The JDR, Japan Double Reed Company, sells them in packages of three different sizes but it's only the longest one that makes sense because otherwise you're on the staple. It goes on the reed before you put it into the oboe. And then you put the reed in oboe and it shows you the way you should not be. You can't go there. The only thing I tell them is if you have top Gs, you should take it off because there you should go in for the top register.

On Throat/Mouth Position

We discussed an exercise that Mr. Indermühle had used several times during the master classes. He first filled his cheeks with air to show the opposite of an oboe playing position, then pulled the air back into his throat as if beginning to swallow. He explained that his mouth and throat were then in a funnel position, with the narrow end at the embouchure, to create air speed.

It's about the pressure that's often in the mouth but should not be in the mouth. If too much air from the lung comes out, more than the reed takes, you will build up a pressure in the mouth, not a pressure in the reed but in the mouth. To avoid that, you try to put the mouth in a certain form so it's pushing back—it's a preparing thing. If you have the pressure in the mouth, the mouth cannot cope with the lungs' power and it gets tired or hurt. But if you push backward, now the mouth has another form. In this form you can play. The pressure goes only to the reed. Because you need the pressure with speed to go to some exit, which is the reed. You don't need pressure to the side or to your tongue.

The lung is made for air pressure. It's the organ for it. The mouth is made for red wine, not for air pressure. In swallowing, in speaking, it's very flexible. But if pressure comes to the mouth that is actually a lung pressure, it's like having the lung in your mouth. Talking, swallowing, tasting, all would not work anymore and you hear it in the slow staccato of people who are pressing to the mouth. Then [PAH, an explosive exhale] they want to breathe but they cannot because they have to get rid of the pressure first. If it's the speed pressure to the reed like a compressor to clean your swimming pool with water [psss], this kind of speed is good. It doesn't go to the sides, just goes to the exit. That happens only in a certain concentrated formations of the mouth. To find out which form that is, you have to do the exercise where you first put the pressure [fills his cheeks with air] and then you take it off [sucks in a little with his lips closed]. So even if you give much pressure to the reed, the pressure won't come to your mouth, to the side. It's an aerodynamic question. You will actually feel the impact that your lung can have in your mouth in a certain mouth form, the lung pushing to the mouth. In another mouth form, suddenly the pressure can go down and you only have the good pressure—the one of the compressor to the reed.

Why use this exercise and not talk about where the tongue should be? I tried it many times before but I'm sure you also go to the dentist from time to time. You know what the tongue does as this poor man is doing his precision work on one tooth with seven mirrors and lights and the small sinks and the patient that is anxious and breathes fast and sweats. On top of that you always put your tongue where you know the tongue should not go because they are working on you. Why would the tongue go there? The intellect says don't go and still the assistant has to come to the patient and take the tongue off so the poor man can work on your teeth without being disturbed. Because the tongue has this instinct. The instinct is there from the first day of our lives. If the brain would have to give the impulse of what to do, we would never learn how to talk nor how to swallow. And the speaking in the first two years of our lives comes through the ear but not through the brain. How do my parents move the tongue to say this word? You listen and you copy so the tongue has a lot of talent in one way and but it's somehow not related directly to the brain by commands—do this, do that—it's more related to the ear. It's more related to taste, to the work that it has to do by itself. When I say, "Student, don't put the tongue so far away," I make drawings. I explain why it's better to have to tongue in front so the pressure focuses to the reed and doesn't open the lower part of the mouth. If the air doesn't go there, you have much more focus but if the air does go there it is really unstable. Just before the reed, you suddenly have a huge chamber so you cannot control the reed because there is something in between your air and the reed. There's room in the lower part of the mouth. They understand this in the first moment and they agree but weeks after, the tongue is still very far away. When I say, "Do this, and now do this," so that the tongue has aerodynamic control of the mouth, immediately the tongue is in the right place. Then I say, "Now in this position you play." Pow, the notes come out that didn't come out before. So, that's just to teach the form of the mouth that otherwise I can't reach through the intellect.

It's aerodynamic: if you have a ship with a point, it becomes aquadynamic and aerodynamic. It's the same laws. It goes fast but a wide ship goes very slow with the same amount of energy. Airplanes fly when they are aerodynamic. In the mouth this is important with the air. This fact and the fact that the tongue is not conducted by the intellect—go there or do this— many people say, "I can't; I want to but I can't—the tongue goes back." I say, "Yeah but when you were a baby and you were born you had to suck the first milk." You could do this with your finger [sucks on his pinky] and your tongue is in the right place and immediately this vacuum that you create in the mouth, this strong power in the mouth. We have to use this instinct, especially for the mouth that is so talented instead of just using it as a tube where the air goes through. It can do things. It can do things well or wrong.

On Air

I use those instinctive things like breathing. First breath of your life: it's not something you can learn. I don't think it should be so different for the oboe. I say many times that the oboe takes so much less air than I need for my own breathing. Why would I take more air for the oboe? If so, I confuse the air speed with the air quantity. You don't breathe for the oboe; you breathe for yourself. You don't breathe for the music; you breathe for your body. The lungs are for you; support is for the oboe; the head is for music.

The air speed is like traffic, air traffic is going through your mouth. You want to speed it up; you want faster air. It is like when there is traffic on the road, if you want faster traffic and you put more cars, it is confusion. You put more air to get faster but more air means slower: more cars means slower traffic. If you put more quantity of air, it is blocking the mouth and it gets very slow and then the note gets flat or the high note doesn't come or it comes late and you actually wanted the contrary. You wanted to speed it up but you put more cars on the street and it's not the right thing to do. Take the cars off and put [on] a fast car and let them alone. Then you get the speed.

On Talent

Between the people who have a lot of talent with the instrument and the people that maybe have to work hard to do things that others can do right away, I wouldn't prefer one side or the other side. If you are one side or the other side, don't feel that you either are really very good or you're very bad because the work that you do to get the thing right it is also a kind of talent. Some people, just by nature they take an oboe and they do everything right, not so many but it happens. Sometimes everything comes to your student without a problem, and you think how does he do it? But I try to create problems in the lessons—problems in difficult pieces. I don't mean personal problems but I mean it should be learned how you can solve something that doesn't work. It can be that those people come into orchestra and the colleague is not nice and then they don't know how to cope with it because everything was always working and now it doesn't work so they have no system how to get things done that don't work.

In one way or the other you have to learn how to make things better and if you are a natural, well-blowing person it can also be that one day something doesn't work in your oboe or in your playing and you get lost. Others have had to work quite hard. Some things I could do right from the beginning but generally I had to work quite hard to get the oboe done. I feel quite safe with that, that if I feel I am not informed I can get informed quite easily in a not-so-long time because I know what I must do. I have done it as a younger person and I have done it as an older person and I can do it. I tell people how to do it, what to do, and what not to do in their playing. If somebody can play naturally well, it should be of course happy to have this talent. Use it for the music; use it to be really more interesting than other people because if you have less problems with the instrument, you can dedicate yourself to being a musician and you don't need to get lost in work about speaking of notes or tuning or sound. Then this should be your problem-solving—the musical things, the style. Because often the easygoing oboists, I mean the young players, they stay there—it's going well and everyone says, "Oh you have talent," but those persons sometimes miss the will to get the best out of it musically. There are exceptions but that's fantastic if someone has this talent and also the will and the projection to go to the edge of the music pieces with that talent. Then it comes to problems because he wants to play more softly and maybe it's not working and he has to solve that.

On Connecting with the Oboe

The other side is that the instrument is very small compared to us so everything that we put in the oboe always gets smaller—the airstream gets smaller, the movement should get smaller. If you look at the reed, that is that actual instrument we have. That is why I work a lot with the reed only to get the oboe away. It is heavy and it's big, but the inside is very small and it is only the low B♭ you see with the oboe so if you look on the inside, the upper part which is down to G, it's about like a Japanese chopstick, so that's what we play on. There's wood around that and then metal around that and then our hands. It seems big but it's really small.

If you have things that don't work so well on the oboe, it means that in between your air and the instrument's inside, there's not a good connection. Then you have to find it but mostly it'll go from bigger to smaller. Look into the bore, see how big it is, and then make contact with your air. This can be learned. It's not a mystery. It's not that someone can do it and the other cannot do it. Everybody can do this. It's the difficulty of an instrument like piano with so many notes and so many manual abilities that I think it's more that one can do it and another one cannot do it. On the oboe, we all can breathe;

the proof is that we are here. We learned how to breathe on the first day of our life and this you have naturally. It's useful just knowing that we are big and the reed is small and that between us and the reed there should be a transition. One can figure this out; another needs a teacher to say how to do it and what not to do and use exercises. It can be learned.

On Starting Oboists

I think the oboe didactic is quite behind others generally. We have exercises, studies, and method books starting in C major and F major and then G major. It comes from the piano. By the time the people get to the left D♯ or E♭, the hand position is already fixed. It is maybe the third- or fourth-year pieces in more complicated tonalities and then they don't know where this damn key is. So this should be first. It's not more difficult to play the long notes that you do in the beginning and integrate the left E♭ position. We should not start in C major. The oboe is not a piano. It does not have black and white keys. The black keys are really more complicated; first you master the white ones. It's a piano didactic that we have. On oboe you can have completely high hand position and you can play C major. Play B major or C♯ major—it costs the same, same price. Then your hand position is exactly right for everything—also for C major. There I think the oboe didactic is a little bit behind.

On the violin, you can see everything. I read this book by Galamian about violin technique and it's fascinating. You can really see as a non–violin player what is good position, what is bad, why it's good, and how to move the hand. They have an advantage in that you can see it. On the oboe you cannot see anything so we have to be inventive and to make bridges.

One of the great things about my teacher (also Holliger's teacher at the time) was that he impressed good hand position from the beginning. He said that I would not use the pinky keys for a while but I needed to touch them at all times. It is problematic when students start with only using one finger and the others so far away.

On Reed Making

I don't really talk about reed making in lessons because I don't have fifteen-year-old children in lessons. I have grown-up persons in the university study and I don't take care how they make the reed. That must be learned by somebody in another moment, another stage, and also I'm not good at it. I was never good in reed making so I had to learn how to play on all kinds of reeds. When I spent fifteen minutes with one reed that didn't work, and I tried to make it work for my air and to improve my dominance of the reed, I learned something. I used the opportunity to get better. When I spent those fifteen minutes with the knife to make the reed easier, then I have a reed that is maybe better but I'm not better. From then on, any time something doesn't work then it's, "Oh the reed, the reed, the reed." When you've got your concert, you've got to take the best reed. And of course on a better reed you can make a better concert. But a better oboist on the same reed probably makes more difference. If you get to be a better oboist, sometimes a reed is too bright and you need to learn how to play dark on it. A reed speaks late and you learn how to make it speak fast, or a reed is very aggressive and direct and you learn how to make it soft through your blowing. It feels like going out with your dog and the dog is doing what you say and not like you are the dog and the reed is the one that tells you what to do.

In the splitting of the activities on the oboe, consider the reed being part of the instrument and a fixed part like for flute. Imagine you have glue on it and it's the only reed and it's for the rest of your life and you have to learn how to play on it. I lost a lot of time as a student saying, "Oh, let's just take a little bit," and then at the end you destroy the reed because you take too much off. You go: "Ah, it was much better before." And you've lost the time for your study and you've lost also the reed. It's not always like that but when you have reed making time, this is not practicing time. And when you have practicing time, it's not reed making time. I decide I'm going to practice on those two reeds. I put one in water and one I play, and when the reed is tired, I take the other one and I go on. I don't want to think at all about reeds because otherwise I cannot grow in the music or in the blowing, in the embouchure, or in the dominance of what I want to do. Then at the concert I take a better reed and everything is more beautiful but it is not necessary that I spend part of my practicing time with a knife in my hand. I think it's a mistake people make.

Some teachers, they are very good in reed making; from them you should learn how so that is not so complicated. I am not one of those people. When they come to me, I say, "On the first day I can say a few things about reed making if you ask me," but I don't want to lose a lot of time in the lesson for this because my specialties are other ones. If you are in big trouble, seek another student, seek another teacher that helps you with that or attend courses. If the students want to use the practicing time to get better, they should decide on which reed they will practice and then put all the others and the knives away in the other room and then take this and say okay, this is my instrument. Accept how it is and not have the thought to change the instrument all the time; don't change the rules. How can you change then your inside dominance? One meter is one meter so if you want to measure your playing, you should measure it with the same meter which is the reed; it's a meter. It's measuring your ability to dominate the air and if when you want to try to improve you change the reed, one meter is 120 centimeters then it is eighty. Then you cannot get really much better so fast. The quintessence of this is don't mix the things. The reed is important—very important for me too—but what you can do on the oboe, your air control, and your dominance, and also what you can do in the music, it should be quite independent of that because the reed will change. When you go from one place to other, you have a different reed. It's a fact.

On Working with the Reed Alone

In those exercises with the reeds you saw today, sometimes I take an old reed and a new reed and we do the exercises—one and then the other and we try to be equal so the difference is not the reed. When your dominance is very big, you get a sound with this reed and you get the same sound with the other reed. But when your dominance is not so big, it's like trying the reed: "Ah, this is like that and this is like that," and so it's not affirmative playing. If you have two reeds, one a bit new and one a bit old, which is actually the reality—you will have always a newer and the new is always too new and the old is always too old. Every oboist in the world agrees I think, so learn how to play on both. This is good practice because it's the reality of oboe.

The reed-alone exercises are my invention. My students are all over the world and use them also in teaching. I tell them there's no copyright on it. [Laughter] I had the idea when I was in the orchestra and I saw the brass players always come with a mouthpiece and I saw they needed it for building up the lip and for the control. I thought, yeah that's a good idea. We should do that also. Especially since for us the reed is more of a mystery than the mouthpiece is for the brass players. The mouthpiece, it's safe. Once you've found one that works, it works exactly the same here than somewhere else but our reed is very relative.

On Language

In observing Mr. Indermühle's master classes, two things struck me strongly: the fact that he played from memory (or by ear) every piece the students were working on and never once looked at the part. And the fact that he conducted his master classes in all the various native languages of the students: English, Italian, Spanish, French, German, and Japanese. I inquired what other languages he spoke:

Well there aren't any Dutch students here but I speak it because I lived 15 years in Amsterdam. I don't speak Portuguese well, but well enough for lessons. More or less I can't really speak well other languages but for the lessons I can mostly come through.

A Sampling of Mr. Indermühle's Reed-Alone Exercises as observed by Michele Fiala

- The students started in a group by playing a long tone on the reed alone with no crescendo or diminuendo and maintaining the same pitch and a good quality.
- When they achieved that, they played short notes on the reed while humming.
- Next they played "D♯, D, C♯, c" on the reed, trying not to use their hands
- Also without hands, at a piano dynamic they played "C♯, D, C♯, C, C♯."
- They practiced double-tonguing on the reed alone.
- 8 staccato notes on each pitch in the "C♯, D, C♯, C, C♯" pattern.
- Mr. Indermühle played entire melodies on the reed, taking the reed in and out using only his lips (no hand), and demonstrated flutter tongue.*

*Author's note: On my American long-scrape reeds, these exercises come out a half-step lower than presented here (i.e., C♯ becomes C, etc).—MF

13

Eugene Izotov

Eugene Izotov is currently the principal oboist of the San Francisco Symphony. He previously served as the principal oboist of the Metropolitan Opera and principal oboist of the Chicago Symphony. He won top prizes at solo competitions in Saint Petersburg (1991), Moscow (1990), New York (1995), and at the Fernand Gillet International Competition (2001). Izotov has appeared over fifty times as soloist with the Chicago Symphony Orchestra, Boston Symphony, San Francisco Symphony, Met Chamber Ensemble, Pacific Music Festival Orchestra, and others. He has recorded for Sony Classical, BMG, Boston Records, Elektra, CSOResound, and SFSMedia. Izotov teaches at the San Francisco Conservatory, Music Academy of the West, Pacific Music Festival, and previously served on the faculty of the Juilliard School and DePaul University. Born in Moscow, Izotov studied at the Gnessin School of Music with Ivan Pushechnikov and Sergey Velikanov and at Boston University School of Fine Arts with Ralph Gomberg. This interview was conducted by Michele Fiala at Izotov's house in Oak Park, Illinois, in January 2009 and was updated in October 2018.

Early Career

When I was twelve or thirteen, I had this silly notion that I would be an oboe soloist and I would be playing all these incredible concertos and fantastic pieces, just like the violinists and the pianists do, in front of great orchestras of the world. And then somebody posed a very simple and absolutely life-altering question to me, which was, "Well, what are you going to be playing? How many Mozart concertos do you have? What do you have in your repertoire?" At that point I very quickly realized, well, really not much. The more time I spent in orchestra—student orchestras and then professional

Great Oboists on Music and Musicianship. Michele L. Fiala and Martin Schuring, Oxford University Press (2021).

orchestras—I realized that I don't have to "settle" for being in the great orchestra. It was a dream to play in the great orchestra because of the way oboe writing goes in symphonic repertoire. It is extraordinarily rich and beautiful, soloistic, and it explores every possible variety of musical expression, something that I would not be able to do with solo repertoire.

National Schools

I think there is still a great divide between what we call the "American School" of oboe playing and the "European School" of oboe playing. That's really funny because what we mean by American School of oboe playing is so many different things and styles. Some of them have nothing to do with each other. There's an ocean of music that's being made here and in Europe. I arrived here [in the] late twentieth century. I feel so old saying this, but things have changed. Since I came here, I was completely impressed by the overall quality of tone production that is so predominant in this country. People are totally focused on it and I fell in love immediately with what was referred to as the American tone of the oboe, whatever that means. It's beautiful, and at the same time I found that many of my fellow students and some professionals seemed to forget that, while it's absolutely crucial to have a beautiful tone, that is really not the end result. A beautiful tone is absolutely necessary to make music; it is a fundamental tool of any kind of expression. You cannot be a great player and have a tone that would limit your musicality, so that's absolutely crucial. But a beautiful tone is only the beginning, and it seemed to be the end result for so many people that I met in this country. They never seemed to get past the instrumental, technical aspect of playing the oboe, limited to what gouge do you use? What is the curvature of your piece of cane? What is the shaper tip and how do you sharpen your knives? All these technical things that are crucial and necessary; I'm not overlooking them at all. But this is really not what this is all about. It seems to be the endpoint and in Europe I would say that it is really quite the opposite. The people from day one are playing concertos, they're playing sonatas, they're playing recitals, they're developing their technique. By technique I don't just mean the ability to move fingers quickly. I mean the ability to control vibrato, nuances, articulations, entrances, releases of notes, general range of expression, in other words, "chops." As a result, their playing is ultimately less inhibited. It is really more about what kind of story can you tell.

It is a generalization and of course there are vast exceptions to those rules. But I really found this to be a great contrast in the early nineties that a lot of my fellow colleagues in Europe would just overlook the very concept of tone, just make music with whatever reed you have. And I would come here and it would all be about reeds and tone, tone, tone, and nothing else. So that was the great divide and I think that's finally changing. We have a tremendous wealth of tradition in this country, in America, with great players who were here before. But we also have the opportunity to go beyond this commitment to instrumental things and to perhaps get more expressive and to get more artistic, more about music, and less about the oboe. That's happening in general.

I think that's why American oboe playing is no longer limited to particular camps, to particularly important cities in America. It is more of a question of stylistic and artistic variety because there are so many players now that don't sound much like their teachers. They sound like themselves, with the very clear understanding that they have been taught and inspired by their teacher, but they really have done something new with what they learned from them. That is something that is very exciting, and that is something that will further American oboe playing.

Audition Advice

People sometimes forget that winning an audition is one thing; keeping a job is another thing. In the process of hopefully both stages of establishing a career—in other words, first winning an audition, then keeping the job—you have to show a variety of musical tools, musical things, and it is not limited to how full and stable your middle C is going to be or how your low C♯ is not going to be flat or how the A♮ in the second octave is not going to be unstable. I as an oboist am aware of all these things and I know how difficult it is to achieve them, but this isn't something that is going to make it or break it for you in the real world. Certain things are very impressive at an IDRS [International Double Reed Society] conference because the audience knows how difficult is to play the entire exposition of the Strauss Oboe Concerto without breathing. While that might impress somebody there, it not only not-impresses anybody at a real audition, but you have to wonder why is it that you have to do these acrobatic, technical things. Is it for the sake of the music? That's the main question. Everything has to be for the sake of the music. In an audition you have about seven minutes to show what you have, both as a performer and as an instrumentalist. An audition is when you have to impress the most people in the least amount of time. That's how it is.

It's easier to win jobs in a great orchestra, in a way, because in the great orchestra you're playing for the musicians who are hopefully looking for things that are truly artistic and if you miss a note they will give you the benefit of the doubt. They will look not only for what you are, but for what you could be in the future. I would not worry as a young kid starting out about how difficult it is to earn a job. I would focus on trying to be artistic, trying to be musical, trying to be in control of the instrument.

There are some very, very common mistakes that a lot of people make. I continue to serve on one audition committee after another and it is truly amazing how common the following mistakes are: bad rhythm, bad intonation, and, even more common, lack of dynamic range. If anybody would concentrate on having good rhythm, flawless intonation, and having a dynamic range, that would already separate that person from, I would say, 95 percent of the people that come to auditions. It is really amazing. Then there is of course the question of "beautiful tone." We can sit here all day and I can try to describe to you in words what that is. My colleague David McGill in his book, *Sound in Motion*, in the first few pages is talking about how he was in the train somewhere and he heard this phrase, "Talking about music is like dancing about architecture." I cannot describe to you what good tone is. I can try, but ultimately it will fail. In Russian we say, "Music begins where words end." That's about right.

Let's just say that we have a similar idea on the area of what good oboe tone is. What happens in auditions is this: somebody comes in and they start playing, and then I find myself making the following comment (because obviously a tone is one of the very first things that you notice about a player). So I might write down, "Bad tone," because I simply don't like it. Then it's discouraging, then it's difficult to recover after that. But there are cases where I write, "Beautiful tone," and at that point I say, "OK, now what? What is the story that person is going to with that beautiful voice?" James Levine is full of wonderful quotes about tone. To those who think that tone is really unimportant—the only thing that matters is what you do with it—he says, "Well, let's talk about singers. Would you ever ask: what do you think of this singer, you know, voice aside?" Right? It would never happen. Clearly it's important. But in an audition, once the committee is sure that this person has a beautiful voice, then you have this great responsibility to deliver a meaningful musical statement with it and if they don't then it's all the more frustrating. Then it remains the only comment after the audition: "Beautiful tone, BUT . . ." Sometimes there's nothing else after that. It is so important to remember that musicians tend to be impressed by musical things, not by instrumental things.

Keeping an Orchestra Job

You have to count your rests and you have to be aware of the overall orchestral texture that sometimes you are a part of and other times you are the leading voice in it. A lot of those things are very basic and they have to do with knowing your part, knowing the music, following the conductor, following your role in the ensemble. More importantly, keeping the job has very much to do not only with what kind of player you are, but it has vastly to do with what kind of colleague you are because you are playing in an ensemble of people. It is very simple. All the jokes aside, like the hatred against a conductor, all those jokes about violists and trumpet players being obnoxious and the oboe players being the bandits of the orchestra and all this stuff. There's a fantastic Fellini movie about an orchestral rehearsal because an orchestra is a little model of society and it's a very fascinating one. But it all comes down to this: you have to make the effort to be a true citizen of the orchestra, as a player, colleague, and with an awareness that sometimes you have a leading role, and sometimes a supporting role. No matter what chair you're playing in—especially being a wind player, sometimes you sit second or third—but above all you're a part of the music.

When you're playing second oboe, you are the principal second oboist in that orchestra. You are responsible for one part that is entirely your part, and if you don't come to work, the concert is canceled. When you're playing a supporting instrument, which may not be the dream of every oboe player, you really have to appreciate the fact that you are a solo or one-on-a-part player in that particular part because you are responsible for one individual voice that is frequently a prominent solo voice. It is a passing tone or that special note in the chord that signifies a tonality. You can bring something really special to the overall sound of the section and when it comes to ensemble playing, it takes everyone to build something wonderful and it takes one person to destroy it. As long as you are aware of these things, keeping a job is just as easy as being a good colleague as well as a good player.

Teaching Philosophy

I want my students to be artists, not instrumentalists. That's a very broad statement and a lot of people abuse that statement because sometimes they think that being an artist overlooks and supersedes any kind of basic instrumental concern. That's very much not true. We oboists have two professions: we have to be carpenters in the reed-room and magicians on the stage. It's often difficult to combine these two worlds, because it's a constant battle between technology and artistry. It sometimes gets to me that I have to sit at home up to hours per day as I make reeds, sharpen knives, calibrate gouging equipment, and then I show up to work and I see a string player take their instrument out of the case and start playing.

On the other hand, I realize how fortunate we are to have so many opportunities to shine in the orchestra writing with all those incredibly beautiful oboe solos. And also, after all that work and suffering at the reed desk, there is an amazing sense of accomplishment in knowing that you have created your own unique voice with your bare hands. And unlike most string players, we don't have to make that incredibly difficult choice between having a great-sounding instrument or a mortgage on a really nice house!

When *Time* magazine did the profile on the Gomberg brothers—1953, I think—Harold Gomberg, my teacher's brother, said that an oboe player must have the tenacity of a bull and the sensitivity of Alice in Wonderland. Those two are necessary all the time to do what we do. We have to be able to switch gears from dealing with hundredths of a millimeter, not to mention all those cuts, and the cleaning the sharpening stones, and the oiling the bush bearings and the gouger and sharpening blades and all this hardly glamorous stuff. And then we have to be artists, and by that I mean that the moment you start playing, even if you're playing a Barret etude, even if you're playing a D major scale, you should really play it in the way that is artistic, that is musical, as if you were playing it on the stage of a concert hall in performance. You cannot be a student in the morning and an artist in the evening; it just doesn't work like that. You're either artistic all the time or not at all. That is a very difficult commitment and the hardest thing for me with a student is to find that balance between the instrumental details—gouging, reed making, and spending enough time on the playing—because it's very easy to get carried away. That is something that you have to measure every day and find that balance. It is very difficult.

If you look at the amount of time that I spend with every student, we spend roughly twenty-six hours per year with every given student. They get to see me twenty-six hours per year times two; that's all the time they see me. Then they're going to go home and that's when they have to be their own best teachers. That's really more important because we cannot be responsible for what they do by themselves.

All we can hope to do as teachers is to inspire them, give them the tools, show them the way. Unfortunately, and maybe fortunately, that's all we can do. And then it takes great initiative and self-control and discipline and ultimately commitment on behalf of each student to develop that advice into something that will be truly their own. Because, aside from some major stylistic differences, in music there's not one right way. I think there are wrong ways, but there's definitely more than one right way in music. That is what's so truly unique and wonderful about our profession. It is really up to the student to figure that out.

Support/Embouchure

While music is a universal language and everybody seems to connect easily through music, in order to find the right connection between people in regards to some very physical things (like the right amount of pressure from stomach and the embouchure in the right position), all of that already differs based on every person because everybody's physiology is different. I simply don't think that one rule applies to everybody. You have to find the right position of the reed and the embouchure for every single student. To show an illustration of a picture-perfect embouchure and say, "Make it look like that," is wrong. It is undoubtedly going to work for some people and it is just as undoubtedly not going to work for other people. The basic rule that is more important and more general is if it sounds good, it is right. It's a question of developing the concept of what that person wants to sound like and that's why, rather than concentrating on the amount of pressure that's necessary from here to lips, I would rather have them listen to me or many of my counterparts who play beautifully and have the concept in the ears of the student to see, "This is what I'm trying to sound like." I will of course help them with some very basic guidelines in every regard, from the gouge, the reed itself, the basic position and the embouchure, overall pressure, the flexibility, etc.

The wonderful thing about the oboe is that every note sounds different, has a different quality. The terrible thing about the oboe is that every note sounds different and has a different quality. It allows for the possibility to build something extraordinary, to change one interval, just two notes slurred, even one note sometimes, and change color on it, change the vibrato, change the intensity, change the basic quality of the note so much that it will be truly exotic and expressive, or not. It is up to the player to figure that out. Barenboim told me right when I started, "On the piano you can never play one beautiful note. You can only play two beautiful notes on the piano." On the oboe you can play one beautiful note! It is a question of how it sounds and then it's a question of how you get there. It is not the other way around. It is a question of finding the right concept, something that's very difficult for a lot of oboists to do. Find the light at the end of the tunnel and then you have to walk there. It's a metaphor that works in so many cases and in moments of our lives.

Reeds

The gouge is so important. A lot of people spend years on trying to make a good reed on a bad gouge and then they pick up a lot of bad habits. I use mostly John Ferrillo gougers and I use the modified Innoledy gouger, which, by modified I mean making it thicker on the sides so that it's a stronger gouge, gives you a deeper tone. It's very easy to use that machine. It's kind of crazy, the whole idea to gouge dry, but it can work. So those are the two ones that I use mainly and there are obviously other ones. Here's a Tabuteau quote for you, "Beware of thin sides." That is just so true. I've paid my dues on having an incorrect micrometer. This is perhaps worth mentioning, that while we're being carpenters and technicians in the process of reed making, you really have to make sure that you have the right measuring equipment. It is important to have the correct micrometer, the right mandrel for the tube and such. Very basic things that can really cause great problems down the line. We have enough trouble dealing with crappy cane. Definitely I would rather have a good gouge and a bad piece of cane than the other way around because if I have a good gouge and a bad piece of cane I will make you an OK reed. If I have a great piece of cane and a bad gouge, it's just not going to work.

One of the things that I learned at the Met very quickly, and it is a very specific technical thing, is a question of pitch stability. I learned that I am not going to be able to play a six-hour Wagner opera after a three-hour morning rehearsal of *Bohème*, after two hours in the afternoon of chamber music in Carnegie Hall or teaching at Juilliard, on a flat or unstable reed. I'm going to die after that. It would not only kill me, it would kill any kind of hope for having a deep, round, full tone, because when you're biting, that's all you get. You compact the tone, it becomes more confining, it is less interesting, and ultimately it makes your playing more labored. You get less and less able to be artistic and free and it's a really bad deal. That's when I had to come up with a setup that would be stable and that would have enough color in the tone but would not require major adjustments for pitch. Being in the Met Orchestra, in terms of the endurance and number of hours that's necessary on that job, and also being surrounded by such great players, of course Elaine Douvas, all of that forced me to find something better. That's when I embarked upon my search for the perfect gouge. I have yet to find it but I found something that works very well.

John Ferrillo's gouger works well for me because he figured out the right curve to make the gouge very deep and very full and very strong, but at the same time it vibrates. A lot of people confuse having something to blow against, having that kind of resistance in the reed, with having a big tone, and that's completely not true. That is very misleading. There are two basic, specific things involved with reed making: stability and flexibility. Those two are very hard to combine, but it's necessary. If you have one or the other, it doesn't work.

Warming Up

Warming up is important. I live in a four-season place. I always have to deal with some sort of a problem weather-wise. It's either cold and dry or it's hot and humid and then the air-conditioning comes in. At the same time, I deal with reeds, which are so delicate and the cane is very sensitive, and of course the oboe itself. You have to warm up both the oboe and yourself. As basic, as unglamorous as it sounds, playing long tones is a really great way to do it. But it is not just the question of blowing into the oboe and holding the note until you pass out. It is a question of having control. I think of every long note, every long tone like a mini solo. I love to play solos; it is a fabulous part of being a principal oboist. If you're playing an A—an important enough note for oboe—as the first note of a warm-up, you really have to approach it as if it's the first note in a Brahms Symphony. It has to come in with beautiful attack, then it has to be controlled flawlessly in a full dynamic. Not a fortissimo, but I don't think there's any point in warming up with pianissimo dynamic. Full tone. Maybe vibrato, maybe not. And a beautifully controlled release. That way you exercise not just your lungs or your lips, but the actual control.

Legato

There's something that has become especially important to me during my ten years with the Chicago Symphony, which is arguably America's most Germanic-sounding orchestra based on its history and traditions. Its massive sound combined with the extremely dry acoustics of Orchestra Hall, made me realize the importance of being able to connect the intervals between the notes and provide both a more significant presence in the orchestra as well as a sense of a seamless beautiful connection. Playing with legato is important anyway because it is something that emulates the sound of the human voice. In order to have legato in your playing, this is something that is achieved not only by your air column, not only the positions and the adjustments between the intervals that have to happen in your lips, but this is something that is also accomplished by your fingers. I call it legato fingers. If you're just blowing your oboe and carelessly moving your fingers around, you will not get a smooth connection, and that's something that a lot of people forget. It's very easy to just be aware of it. All of these things are very difficult to talk about and sometimes they're even difficult to grasp right away. But the good thing about all of these things that we talked about is that once you understand what they are and once you start paying attention to them, all of a sudden, they just become a part of how you play and they happen naturally. That's the wonderful thing about it. At first it is a conceptual idea and you try to focus your practicing and your playing on it, but then all of a sudden it just becomes how you play.

Inspirations

We are musicians, not oboists. We can learn so much from other musicians. I learned a tremendous amount from so many players. Jascha Heifetz, because the way you combine such high intensity of expression with flawless technique and at the same time the playing is really for the sake of music; the dark, intense, full sound and the absolute, immediate, perfectly controlled adjustments in the tiniest amount of time happen. It is just uncanny.

It's wonderful and so useful that string players try to think of breathing and we often think of bowing when we play. Of course everybody thinks of singers when we think of the most perfect and natural way to make music, even though some singers, well, think of nobody else but themselves! But, you know, that's just the way it goes. My time in opera influenced me in every possible way. Because every instrument, no matter how technically flawless it is and how well it is designed, is still not as perfect as the human voice because that is the perfect instrument. Being able to hear Plácido Domingo, René Pape, Susan Graham, every other day, at first it was both thrilling and kind of depressing because you're overcome with this immense joy and frustration that you just cannot possibly emulate that kind of beauty. But then you learn to find ways to bring that kind of expression to what you do. And what we do is something very special. The oboe has a very unique voice, a very exotic voice, and the great composers, they really use it wisely. Even Hollywood has figured out that the oboe communicates sorrow really well. Whenever there's a love story and something goes wrong, in Hollywood that's where you hear the oboe solo. If you hear the English horn, both in Hollywood and opera, somebody's going to die! That is absolutely guaranteed—bad news if you hear it. But seriously, the oboe is also capable of a variety of emotions.

On an instrument like the piano, where they cannot sustain or cannot use vibrato, it is really amazing how somebody like Murray Perahia is able to sustain, seemingly float this beautiful, ravishing legato phrase like that in a second movement of a Mozart piano concerto. I learned from that tremendously because it is really interesting to see how any singer or instrumentalist sounds up close and then if you hear their records, it is really very different. When you're playing on a stage, I always found it very different, very fascinating how I would listen to my recordings of a broadcast or something after a performance and how different it would sound to me. It would not sound different only in tone, because that could be adjusted by knobs and all that stuff. But our sense of timing as performers is very unique on the stage. Our sense of dynamics is very unique and I learned, not just from musicians, but I learned from actors. It is really interesting to see theater. I do not mean Broadway; I mean an actual theater. The way they deal with time and volume, they project intensity, certainly not in decibels but they use time to communicate that sort of expression and intensity. If you hear an actor up close, the way the voice resonates, sometimes it is really too much. But you have to re-member that whatever you're projecting into the audience is for the sake of the audience. It is not for here; it is for there. And that is a concept that is very important to remember in both auditions and real life, in the performance.

My dear friend and conductor in the San Francisco Symphony, Michael Tilson Thomas, he learned this from his grandmother, who was Bessie Thomashefsky, this great, great Broadway superstar in those days, it was re-ally huge. She took him on the stage once when he was a teenager and she pointed to the exit signs, the very, very far end of the hall. She said, "Do you see those exit signs?" Yes. "The people who are sitting out there paid the least amount of money for the tickets, but they care about the show the most. Make sure that whatever you do here is obvious to them. You have to aim for the exit signs." This does not mean that everybody should be playing every-thing louder, absolutely not. It just means that you have to exaggerate your expression so that it carries across and it goes the distance. So your pianos are softer, your fortes are louder, your climaxes are more apparent. If you're playing something cold, it really has to be absolutely still and if it's something hot, it should be just burning with passion. That's the only way it is going to come across. It's a general rule in "show business," but we are artists, we are on the stage, and we have to bring something to people who come there, to a symphony concert, to an opera concert, to theater, whatever it is, something that they often don't get to experience in everyday life—something that is truly magical. Whatever analogy you would use, we must always bring our audiences something that is out of the ordinary.

14

Sarah Jeffrey

Sarah Jeffrey is principal oboe of the Toronto Symphony Orchestra. A regular soloist with the TSO, Jeffrey has also appeared as soloist with numerous orchestras across Canada, performing works by Bach, Mozart, Vaughan Williams, Marcello, Haydn, and Mozetich. She is also an active recitalist and chamber musician; making frequent guest appearances with the Amici Chamber Ensemble, the ARC Ensemble, and Trio Arkel. A devoted performer of new music, Jeffrey has commissioned several chamber works, including Chaconne for Oboe, Horn, and Piano by Erik Ross, and Rhapsody by Ronald Royer. Jeffrey is a recipient of the Ontario Arts Council's Chalmers Award for Creativity and Excellence in the Arts. Jeffrey is on faculty at the Glenn Gould School at the Royal Conservatory and the University of Toronto and spends her summers at the Orford Arts Centre and the National Youth Orchestra of Canada. This interview was conducted by Michele Fiala in June 2018.

Start in Music

My parents are both musicians; my mother is a pianist and my father plays horn. Naturally, I began on both violin and piano at the age of three. I loved the piano, but never really found my voice on the violin. I was never very good, never really practiced, and after years of it began to beg my parents to quit. But I *loved* music, did lots of dancing and sang in a wonderful choir so I always knew it was in me.

My dad is a wind ensemble conductor, and after years of hearing me beg to quit the violin, my parents agreed that I would make a good oboist given that I had a good ear and suggested that I pick up the oboe if they let me quit the violin. I quickly discovered that being one of only a few oboists in a school or an orchestra presented many more opportunities and gained much more

Great Oboists on Music and Musicianship. Michele L. Fiala and Martin Schuring, Oxford University Press (2021). © Oxford University Press. DOI: 10.1093/oso/9780190915094.001.0001.

attention than always being at the back of the second violins! I knew that I had found my "voice."

North American Styles

I studied at the University of Toronto and at the New England Conservatory for my master's and at Tanglewood. Being Canadian, I found it profoundly important to immerse myself as a student in the American music scene. It is a much bigger scene with so many more people, and it gives you a sense of what the expectations are, and therefore what the stakes are. I went to as many concerts as I possibly could to hear as many sounds and ideas as I could soak in. I woke up hours earlier to practice when everyone was practicing and stayed as late as everyone else was. It was a different level of expectation. As a teacher in Canada, I do encourage young Canadians to study in the States, but mostly to not feel like [a] big fish in a small pond, and to take advantage of all there is on the continent. One's eyes and ears must be completely overwhelmed at this stage in the game.

As far as a national school, there isn't one. Almost all of the teachers in Canada, except for a few, studied with the great American masters: John de Lancie, John Mack, Ray Still, Robert Bloom, Ralph Gomberg, and more recently Richard Woodhams, Elaine Douvas, [and] Eugene Izotov, to name a few. There are people in the province of Quebec who studied with European teachers and have kept that style of playing, but in general it is the American School.

Warming Up

My warm-up routine is gold to me. It keeps me grounded and focused and consistent and fresh. I do a warm-up every day. I am married to a horn player and have learned the value of practicing consistency and spending daily time on fundamentals. It is the long game, and boy does it pay off. A little bit every day pays off, big time!

First, I move my air and focus on my general set-up, which means slow scale patterns which I change up, concentrating my embouchure set-up, body set-up (namely my posture and fingers), and my air. Next, I play long tones, focusing on the reed beginning a note as softly and smoothly as possibly, a seamless spin in my air and vibrato, as big a contrast in dynamics as possible, and as elegant and delicious a taper as I can make. This improves one's reed making tremendously as well. Then I move on to some fast finger motions, such as trills or other Gillet-related exercises for fast "action" in the fingers. Following that, articulation exercises for clean tongue action, consistency, and coordination. And to put it all together, an etude or two!

Reeds

Bar none, my priority in reed making is to make a reed that has the following, in the following order:

1. Balance: tip and plateau vibrate together so as to not have one more pronounced or inhibiting the other in any way (not a spitty or tippy tip, or a tubby plateau that doesn't vibrate).
2. Response: the reed must respond when I want it to, and exactly how I want it to (from the corners—projecting a dark and delicious ppp sound from the corners of the tip at any range of the instrument during my long tones).
3. Intonation: a good scale, the flexibility to color different degrees of different scales as needed. I.e., an F will be in three different colors depending on which scale: F major, B♭ major or D minor.

When all three of those things are happening, the tone will be just right! Happens each and every time—almost!

Learning Technical Passages

Slow work first, seamless integration of notes, and careful finger work or coordination with articulation, followed by very short bursts of quick action to practice the *action*.

Improving Articulation

Slow and steady, and consistency up to fast. Listening for a relaxed, but controlled action.

Inspirations

I am tremendously inspired by different artists for different reasons, so I try to incorporate many of them into my listening to achieve everything that I want in a passage! For instance: the silkiness of John Mack's tone, blended with Francois Leleux's unbelievable facility and lightness; Eugene Izotov's richness of tone, and Jonathan Kelly's endless vocal phrases. Alex Klein's bravura, and Gordon Hunt's singing vibrato! So many artists offer so many ideas; pick and choose what you hear and what you can try to emulate to find the process of what makes them play like they do!

15

Richard Killmer

Professor of oboe at the Eastman School of Music, Richard Killmer was principal oboist of the St. Paul Chamber Orchestra for eleven years. In 1960, Killmer received a BA in music education from Colorado State College (now the University of Northern Colorado), where he studied with William Gower. Upon graduation, he became orchestra director of the Longmont, Colorado, public schools, a post he held until entering the US Army in 1962. During his three years in the army he was principal oboist with the NORAD Band and baritone saxophonist in the NORAD Commander's Dance Band. After the completion of his service duty, Killmer attended the Yale School of Music, where he studied oboe with Robert Bloom and received his MM, MMA, and DMA degrees. This interview was conducted by Michele Fiala in December 2011 in Mr. Killmer's studio at the Eastman School of Music and was updated in November 2018.

Early Career

I started music lessons when I was in the second grade in Garland, Texas. I sang in a choir and took piano lessons. I have a twin brother and in the fifth grade when we had the chance to select our instruments, he chose flute and I chose clarinet. For a week or two, I tried the oboe and the band director had given me an oboe with this full-of-lipstick reed, just a grotesque thing. I got the fingerings and then played it in the band to try it out but when I took it home my mother just recently had given birth to one of my brothers and he was not well. He was having some tough times and she and he needed to sleep. She said, "Get that thing out of the house!" So I took it back and then we moved.

My father was in the army and was called back during the Korean War, and we moved to El Paso. I was playing clarinet in the junior high band which

Great Oboists on Music and Musicianship. Michele L. Fiala and Martin Schuring, Oxford University Press (2021). © Oxford University Press. DOI: 10.1093/oso/9780190915094.001.0001.

was conducted by the orchestra teacher who was a cellist. He recruited my brother and myself to play cello and two of the other band members—a clarinet player and a baritone horn player—to play bass and we started playing string instruments. I was in the third clarinet section and he said, "Does anyone want to play oboe?" I said, "Ok, I'll play oboe." So the eighth grade was when I started the oboe and then studied with the orchestra teacher and then studied with my band director. The band director played first bassoon in the El Paso Symphony and a fellow named Richard Henderson had just recently come to town to teach theory and composition at Texas Western College, which is now the University of Texas, El Paso. He had studied oboe; he had been a saxophone player but he was mainly a theory guy. He was the new principal oboe of the orchestra. My band director said, "Why don't you go meet Richard Henderson?" I went to take my first lesson and he said, "How would you like to play second oboe in the El Paso Symphony?" So I started as a high school kid playing with my teacher in the El Paso Symphony. He was in fact the father of Rebecca Henderson, who's a very well known oboe teacher [now retired from the University of Texas Austin]. She did her graduate study here so we kept it in the family, so to speak. Her father passed away but he was a wonderful man and a great influence. He and I had just a great time as a kid playing in the orchestra with no thought of ever being a professional oboe player.

I had no place to go to college. I had been invited to go to Oberlin by David Robertson, who was the orchestra conductor there. At the time my father was in the army and he had just been transferred to San Antonio. He had already moved down there and my mother was trying to hold our family together in El Paso so my brother and I could graduate from high school. Bill Gower called me—I had met him at a summer music festival—and he said, "Are you going to Oberlin?" I said, "No, I can't afford Oberlin." I didn't even apply. I didn't know about applying to college. I didn't know anything about that stuff. He said, "Well, come to Greeley." So I got on a bus with $90 in my pocket and went to Greeley. I started in the summer band and then was there for four years although I did my student teaching my senior year in Longmont, Colorado, and then was hired to take the job that I was student teaching. My mentor Kenny Evans—who's also an oboist—was going to Iowa to get a PhD.

I took the Longmont job and I had that for two years, during which time I played in community orchestras a variety of instruments: viola, cello, oboe, contrabass clarinet (as substitute for contrabassoon), and so forth. When I was in Longmont and I taught, I had the whole string program. We started the program the summer between fourth and fifth grade. We had three schools; we had the sixth grade orchestra—sixth, seventh, and eighth, and then the high school. It was a town of 13,000 people at the time. I had one hundred string players. We had a seventy-piece junior orchestra and a sixty-piece high school orchestra, and it was something else. It was really good. I loved it and I would have stayed except the army came along and took me away from that. I even thought about going back to that after I had finished the army. That was one of the options but the oboe was gnawing at me. It's like a virus that you catch that you can never get rid of.

I loved teaching in Longmont. I loved that public school experience and I wouldn't have traded that for all the money in the world. I wouldn't have traded going to Greeley, which was Colorado State College of Education when I went there. Now it's the University of Northern Colorado. I'm proud to be a music educator. My philosophy is wherever you are, if you turn that into the best thing in the world that you can be doing at the time, there will be other opportunities. In the meantime, if there aren't, you are happy where you are. If you're waiting for something good to happen and not taking care of where you are, it's not going to happen.

I met my wife [of over 50 years who passed away in 2016] in a community orchestra in Denver. I went into the army and during that time met professional musicians both from New York and Hollywood. I really enjoyed playing but I didn't know which instrument I would play, whether I would go to Hollywood and be a doubler or whether I would go to Yale. I had been accepted into Yale to study oboe with Robert Bloom. My wife said, "I could relate to you best as an oboe player," because her father was manager of the Dallas Symphony at that time. She said, "That seems like the right thing." I said, "Yeah, but I'm no good. I don't think I can do that." But she said, "Well it seems to me that's what you should do."

I valued my teachers Bill Gower and Dave Abosch when I was in the army. David Abosch was the principal oboe in Denver who replaced my teacher Bill Gower in the Denver Symphony. Wonderful influence on me while I was in the army, and he helped me decide that I wanted to play the oboe. He played a huge role in that encouraging. I said, "Well, I have to give it a try. I have to see where it goes." I just did it. I never said, "What if it doesn't work? What if I can't get a job?" I was so naïve. I never thought about that. I just said, "Ok, here we go; I'm going to work," and good things happened.

I went to Yale. At the end of the two years we both were hired by the Oklahoma City Symphony. It was our first job. I was there three years and went back to school to do the MMA, which led to the DMA at Yale and then I got the St. Paul Chamber Orchestra job. I was there eleven years, loved it, and then this job came open. I said, "I have to. I can't wait another 45 years," because Robert Sprenkle had been here 45 years. I said, "I can't wait that long for the next opening; therefore I'm going to take it." That was 1982.

I still play the cello from time to time and I recently bought a baritone sax. We have a holiday double-reed concert and one of my graduate students and I played Christmas carols on two baritone saxes as a duet. I just like instruments. I have never felt that I had the technical skill—certainly artic-ulation skills—that my best students have. They have tremendous skills. But I've always been able to do what I need to do and I enjoy playing. That is the main thing. I really enjoy playing and teaching.

Evolution of the Oboe World

The mechanics of the equipment has changed. The mechanics of making reeds, thanks to some very generous people who've spent a lot of time dealing with it. I think most notably of John Mack and what he did with reeds, but a lot of people. Certainly Tabuteau from the beginning because he was always seeking something better, always seeking a solution, always trying to find the gouge that was going to do the trick, and that equipment level has changed in my lifetime unbelievably. Not that we were hand gouging—scooping it out with a spoon—but it was a whole lot less precise and useful than it is now. From an equipment standpoint there are so many options to solve problems. The instruments clearly are better and the competition between the instru-ment companies has been nothing but good for all of them because they've had to stay on top of it. There are many brands of oboes that are excellent. They're all being used by people who are making their living and that's very good, but the most important thing is that teaching around the country is better, maybe around the world. I've had students who've studied in Germany, who've studied in Paris, and the teaching is excellent everywhere. It's just a high standard. In every small school, large school, you find a level of teaching that is far beyond what I think was happening forty or fifty years ago. Fine playing is happening everywhere and young people hear a higher standard and they just do that. You can't avoid it. The teaching is excellent, the equipment is excellent, and now there are so many more examples for young people. The International Double Reed Society played a huge role in spreading the word so information is now readily available, which was not the case fifty years ago.

On Unfilled Orchestra Positions

That's an odd occurrence in this upgraded level and I'm thinking there were years when anyone who came to that audition would have been satisfactory and now no one is good enough. On the audition committee side we've kind of grown to expect a certain kind of perfection that is actually not possible. It's an unreal expectation because we are still all people and we still have to make a reed every day and we still have to play. We're subject to our own limitations so there is no one who's perfect.

It's odd that there are jobs that remain unfilled. In the end, orchestras are finding people who are playing very well and sometimes they are people who have been rejected in earlier rounds. Very important oboe players, some of whom are playing in their orchestras today, came to the audition and were eliminated the first round. For one reason or another, they were brought back in and they were the winners and had distinguished careers in those orchestras. This has happened quite a few times where a person who might not be invited insists on coming and they win the job but they were deemed lacking the necessary credentials to even be invited to the audition. They say, "But I really think that I can do this," and then they win the job. So, sometimes just stick to it. Believe "I am the person" and go after it. You can't win the job if you don't go to the audition. That's the only thing that's a guarantee.

Teaching Philosophy

In my studio, everybody helps everybody. Everybody is a star and nobody is a star. We all are in this together. And they're very, very good. There's no competition among the students so that means everybody gets better. Every one of my students is eager to do well and they work hard. The motivation is all around them. The older students, when they hear the freshman, say, "As soon as class is over I'm going to go practice." The motivation is there all the time. It's in the room. It's at every concert. The students all hear each other play as often as they can and then they gather outside at the concerts and the whole oboe class, they salute the players. This is oboe class behavior which really pleases me.

Breathing

I don't really talk about techniques of breathing. I will say things like, "Get to the fundamental of the sound," and then, "You're breathing shallow. Take a breath and now use that air to support the tone." When you get nervous you'll notice that the tone is from here to here and so I'll say just get back to the fundamental. I heard Wayne Rapier say that once in a class and I said, "That's a great way to get to the fundamental breathing mechanism without saying, 'Ok this is how you breathe.'" We talk about a science beaker instead of filling up in the chest, filling up in the abdomen. I feel that I'm pushing out in the back and I'll use that if I feel a person is breathing shallow. I'll say, "Just feel like you're pushing your back right out, the small of your back out."

I don't get super involved in the mechanics of breathing or embouchure but I will offer advice and, particularly with embouchure, simplify what the face does, what the mouth does to control the reed. We talk about keeping the teeth open and the mouth closed but the control is best toward the tip of the reed rather than toward the winding. So we'll find the optimum place on the reed where the tone is most resonant. It's making a more stable reed that allows the embouchure to not have to take so much reed and those things take care of themselves. We talk about keeping the chin down but we don't stop playing until the chin is taken care of. We evolve and by the time a person graduates, those mechanical things have really sorted themselves out because in a lesson I'm saying, "That chin's back up again. Stop playing when you lose your face." When you're playing long tones it's the end of the note that gives you what you really need, which is the control, and then you're able to keep your chin down.

Intervallic Placement

I had a conversation with Linda Strommen at the convention and she said she really enjoyed hearing the way [my student] elevated and I said, "Wow, I want to use that word," because that's the placement of voicing. She said,

"He elevates." And I said, "I'm going to use it but I'm going to cite you. I will always give your name when I say that." That's a wonderful image of elevating to the right place. They do interval studies all the time. It's not necessarily that they have a technique for doing it; it's that it must be done. It's more, "You have to play intervals," rather than, "This is how you play intervals." It's a combination of where you are on the reed and also the placement of the tongue. If the tongue is low you can't play in tune. If the tongue is high, you have all the options available to you for playing. I find that's very helpful just to make them aware.

There's a mechanism for placement. There's a place to put that note, and with almost any reed in any oboe, you're still capable of getting to the right place within a certain limitation. You are capable of getting to that place with just being aware of the placement. Low C♯ we voice very high. High B♭, same thing. E can't be voiced high. E to G is a feature interval for placement of distance: the G higher, the E lower. Same thing with D to F, which occurs in the Beethoven 3rd Symphony and also in *La Scala di Seta*. Those are feature intervals that I use to help place the note regardless of the oboe. F to G♭, half step—Shostakovich 1st Symphony—it's a really great chance to really play a half step. Mozart Concerto, first movement, B to C. The B is often flat and the C is high so we place that interval. Being aware of those half steps that are vulnerable on the oboe changes the perception of your ability to play in tune rather than "the reed does everything." It helps certainly. The oboe helps but it's a combination of all the things that you have at your disposal rather than, "This oboe is out of tune. I can't play it." There's no such thing as an oboe that's in tune completely because you can't cover all the bases. Every possible use of that one note in every interval that it could be used—there's no way unless you play the pitches that are necessary. That's voicing and placement: a mental concept of the pitch and then you play that interval. In class, I'll take their instrument where they played D really high and F really low and I'll play it and I'll turn the interval around and they say, "Well, how do you do that?" I say, "Because, those are the notes that I want to play. I don't want to play the notes you play. I don't hear those notes as the right notes." Does that mean we always play in tune? No, that's impossible. We are human. We are limited to what we are able to do, physically and mentally. Everybody doesn't hear equally but striving to play a good interval is important rather than accepting what the oboe gives you and blaming the oboe. The oboe is an inanimate object. It can't fight back. Don't blame the oboe.

Long Tones

I do an exercise I call the B-C exercise. I got it from David Abosch in Denver, the first oboist. It can be used starting on any note, anywhere from low B to G actually, but we take a two-octave range and we play every single interval within the two octaves, so B3-C4-B4-C5-B5, back to C5-B4-C4-B3, diminuendo. Start very soft, crescendo, make the crown of your oboe ring and rattle and get down to nothing again. At the very outset if you can't play low B, your reed is not playable. You have to be able to play low B and that's a good note to start on because you want to come in soft on it just like you have to do in Ravel's *Pavane*. You have to play a low B; you have to come in soft. Barber 1st Symphony, you have to play a low B. So, it's a great way to start. And then, B3-C♯4-B4-C♯5-B5-C♯5-B4-C♯4-B3. B-D, B-D♯, B-E, B-F and that. Then you have to figure a way you're going to play that forked F because you can't—some hands can slide—but you've got to find a way to play from B to forked F. You need it in *Das Lied von der Erde* and you need it in Samuel Barber. The forked F doesn't always sound good. You have to learn to play that note. You're finding a way to make that note fit in the tonal context of your oboe. People avoid it and I say you can't avoid it; you've got to use it, so you have to find a way to play that note. When choosing an oboe, I'm playing that B to F to see how the F is. They're so much better now than they used to be; when they first added the resonance key they were so sharp and we'd stuff them up and put cork in. Now it's much better. My teacher Robert Bloom didn't have resonance keys and his F was super stuffy and he loved that sound because he said that's the way people would know it was him. It was like putting his signature on the music because they could hear that foggy forked F and he loved it.

Anyway, if you crescendo through the large intervals [on the ascent] and then maintain even, smooth in the small intervals, and then coming down diminuendo through the small intervals but maintain through the large— for instance you're up on high B and we want to go to the third space C, you don't want to cave in, you want to play to that C and then small diminuendo and then from that B to low C you don't want to diminuendo because you want that note, so then you diminuendo and taper at the end. If you do that slowly, very thoughtfully connecting those intervals, it's a great long tone exercise. Then taper at the end; the most valuable part of a long tone is the taper. The walrus tusks which I talk about and the "ooooh" factor—getting the upper lip to the reed—some people call it getting the corners in. It's the same gesture but Roger Rehm, who used to teach at Central Michigan, mentioned that to me, walrus tusks. It's the "oooh," it's that control that comes down towards the reed rather than just letting the upper lip be flabby. That's where the warm color comes from; it's the upper lip control.

As your interval gets larger at the bottom [on the ascent], then you're crescendoing more through the larger one and then the smaller one you're not, so basically crescendo through the big intervals, diminuendo through the small ones. The main thing is to get the crown of the oboe, the top, vibrating and very small at the bottom. I use that as a vibrato exercise in using the appropriate vibrato for the range you're playing. I use an example of a string bass player. If the string bass player is on the low E string playing a vibrato that he would play if he were playing the E string of a violin, it's out of context. It won't work. It's not going to be fast and wiry; it's going to be very slow. On the oboe, a very fast vibrato on low C seems inappropriate whereas on high C, the vibrato is going to be much quicker. That's not to say anything about the mood the vibrato is creating where there is a note that is slightly pressed and becoming a note and then the vibrato shows later down the road. That's all the wonderful way of using the vibrato to create mood and magic. But, just in basic terms, is the vibrato consistent with the size of sound? With the size of the note? Is it too fast for the note? Is it too slow for the note? We use that B-C exercise that way too—is the vibrato appropriate?

Then, start the whole thing on C, then the whole thing on C♯, then the whole thing on D, until you get to G and then of course high G will be your final one but it takes about a year to get through all that. It's a great way of doing long tones without counting seconds (which also is valuable sometimes). What I'll do with that is I'll say, "How long can you hold the tone?" Innocently I'll say it in a lesson. I'll turn on the metronome at 60 and we see. About 30 seconds to 40 seconds later they'll say, "Well, how long do you hold the tone?" And I'll say, "Well, about two minutes but that explains my brain damage and oxygen starvation. So, if you think I'm weird it's because I hold the tone for two minutes!" The point is that you build up a tolerance for distribution of the air so that you can extend the length that you hold the tone. You're using your air efficiently and you're keeping a contact point with the reed but you're not overblowing the reed.

Technical Practice

Sing it. Spell it. Transpose it. All of the above. But the main thing is slow and deliberate and memorized. Memorize the bits and pieces. You train your fingers. John Mack said that to me once. He said, "When I'm in trouble I just close off my brain and let my fingers do the walking because they've been there so they know what to do, but if I think about it . . . oops, crash and burn." I'll do that; I think, "Which F am I going to do here?" And then I play them both. Have you ever heard left hand and forked at the same time? Wah! Sometimes thinking is not a good thing to do.

I don't have any secrets. Just slow and don't practice mistakes. Don't keep playing the same mistake. They say, "I keep playing that; I keep making the same mistake." And I say, "Of course. Now you're really good at that mistake. You can't miss it now; you can't miss that mistake!" Just play it perfectly as slowly as necessary until that's the habit. You're building a habit and if it means three notes then just do three notes. Whatever it is, pick out the note that you think is the trouble spot. If you don't know, start going through the passage and concentrating on a different note each time and see which one in concentrating on it solves the problem. Or articulate the note that's giving you the trouble in a slurred passage. Tongue the note that's giving you the problem because you focus on that note.

Articulation

I've been through all the technique of improving my tonguing. When I was in junior high even I noticed everybody could tongue faster than I could and I'm wondering, what are they doing? My brother played flute and he said, "Oh, well I go, "ta ka ta ka," so I started going, "ta ka ta ka ta," when I was fourteen and it was a mistake. I never developed single tonguing like I should have, although as an adult I did practice. Pay attention to the tip of the reed, know where the tip of the reed is, and close the opening of the reed, whether it's the tip of the tongue or just above the tip of the tongue. The problem when it's below the tip of the tongue is the tongue can't be in the right place to play in tune. I've had students who tongue the roof of their mouth and didn't realize it and we caught them somewhere along the way.

Be aware of the tip of the reed and then practice with a deliberate closing of the opening of the reed. For developing fast tonguing, practice legato rather than staccato. For many people, as they learn from their metronome where they are and they're working gradually to increase—and it's got to be a daily thing for a person who's tonguing challenged, it's got to be every single day you're in touch with that mechanism—for most students who have tonguing problems, there is a day where their tongue seems to go into a second gear, into overdrive. All of a sudden their tongue can move and I can't explain it physiologically but if they keep after the deliberate, every day, keeping track of where they are with their tonguing speed, it seems to always get better. If they think it's just magically going to get better because they wake up one morning and it's there, it won't happen.

Vibrato

For the students who have vibrato problems, they have to pay attention to every single interval. Sometimes it's a matter of playing three notes and having the vibrato be a part of your airstream rather than assigning a vibrato number to each note. If they're having a real problem with it, I'll go back to really mechanical production of it in order to get the mechanism going. I'll use a metronome. I'll do anything I can to get the mechanism, which is a moving of the airstream, pulsation of the airstream, going. For most people it's a matter of making them aware of the appropriateness of the speed and the ability to go faster and slower, to have control. I don't say where it happens. If I can hear it, I say no, that's not vibrato, that's choking. Or I say no, we have to get it in the airstream. Move it where it works, but short of saying it's exactly here or there, I tell them it's different. It's all over the place. It depends on the reed, depends on the music, on all kinds of things.

Reeds

When I was playing four concerts a week, I muscled those reeds in a way that I can't now. I make a better reed now because I can't play a reed that doesn't have certain stable qualities that are absolutely essential and closing on the sides. I find the reeds that are so completely stable that are totally in place and up, unplayable. I get so tired that I can't play because I can't keep the pitch down. I can't keep it resonant. On the other hand, a reed I have to close to play, I can't play that kind of reed either. I talk about it as being from super stable and closed and tight at the extreme to super loose and too free at the other extreme. Every oboe player, their tolerance level for those aspects of the reed is in a different place. Finding that up-to-pitch or down-to-pitch reed is really crucial so that the person can pick up the oboe and without undue stress or clamping, just honest pitch comes out of your reed. If, when I play that reed, it's 448 [Hertz], I say, "I don't know how you can play that reed." Or if it's 432. Within certain parameters everybody's going to be able to play something that's different from what I can play. I've got big lips. I cover without even trying to cover. Therefore, I can play it out of the side of my mouth and still play it. When the freshmen first get here we have a reed day where I show them how I process cane, how I select cane, split it, guillotine it; we take every step and then I make a reed. So, I made the reed and I handed it to the two girls. Both of them had been my high school students, one of whom was a very good reed maker and the other is just learning to make reeds. I gave it to Alina, she played it absolutely in tune. I handed it to Nora. She said, "This is a really nice reed." John played it and he said, "What I like about your reeds is that they're really up to pitch." And then Matt said, "I don't know how you can play this reed. It's so flat. I can't play it." That's a freshman too. And then the DMA student played it and said, "That's unplayable." Then he looked at the three freshmen who could play it and said, "How do you do that?" and they said, "It just works. It's a really good reed." I said, "From my standpoint that reed is not finished at all, but three or four of us just pick it up and play it and two of you can't." Now those two have moved much further towards a reed that's more resonant and that they can play in tune without undue stress. It's a change in balances as the reeds change their embouchure. What their embouchure does changes; how they're using their air changes; the voicing changes as it evolves. They're now able to take my reed and just play it. But a year ago they couldn't do that.

I'm not saying that my reed is right. What I'm saying is that four of us were able to play it and two were not and now all can more or less play everybody else's reeds. At least they can all play what each other considers a good reed. It's a matter of expecting it. That's what the DMA student said: "I always expected a reed not to be good instead of expecting a reed to be good and then playing it like you know it's good. I expected it to be bad because that's the way I was brought up—that reeds are evil. Reeds are bad. Gougers don't work. Knives aren't sharp enough." "Everything is wrong" instead of "let's make a reed and play." I've changed his attitude toward reeds. It's amazing how that attitude changes as our playing changes. I try to guide them through to different perspectives of reeds. I don't claim that I have all the answers about reeds, but as I've taught longer, more of my students can play my reeds than when I first came here. They are more aware of the value of certain aspects of a reed.

Gouging Machines

I want to be able to play the reed with a consistent tone, response, pitch I can deal with, and I have to be able to taper. I have to be able to come in soft and I have to be able to end the notes. Almost every gouge I've ever owned, I could make a good reed with. If I have a student who is very happy and they're using a particular gouge I don't say a word. I say, "That's great. Give me some cane off that." Anything that's working, I think that's terrific.

What's been fun with the Ross gouge is that Dan came here my first year to hear his student's master's recital. We were in my studio and Dan looked at me and he said, "Are you interested in dealing with a gouging machine? I'd like to make a gouging machine." I said, "No way." I was using a Gilbert gouge which I thought was fine. I made my career with that gouge. I loved it. I said, "I don't want to get into that. All I hear about from people is that they're having trouble and I'm not having trouble, therefore don't talk to me about gouging machines." "Well if I made one would you pass judgment on it?" And I said, "Well, yeah, but I'm really not interested in changing my gouge." So I went down to Arkansas and we spent a long time, I think we spent a week, and did not get one reed. I went home and he figured he'd never see me again. Little by little what we used was a gouge I liked a lot, comparing reeds from that with his gouge—and he was doing the blades by hand—until he got something that I thought was workable and then I said, "Ok, I'll take that." I took it home and made reeds with it and found that I was successful with it. I thought it was a mysterious piece of equipment and I didn't touch it, wouldn't turn the screws, wouldn't do anything with it. I was afraid of it. It was mystical, whereas with the Gilbert gouge I would adjust all the time. Through the years it's been refined and I've had fun in the process of seeing that gouge become more and more a wonderful, wonderful gouge. The things that have been mistakes or difficulties, each one of those has been a learning step which has made the gouge more reliable and consistent. When it's not working, we learn. If there is something about the symmetry of it, we learn. It's the process with working with this and passing judgment and evaluating the gouge that has been fun for me. When it's not right I'll say, "Dan, that's not a Ross gouge." And he'll come here and he'll set a blade and give me a piece of cane and I'll make a reed. And then he tweaks the blade a little. I say, "That's a Ross gouge." That's been fun. I don't insist that anybody use any particular thing. If it works, keep doing it. I tell my freshmen don't give up whatever it is you're doing that's working. If you're having a problem, I'll offer a suggestion but I don't have any wholesale, "Everybody does this; everybody uses this shape; everybody uses this gouger." I can't say that any gouge is the best gouge because every gouge that's sold is being used successfully by somebody.

Listening

Most importantly, singers and violinists and cellists. Piano in some ways but it's more clear on the string instruments because with the string instruments you have the bow, you have the nuance of moving the bow and the pressure and letting it up on pressure. On violin you would never play "AHHH AHHH AHHH," but on the oboe, we're sometimes taught "blow through, press!" I say, "What are you going to do with that?" There are times when that's appropriate but the other 999 times it's not appropriate because it's a crude musical device. You listen to a violinist and you're not going to hear that. You're going to hear how the bow creates legato as well as nuance as well as commas and phrasing and obvious grouping of notes and then we've realized that that's our air. Our air is the bow and you just don't turn it on and blow until you get to the end. You use the air in the way that you're singing. Singers have words to sing. They are speaking logic. I want the air to be used in a way that you could make a logical musical phrase rather than just blowing until you get to the end and then shutting off your valve. Some people say, "Well, it's this pressure." I say, "No, it's the absence of pressure. It's using the pressure and release, so the release is just as important as the pressure." It's that neutral of moving from one to the next that I find strange unless it's the aesthetic that is required and there's an austere quality that's very attractive in certain phrases. You want to use that when it's appropriate but you don't build your playing around neutral.

I listen to any player and then react to the way they play—not to criticize. It's to react and relate to the way that person plays. What is it about their playing that you admire and what is it about their playing that, if you could have them do something different you'd say, "It'd really be great if you could do this?" It's so you become discerning to some of the ingredients that go together to make wonderful playing.

On Teaching

I just I love it. I'm obsessed and it's enabling when you can see the results of your work and they see the results of their work. It feeds on itself and no motivation necessary outside. We just go to town. I feel privileged to be in a school where I have those kinds of applicants, although I felt very good about my students at Oklahoma City University and some of them are out there teaching. In fact, I've had students of my students from University of Oklahoma, Oklahoma City University, Macalester College, and Central State. There were students from every one of those schools that got into the profession. It doesn't matter where you are. There are going to be people who can do it.

16

Nancy Ambrose King

Nancy Ambrose King is professor of oboe at the University of Michigan and first-prize winner of the Third New York International Competition for Solo Oboists, held in 1995. She has appeared as soloist throughout the United States and abroad, including performances with the St. Petersburg (Russia) Philharmonic, the Prague Chamber Orchestra, the Janáček Philharmonic, the Tokyo Chamber Orchestra, the Puerto Rico Symphony, the Orchestra of the Swan in Birmingham (England), and the Festival Internacional de Musica Orchestra in Buenos Aires (Argentina). She has performed as a recitalist in Weill Recital Hall and as a soloist at Lincoln Center and Carnegie Hall. She has recorded eleven CDs of works for the oboe, on Boston Records, Cala Records, Equilibrium, Naxos, and Centaur Records. This interview was conducted by Michele Fiala via email in September 2016.

Teaching and Playing

Teaching a lesson is not only beneficial to our students; it is a continuous learning process for the teacher, too. I have learned so much about the oboe from teaching others, and the constant reminders of fundamentals carry over into my own playing. Every time a student comes to a lesson with a certain difficulty, it forces me to think critically about the cause of the problem and the eventual solution, which can be different for each person. The creativity needed to problem-solve, and the reinforcement of fundamentals and good practice skills continue to inspire my own practice and attention to detail in my playing. At times, the scrutiny of an item in my own playing may or may not come easily to me. Figuring out why that's the case, and how best to describe that particular process to a student, can deepen an awareness in my personal performance.

Great Oboists on Music and Musicianship. Michele L. Fiala and Martin Schuring, Oxford University Press (2021).
© Oxford University Press. DOI: 10.1093/oso/9780190915094.001.0001.

I am continually inspired by my students! I learn every day from their musicianship, creativity, and technical feats that they bring to their lessons. My students have inspired me to learn new works that they've found in their library or internet searches; they've inspired me to learn to triple-tongue and improve my flutter tongue, and they continually enlighten and refresh me with their exuberance, excitement, and love for the oboe and its music. The most wonderful part of my job is that each year it becomes new again: new students with new strengths and areas of concern, new personalities and ways of learning. The challenge (and excitement that represents) keeps me motivated and eager to teach. I believe in the importance of continually learning each and every day, whether it's about the oboe, music, or life in general. Since that is what I stress so strongly to my students, it only makes sense that I try to emulate it for them as well!

Reeds

We need a reed which is an equal partner to us. We can't be making constant adjustments in our playing to adapt to a reed that won't play in tune, respond, or be able to play easily in all dynamic ranges, but we also can't expect the reed to do all the work involved while we just blow and finger the notes. It's a collaborative experience; our reeds should react positively as we challenge them with our air or our expectations of a beautiful diminuendo, flexible leaps, a more diverse color palette, etc.

In most cases, a reed that is in tune and responds well will accomplish the other things we desire, and we can't sacrifice pitch or response in search of a deeper tone quality, especially early on in the reed making process. I've seen trouble in my students' reeds come from their search for a specific tone color before they have made the reed stable in pitch and response. Keeping to the goal of a good crow of octave Cs, and a reed that passes the "C test," meaning the ability to respond immediately with an extremely soft 1-and-1 C [C5], is crucial.

What am I looking for in a reed? A reed that is stable yet flexible, that responds easily yet challenges us to be engaged in the process of changing the color palette, that is covered and pleasing in tone color yet projects to the back of the hall, that takes the air yet doesn't require biting or undue effort, that is substantial enough to last through a two-hour recital yet allows me to actually *play* a two-hour recital. That is what I'm looking for in a reed!

Learning New Repertoire

I find learning a new piece of music extraordinarily fun. The challenge of digging into a new and difficult work is gratifying and rewarding, though it can be understandably frustrating at times, too. I have a few *dos and don'ts* when learning a new piece of music:

1) If a recording or midi-mockup is available, it's fine to listen once or twice before starting to learn the piece for general context and a starting point. However, I don't advise too much listening to other performances before our own interpretive ideas are formed.

2) Start slowly! This is "Level 1" learning . . . just the basics. Concentrate on notes, rhythm, and articulation. One of the biggest mistakes I find my students make is only learning the notes and rhythm first, ignoring the articulation! Eventually they need to go back to Square 1 to correct all the articulation errors that they made along the way. Go slowly enough in this first level of practice that all three basics are learned simultaneously: notes, rhythm, and articulation. At this level of learning, I advocate not only slow practice but also many, many different rhythmic patterns for the tricky technical passages. Long-short, short-long, long-triplet, triplet-long, etc. Write your goal metronome marking on the side of the page, along with the speed currently playing with accuracy, and fill in the numbers each day until you've reached the speed of your goal tempo.

3) Stage 2, add dynamics and extra-musical markings such as sforzandi, tenuto, etc.
It should now be close to tempo or just a bit under.

4) Stage 3, overall architecture and nuance. Think about your phrase direction and musical goals on a variety of levels: a short-term goal in a four-measure phrase, but also how the phrases interlock to create larger musical ideas. Incorporate the piano or orchestral line into your architectural study. Link the notes together to form your phrase architecture; link the phrases to form a larger idea, and think on an even larger scale—how will the recap differ from your interpretation of the exposition? How will you recreate a theme that reappears in a later movement?

Only after you have firmly committed to your musical, ornamental, and architectural interpretations do I suggest listening to others' recordings once again. You may find them inspiring and helpful at this point, yet not exerting too much influence over your own creativity and musical purpose.

Inspirations

As much as I love the oboe, I feel we can gain our most profound inspiration from listening to vocalists and string players. We are trying to emulate the human voice in our lyricism, and our air (and articulation) is the equivalent of the bow. I am personally amazed by the artistry of Cecilia Bartoli and inspired by the expression of the late Jacqueline du Pré. Yo-Yo Ma is a shining example of musical flexibility in all genres and the value of expressing ourselves in a variety of musical genres. Glenn Gould was the pinnacle of clarity in his performances of J. S. Bach, and a testament to the ability of modern instruments to perform early music with intelligence and respect for its authenticity.

On Winning Jobs

Although the musical world is extremely competitive, I have found that my students who are extremely committed and willing to think creatively as well as work diligently toward a goal are successfully supporting themselves in the field of music and the arts. I am happy and proud to say that their love for the oboe continues to be strong even if they have pursued another field for their "bread and butter." The ability to persevere and be creative in carving out a niche for themselves and their career is crucial. There are more opportunities for musicians now than ever, yet it is a changing musical landscape out there and students must be prepared to do everything: orchestral, solo, chamber music, new music, Baroque music, English horn, pedagogical knowledge, reed making, speaking to an audience, and the openness to ideas that haven't even occurred to us yet. They are all necessary skills to have in today's marketplace. I believe that collaboration and entrepreneurship are extremely important for today's young musician. And of course, impeccable playing!

College teaching positions are becoming as competitive to secure as orchestral positions. The well-rounded musician who is vibrant, energetic, able to recruit and encourage young oboists to study with them, and who is a positive and supportive collaborator will be a fine colleague and one with whom a search committee would like to work. I also recommend the ability to teach in a secondary area, whether it be bassoon, music theory, music history, etc. My first teaching position required me to teach the oboe, oboe methods, chamber music, class piano, and music history to the entire freshman class of 150 majors! Needless to say, I was very busy, but the flexibility and willingness to accommodate the needs of the school served me well. In a nutshell, be open to new experiences, be confident in your ability to do the job, be a well-rounded and curious musician interested in furthering the advancement of the oboe and its literature, and be a good, supportive colleague!

Reminiscence

I've had the opportunity to perform with some of the finest musicians of our time and wonderful friends and colleagues. I am very fortunate to have had these many experiences! I've also had several unexpected performance experiences, sometimes humorous and sometimes not . . . such as a large wasp flying around and finally landing on my knee during a concert, getting a swab stuck in my oboe only seconds before walking onstage (lesson learned: not to use a pull-through swab again!), etc., but I will convey two performances which are still very memorable to me for different reasons.

The first was in 1995 at the finals of the New York International Oboe Competition, held at Lincoln Center. The competition had come down to just three of us and I was profoundly honored and surprised to find myself still in the competition along with the phenomenal oboists Rebecca Henderson and Eugene Izotov. The three of us had reached the finals of the competition and were each playing the Mozart Concerto with an orchestra of Juilliard musicians, with Mitch Miller conducting. When I had first learned that I was one of the twelve oboists selected to compete in New York City, I didn't think I had a chance of making the finals, and with a three-year-old son at home, I had actually booked a return ticket before the final round of competition was even scheduled! Needless to say, I hadn't put in much practice on the Mozart Concerto but had focused on the large amount of repertoire needed for the previous rounds of competition. After making the finals, I changed the ticket and practiced Mozart for hours. It wasn't enough, though, and I was disappointed with how the first movement was going during my performance. I mentally criticized my trills as being uneven or incomplete, and didn't feel my technique was smooth enough to warrant my being selected as a finalist. For a minute, midway through the first movement, I became discouraged. The cadenza went well, however, and I collected my thoughts before starting the second movement. I decided that no matter how things turned out, I would pour myself into the music and at the very least feel that I had played that gorgeous slow movement with an emotion and sensitivity worthy of Mozart. The connection I felt with the music at that moment and with Mozart himself was transformative. It was a very profound experience, and the confidence ensued into a fun and rollicking Rondo finale. I learned from a judge following the announcement that it was the slow movement that determined the outcome of their jury selection. I really was shocked when I won first prize in the competition, and of course thrilled, but the lessons I learned during that performance continued on for years: 1) Never give up or look back when a performance may not be going as well as you hoped, but instead continue with a determination to play your most beautifully on the next entrance, phrase, or movement. 2) A slow movement played with your deepest emotion, sensitivity, and nuance can connect with an audience in a profoundly personal way. That is easy to overlook, as the bulk of our practice revolves around the technical accuracy and speed necessary for the outer movements.

The other concerts that come to mind as especially meaningful were the two that I played the nights before each of my children were born. The first, in 1992, was actually a dress rehearsal. I missed the performance the following night as our son was born. The next was a concerto in February 1997. With his due date not until February 14, I had committed to play the Handel G minor Oboe Concerto and J. S. Bach Cantata #82 with a Baroque orchestra on February 3. I had my graduate assistant learn the music just in case, but all seemed fine and the rehearsals went well. At my last appointment, however, the determination was made that the baby couldn't wait until February 14; the doctor would like me to deliver on February 1. Well, with a performance on February 3, I requested February 4 for the delivery date! The concert went fine, although it was a bit of a struggle, and I felt quite enormous, uncomfortable, and not too attractive up onstage. The audience seemed in awe, probably in fear of the ramifications of an extremely pregnant woman playing the oboe for an hour. Following the concerto, instead of flowers, the ladies' league presented me with a large package of diapers and balloons! It made for a memorable topic of conversation, and the evening did become a symbolic representation of the many years of my life spent juggling my performing and teaching career with my children and family life. Both my career and my family have brought me boundless happiness and gratification, and I continue to be profoundly grateful.

17

Alex Klein

Brazilian oboist Alex Klein won a 2002 Grammy Award for Best Instrumental Soloist with Orchestra as well as first prize at the International Competition in Geneva, the New York International Oboe Competition, and the Fernand Gillet International Competition. From 1995 to 2004, Klein was principal oboist of the Chicago Symphony Orchestra, a position he left after struggles with focal dystonia. He is currently artistic director of the Santa Catarina Music Festival ("FEMUSC") in Brazil, principal oboe of the Calgary Philharmonic Orchestra in Canada, oboe instructor at DePaul University in Chicago, and a regular performer and faculty with the Aspen Music Festival (Colorado), New World Symphony (Miami), Sunflower Music Festival (Kansas) and Saint Barts Music Festival (French Antilles). He taught at Oberlin College, where this interview was conducted by Michele Fiala in May 2009. Klein was hosting an oboe cleaning party for his students and spoke to me while seated at a table of disassembled oboes and bottles of Tarn-X.

Early Life and Career

I was a little bit of an *enfant terrible*, not that you would ever know. [Laughter] And if you are about to be expelled from school in fourth grade you'd know that things are not going well. At the time the school counselor said to my parents that I was going to go into sports or the arts because they were high-energy activities. And I was the sort of kid who had too much energy to offer and was just not fitting in to the rest of the curriculum there. So, music it was. We did some trials. We tried some sports and I was kicked out of those, too. And eventually, we went—there was a music festival in town—and my parents desperately brought me to this thing to see if something there would hit. And I pointed to the middle of the orchestra and said, "I want to play that

Great Oboists on Music and Musicianship. Michele L. Fiala and Martin Schuring, Oxford University Press (2021).
© Oxford University Press. DOI: 10.1093/oso/9780190915094.001.0001.

one." I specifically remember seeing that sea of violins onstage and it creeped me out that so many people were playing the same thing. But there was something about the oboe—I think it was Lido Guarnieri, an Argentinian who has been in Venezuela for a long time, who played the Mozart Oboe Concerto and I just was just amazed that such a small opening could fill the hall. And I got interested in the science of it. Little did I know we were talking about reeds, but it just amazed me what the oboe could do. And I decided to do that, and I had no idea what it was, what it was called. And it worked. From then on, I improved in school. Everything went beautifully.

But in my hometown there was no oboe. It took me a year and a half to get my first oboe. During that time I started playing recorder and learning music theory, reading music and stuff like that. There was a symphony in town. The oboe player, João Ramalho, was self-taught, so he wasn't about to teach me Barret or some of the other canonical oboe things. In a way this was a disadvantage because I didn't get the beginning on oboe like everybody else did, that already went into a method—"this is what you do."

I started having oboe lessons six months before I got my first oboe. I did one year of theory, recorder and all that, and then I enrolled in a music school that had an oboe teacher, but I still didn't have an oboe for another six months. And he told my parents he would not teach me unless I got a new oboe, that the oboe was hard enough to play, to start on a bad, old oboe with all sorts of problems. And so for those first six months, I took the reed home and practiced on the reed alone, to the desperation of all the neighborhood dogs [Laughter] and my family. And once a week I would play something in the lesson on his oboe. Then I would play something and not practice for a whole week, just come the next one and let's try something else. So, to keep me interested, he would just give me different sounds to make on the reed. "Just go home and try making this, and then try doing that rhythm. What if you played that sound? Wouldn't that be cool?" So this is very far away from the normal canon. Once I finally did get my oboe—it was a very good new Puchner—then we started actual lessons, but again it was not according to the canon. I was ten years old and he was telling me, "Play like you just lost your girlfriend. But then, you haven't had one yet, have you?" [Laughter] He was a delightful old man. I really miss him. So I was being instructed in music and not in oboe and to this day I really don't feel like I belong with a method of oboe. I feel like I'm tied to the music. All through my teenagehood I was more friendly with violinists and pianists and cellists than I was with oboe players because there were very few of us, very few oboe players. There were probably two or three oboe players in our hometown of a million people. So there's no oboe society there, oboe culture. So I just hung around violin players. We were listening to Brahms Violin Concerto, Wieniawsky and Paganini, and such for our gatherings. Not John Mack or Strauss or Holliger.

On Teaching

I'm very critical and sometimes suspicious of the existing models of oboe playing and oboe teaching that don't always serve the interests of music. It's something that needs to be changed in favor of music. There are many, many excellent teachers who do worry about music and they make oboe work toward music. There are many of them, excellent players and teachers, but also there is a certain culture that says if you just do this, this and that, you're going to be a great oboe player. And that's a lie. That's simply not true. The only way that works is when the teacher and the students are tied to what is above oboe.

My quest right now is to investigate how above music there is thinking. There is philosophy; there is a decision-making process. I'm very curious about what is it that makes people think. Let's consider that the DNA difference between human beings is very small—insignificant. What is it that makes one person know more than others or perform better than others? Is somebody just born with it so if you don't have it, too bad? Or is it a thought process that opens people's minds to certain possibilities? And once they feel comfortable in those possibilities, they will be better performers. So I realized then that just as oboe playing is above reed making is above cleaning is above the kind of blade you have in your gouging machine, there is something above oboe that is art, music, that's creating something. There is also something above art: that is philosophy. There is a part that decides how we think about music, how we feel, how we describe it, how we go about expressing it, with what standards do we understand music? And above philosophy we find self. We find ourselves, our person, our feelings, our true, original self. And above that is community. I think there is a point that even self is no longer as important. That we give ourselves to a greater cause and that's community. But the self is sort of a pride thing. What is above philosophy? There is an element of pride, of defending oneself. You think this way because you believe that it is correct to you. So you then bring this down one level to music and you apply yourself through philosophy into art. And you think in a certain way. You're proud of the way you think. You're proud of your decision making. And you are then going to express it through an art. In order to express that art you're going to need an oboe. In order to play the oboe, you're going to need a reed. And then it keeps going down the scale. So the little techniques of oboe—you know—buying a plaque, what kind, do you have a round or a straight cutting block? This is really mundane. And it has to stay in its place in order to allow the person to grow up in the scale. So my interest now is to try to analyze what is it that makes people think in a way that makes them better artists? It's that philosophy that's just above art itself.

On Musical Activism

I'm a musician and therefore when I want to do social work, the first thing that comes to mind: what can I do with my oboe, with music that's going to make that difference? So I use music as a tool to do social work. But the social work itself is a separate category of activity that I do in my life. It may seem like it's the same thing but it's actually very different and there are different principles that apply to it.

I grew up in a city that is a very nice city, really lovely, but I had to fight to get every piece of knowledge that I was looking for. I suffered from the complex of inferiority coming from a colony, or from a secondary town, from a little town in the middle of nowhere. Which this wasn't really—it was a state capital, Curitiba, Brazil, but still there was a feeling that when I went to the big festivals, I was not part of the crowd. I was sort of squirming my way in. Even to come to Oberlin, it was sort of a very faraway dream. I was really out of my league coming to Oberlin. But that made me practice really hard here to beat what I perceived as being my drawbacks. While for everybody else I was doing pretty well, I still perceived myself as an under-player. In the end it kind of worked to my benefit. But today I see many young people in several different countries, not necessarily poorer countries. There are a lot of people in Europe and Japan and here in the United States who have that same feeling: how do I fit in? Where do I go? And I see myself in them. And I try to, now from a different position, find better answers. Maybe it's one of the reasons I like to teach.

On Mindset While Playing

The principle is that when we play we have too many things in our mind that we have to concentrate on. To play one note you need about forty muscles that have to be in a specific position with a specific tension doing something at a specific time. We have breathing, we have pressure, we have standards to meet. We have our reed that's outside of our body and technically outside of our control, really. We have an instrument that may or may not respond according to the color we want at the moment. If the temperature or humidity are different, that reed will respond differently and not always to our liking. So these technical problems distract us from having more worthy thoughts such as art. So often oboe players will become mechanic players, not because they're not musical, not because they don't like art. It's because of the burden of having so many things to consider at the same time.

So it's a good exercise to do alternative art expression. You pick another art form that you can explain the same general emotion that's going on in that part of the music you're working in. So you can go to literature, you can go through theater. You can describe a scene from a movie, even architecture. Architecture I find very useful in understanding Baroque music. Architecture is the recordings that we don't have from actual Baroque music. The Baroque art expression is recorded in architecture and in paintings. And those Baroque churches are so amazingly beautiful that just looking at them we know about structure, we know about symmetry, we know about ornaments, we know about an order to the phrases, an order to the elements that are important to that building. And we transfer that easily to music. Usually it gives me and students an easier understanding of the music if we can transfer momentarily to another art form, understand what the emotion is, and then bring back the message to music with a little more power. And then that power, that musical power hopefully will overwhelm the technical issues and allow us to be expressive even though we are thinking of so many different things at the same time.

On Technique

Technique is everything that's mathematical about oboe playing. So fingers, breathing, rhythm, posture—everything that can be understood in essentially a binary system: it can be zero and one and done. It's easy to understand and simple, and we can get to a final understanding of it by simple mathematics.

For me there are two kinds of technique: there is instrumental technique, so there is the math in handling the instrument, in making a reed—there is no music there, just an instrument that produces sound. The other kind of technique is the technique of music. When we make a crescendo, when we make an accent, when we create a round phrase, when we keep tension in the phrase. None of that is actual art. It's just things we learned that make music more interesting. While it is possible to have a brilliant career just playing the technique of music, I don't think you would be completely honest to call that art. Art is our ability to imaginatively create manipulation of the sounds so as to provoke a response or provoke an emotion in those that listen to it—that is music. That's a very different analysis altogether.

Since developing focal dystonia, I realized that we have some work to learn in our brain and I learned a lot from neurologists about what's going on up there. And it's fascinating that we have a certain separation in the brain that we loosely call right brain or left brain—right brain meaning intuition and left brain meaning reason—but it's not as simple as that because the gray matter connects. It's distributed in both sides, but it allows us to concentrate on these two areas separately. Everything that's technical, including the technique of music, is mathematical, is reasonable, something we all respond to—whether you are a teacher or a student, you respond to the same standard. And everything that's artistic is sort of what we would call the right brain or the intuition. And it's something that's personal and imaginative of the moment—the spur of the moment. Your intuition has to be developed and studied but it cannot be analyzed in the same way that math can. In the end it is all calculations but the calculation done through intuition is very different than the one done through reason.

So, for that to truly work a person needs to be left alone to develop whatever they want. In that regard everyone at this table makes reeds in a different way, and none of them make reeds the way I do, because they're all looking for something that's unique to them. I get concerned when I see people merely copying a famous player. I see students saying, "Well, that person did very well doing it this way" so they are just going to do that. That is technique. Copying is a technique. That's not art. So we're not serving the musical world very well if we simply copy what other people did.

On Focal Dystonia

There's no prevention. Nobody knows how we get this thing, so we don't know what to do to prevent us from getting it. From what we know it's a little bit of a burp in the brain and a couple brain cells died in the wrong place at the wrong time and then the fingers don't get the entire information, so they tend to have spasms. They will either refuse to work or they'll work when you don't want them to. I'm lucky that I got it in the fingers. Some people get it in the embouchure and then you can't do much. They have to really stop playing. I think the best advice I can give to people who are dealing with those things is first of all to accept that they'll never play like they used to again, ever. Just accept it. And then right away remember that they can become very good players again, but differently. They are going to have to follow a different path. I think of it like a foreign language. From one day to another you can never speak your mother language again. But you can learn to express yourself very well in another language. You will do very well, but you'll never do things, express things in the way you used to. That's gone. If you use that, your brain then goes in the old pathway, and that pathway is defective. It's not going to work. So as far as my brain is concerned, I don't play the oboe. I play the saxophone. I'm very careful not to do certain things that will confuse the brain. The more time passes, the more this saxophone gets developed. I play sideways. My left hand is sideways like a saxophone instead of being straight like an oboe because if I go straight, my brain immediately points to a pathway of oboe playing. The pathway of oboe playing is my old language. It's gone. I cannot play more than five minutes and my fingers are all over the place. It's depressing. For those who hear, it's maybe a little bit funny because I start tripping all over the place. But for me it's depressing. It's miserable. If I play sideways, my brain thinks I'm playing another instrument. As funny as these things are, it took me a long time to accept that focal dystonia is task-specific—that I can have focal dystonia on the oboe but I can play the flute just fine or the clarinet or the bassoon, for that matter, or piano. And at first I thought this is the greatest nonsense ever invented. How could that be true? But it's true! That's how the brain works. Once I accepted that I started seeing—well, if the brain works in tasks, in pathways that are that specific, let's create a pathway that helps us play a certain thing very cleanly and very organized and we will always have it. We'll always have it. So I started questioning myself: what if we were to reinvent the way we teach music and teach instruments based on the latest advances in neuroscience?

The little I've discovered from them is fascinating in many ways—it tells us we've been doing it all wrong in teaching instruments.

One of the worst things I've found is the idea of starting to learn a piece very slowly and do it several times slowly and then a little bit faster. Do several times a little faster and then a little faster. You end up learning the same piece five times and then your brain creates five different pathways. Which one of them are you going to bring to the stage? The question of how can we practice slowly has to be answered from the point of view of neuroscience, not from a textbook that was written before neuroscience helped us.

The brain requires specific information about what muscles have to move in what order and how long they will stay in that position. You can vary a little bit but the brain is very specific. It wants very clear information, no variation. Well, our heartbeat varies a little bit—let's say, during the day, 15 percent either way. So, let's say that in practicing music we can vary the tempo 15 percent either way. So if the music is written at 120, maybe we can practice at 138 and down to 116, 112, but we shouldn't go beyond that because that will force the brain to consider a different pathway to deal with it. So we have to learn from the beginning in tempo. Well, we can't play a very fast piece in tempo right away, so how do we do that? You divide it into groups, each group to be played up to tempo. In between groups, we freeze. Don't move a muscle. Don't twitch, don't scratch behind your back, don't raise any muscle that might be added to that pathway. So we will organize the phrase like that. And then eventually the brain will realize that these things are together. We're telling the brain that these sections are together, and they will slowly bond together. There will always be a little bit of a curve in between the groups but the brain will put together the groups and allow us to play very fast. I found that once I do it that way, my brain only knows one way to play the piece, instead of five. So my brain is not going to question whether I can play it at this speed or not, because that's the only speed I've ever played it. I can learn music better, faster, in a shorter period of time than I have ever been able to. And practicing very little. I practice so little! It should be shameful by certain standards, if not amazing by others. And what I've found through questioning the pathways and devising pathways for things, that there's a whole world of music performance we have not yet explored.

Your fingers should go to the next note even though you don't play it, so you freeze at the moment that your fingers are ready to play it because what really begins the process is the beginning of the note or the articulation. That should be the last thing you do. So you freeze before the articulation. It is very important that your fingers all move in a predictable, organized manner like a robot. We're talking technique, we're talking math, we're talking robot. Always, that way it's scientific. If you move it this way, you're going to get that result. It's a scientific process. You get a theory, you test it, and if you put three fingers down, you're going to get a "G." That's the way it is. If you get some other note, your theory is a mess. We need security in technique. We need to get these things down, so for a group, it would be the same thing. If you move this finger going to that, you should always get the same result. Pretty soon the brain accepts that very quickly and can move all of the forty muscles in a precise manner and be waiting for the next signal. When you have security, you can play the next note and it should be the same thing: robotic. Technique is robotic. Music is a different thing, but we need the robot in order to get the music out, so we've got to go through this.

The groups must be organized in a way that's musically appealing. Often if we just go on the beat [he accents every syllable] we're going to end up with a piece that has everything emphasizing—we don't want that. But if you look at the cadence of the phrase and look at what is leading to what and divide the groups usually across the beats, so that you always put the emphasis in the middle of the group, it helps us to bring that emphasis to the group as well. But that group, we're sending a message to the brain, and if you repeat that many, many times, the brain will take that as a priority. If we think it is very important, we are deeming it to be of great enough importance that it will be passed on the next night into more permanent memory.

The brain has three memories. There are three ways of understanding that, from the latest I've read anyway. I'm not the expert in neuroscience, I'm just grabbing information. There's one kind of memory that disappears very quickly and if you give it a few seconds it will be gone, and we'll never remember it again. We're walking around and we see a nice car and think, "Oh, that's a very nice car." For two or three seconds you remember that and then nevermore. It's gone. Or we see a nice, interesting license plate. "Oh, that's really fun, I should write that down." A few seconds later it's gone and you never remember that license plate again. And then there is a temporary memory of things that are maybe of certain importance. If you sight-read something today, you play that and if you play it again tonight before you go to sleep, you sort of learn from that but if you wait a few days and you go to play that piece again, it's like you've never played it. Because it was not deemed important enough to be passed on to a permanent memory.

Then there are those things that we repeat several times (or only play once but with a lot of emphasis). For example, the time that Tchaikovsky heard a piece and a long time later he could still write it down. When I won a prize in the Prague competition, we went into the prize ceremony in the Karlova University, which is a very old university in Prague. I felt like I was walking into the sixteenth century because of the way everybody was dressed. There was a fanfare played—I couldn't see the musicians, it was in some back hall above and they filled the room with music. I can still remember the tune and the harmonies, everything and what each person was playing because at the time it was shocking to me. They played that once or twice or three times for everyone who got a prize. I forgot how many times they played but it was just in that hour that we heard it and that was twenty-three years ago. There are things that we experience only once but they go into our permanent memory, but what we practice several times, that we want to do well at this concert, that will go into our permanent memory. What is that information that's going to go? It can be at 120 or it can be at 100 or it can be at 160—what is that information? For the brain, telling the brain that you are going to spend .001 or .005 seconds on each note is a big difference and may affect our security in the moment we're going to play. So we've got to be able to give the brain the most specific information possible. If there is something that we may be able to play in very different tempos, it's OK, we can create two pathways and do it very well in different tempos. We can do that. But it's better for us to be aware of that than to send random information into the brain that's going to be recorded who-knows-how and then the minute you walk onstage our brain is having to ask which version do you want to do? What do you mean, what version? And we get into conflict, we get nervous because we begin to have self-doubt. We don't know if we can do this or not. And of course the brain is going to go toward the slower one because it's the easier one to decode. You spend more time with that key, so of course your brain is going to do that. But if we always learn it at breakneck speed if it is a breakneck speed piece, the brain is only going to have one option—play that speed and that's it. If you can't play it, you can't play it but then you know about it and you practice before the concert.

On Air

I would say that air is something we can count on because we have control of it while it is inside of our body. We have a certain control over it. And it is therefore more reliable than having to count on a reed or on acoustics or on our embouchure, which sometimes involves very sensitive muscles that don't last very long. If we base our support technique and our sound production technique more on air than on anything else, we're bound to have a little more steadiness in our playing and practicing.

I'm not in favor of blowing too much. I think we need to use a lot of air but once we realize how much air we need and are able to do it, it should be our goal to make it more efficient and reduce the amount of air to the minimum necessary. That minimum necessary may feel like a gigantic wave of air for somebody who's beginning to play the oboe, but we shouldn't continue to blow our brains out forever. At some point we need to realize how much air is really needed and what is the most efficient way to do that. So we will overblow and then we will bring it down to a level that we can get everything done with an efficient amount of air.

On Vibrato

Vibrato is a color and as a color it should be used in diverse amounts according to the will of the performer. It should not be a matter of school; it should not be a basic technique. It's a technique of music. In the basic technique are all the things that we live and we respond to in the music market. We've got to play in tune, we've got to play in rhythm. We've got to have technical control of the instrument. Our scales have to be straight. But vibrato is not one of those. I don't think vibrato should be taught as a basic technique— you always do it this way, just turn it on, turn it off. Color is a technique of music. We're going to apply it when it's necessary.

On Solo Performance vs. Orchestral Performance

The difference is no bigger than what it is between Stravinsky and Bach and Brahms. There are different principles that govern the style, both for the style of music we play and for the setting. Certainly, for solo music we have different responsibilities and different limitations than for orchestra. But there is no impediment to a player being completely at home in both settings and in chamber music or in contemporary music or anything else that we can do with the manipulation of sounds. We just have to know what those limitations are and be responsible for them. But it's an error to believe that some people will be soloists and some people will be orchestral players. Or some people will only do first oboe, others will only do second oboe. No. Or others were born English horn players. I don't believe in any of that—we should be able to do everything. I love playing second oboe. Love it. If I'm playing next to somebody I really admire (and there are many, many people that I admire, including many of my students) I just love playing second oboe. I just did it this afternoon during the recital [the senior recital of his student, on which he performed Isang Yun's *Inventionen* for two oboes]. Being there to support somebody in what they are doing, I love it. And playing first oboe in an orchestra carries a certain responsibility. It's incredibly fun to play all of the melodies but there is also a big weight to it. As a soloist there is a certain responsibility to lead everyone and to be at the forefront of musical provocation and imagination. You need to create something that the audience is going to remember. As a first oboe you are responding to whatever the conductor is going to do because the conductor is in the position of being the musical creator. And we are responding to that and if we have a very, very big solo maybe we can participate in that decision making, but as a soloist we have that burden. So I don't think there is one way that I would prefer. I would be very happy doing anything.

On Memorable Concerts

Oh, there've been many, so many. You never know what's going to take us into remembering something. There are certain concerts I remember well because they would be memorable for anybody. Playing the Bach double concerto with the likes of Pinchas Zukerman or of [Itzhak] Perlman—undoubtedly, it would be there. My first concert with the Chicago Symphony would be memorable. But then sometimes there are other things that catch your attention depending on what our vision of the world is. There are concerts that we play for all those of us who worry so much about reeds and what we play, how we play, if it's in rhythm or in tune or not. The concerts that we play for people who couldn't care less what kind a reed we are playing, but they cry. They cry because that changed their lives. So those concerts too are very important for me. It's one of the reasons I like to be involved in different countries, in different circumstances with young people. Often, what would have been a routine performance with the Chicago Symphony is something completely unique in their setting—for people to hear Mahler 5 for the first time is mind-boggling. So it's very difficult for me to say what kind of super-experience I would prefer because there are a lot of highs out there.

On Future Research Interests

I would like to put these ideas down someday, as we develop these theories and maybe get people from neurosciences here involved. We would do controlled experiments to prove what we're trying to do. What would happen if we give a Pasculli piece for David to perform and he practices for four weeks the start-slow-and-get-faster way? And how would he accomplish that? Every week we'd measure brain waves as he's practicing to see what parts of the brain he's using. What is the security part of the brain telling him as he's playing it slower?

Then we're going to have Sumara do it the other way: start fast right away, do it in groups. Then, every week as she practices we're going to be measuring to see which parts of the brain are being used and why. And then in the following month we'll exchange that—so, David's going to learn yet another Pasculli piece the fast way and Sumara is going to do the slow way. And then, eventually, these pieces get performed in a controlled environment. Let's measure what's happening in the brain while people play. Does it really make a difference? I'm interested in motor control, security, and fear, because any time you are talking about a Pasculli, you are talking about a fear factor. No matter which way you learn it, you're going to go onstage thinking, "Oh, my god, what a stupid person I am to go in there and play this thing," because it is hard! It's a lot of concentration to do. Then, we'll be able to test and see—is it really more effective? So these are things that we would organize with the whole studio, so the whole studio would participate and give opinions and offer possible solutions.

We will need to organize this with the neuroscience department and see if we can get to a conclusion about what it does because for me, I learn music so quickly. It used to be that I was nobody if I didn't play for two days: my embouchure was lost, I didn't have endurance, it was just miserable. And now

I can be without playing the oboe for two months, and then I pick up the oboe and in two days I'm playing a recital. Where did this come from? I really don't understand. I really don't get it. Like this afternoon [May 9], I just played for the first time since early February. I did Baroque oboe, I did other things here and there—certainly playing in lessons a note or two, but not going to perform something. I don't have to worry about air, I don't have to worry about support, endurance, embouchure. Where did it all go? What did I do right that for two decades I didn't? I don't get it. So I'd like to explore to see what that is and if we could analyze it and duplicate it, then all of them are going to have that knowledge. If you say I want to play Poulenc Sonata tonight, OK, I can. Give me the music—OK, onstage—now play. A lot of that is eliminating the self-doubt factor. I don't do self-doubt. I don't question if I can or cannot do. This afternoon I was not questioning—really can I do this? Can I really go onstage? I haven't practiced it that much. No. What do I have to do? Oh, that's a high F#? How do I do that? OK, done. Go and play. Now stop thinking nonsense, just go and play. It works. But how do we quantify this and pass it along like a Barret etude to everybody: if you do this, this and that, you are going to get that result. I don't know. It would be fascinating to take this farther so we can understand and prove scientifically. The theory should work for everyone or the theory is not good. For less advanced students, we could give everybody a Mozart sonata or a Ferling etude. And we don't do one month with them—we do a three-hour practice session. Or one hour for them or half an hour. And then we test what does it take to get from point A to point B. I'm convinced now, regardless of what we do and when we do this, I'm convinced that it's time to evolve the music learning process, because now we know. We have tomography, we have CT scans, we have MRIs, we've been able to measure things inside the brain even doing experiments with animals. It's really cool and shows how the brain works—you can't rely on other science.

18

Humbert Lucarelli

Humbert Lucarelli has appeared as soloist with orchestras and chamber music groups throughout the United States, South America, Europe, Australia, and Asia. He also has performed and recorded with leading conductors, including Leonard Bernstein, Kirill Kondrashin, Josef Krips, James Levine, Dimitri Mitropoulos, Artur Rodzinsky, Sir Georg Solti, Leopold Stokowski, and Igor Stravinsky. He has recorded for Koch International, Vox, BMG Classics, Lyrichord Discs, MCA Classics, Well-Tempered, Stradivari, and Special Music. Among the recordings to his credit is the Concerto for Oboe and Orchestra written for him by John Corigliano. Lucarelli is the recipient of a Solo Recitalist Fellowship, Consortium Commissioning, and Music Recording Grant from the National Endowment for the Arts. He held positions as Professor of Oboe at the Hartt School in West Hartford, Connecticut, the Steinhardt School of Culture, Education, and Human Development at New York University, and as a faculty member of the Yale School of Music Chamber Music Festival in Norfolk, Connecticut. This interview was conducted by Michele Fiala at Lucarelli's New York apartment in May 2009 and updated in January 2019.

Musical Training

I was trained as an orchestral player, having studied with Ray Still for about seven years and Robert Bloom for another five years. My lessons with them were on orchestral excerpts. I never played an etude for either one. It molds my attitude about lessons because I don't teach via etudes, either. Facetiously I joke that etudes are make-work. They teach you some facility, but you can get that by working more with abstraction—more with scales, etc. Ray Still said to me, "Why do you want to practice etudes and develop your facility with them? You should just practice scales and arpeggios for that, which

Great Oboists on Music and Musicianship. Michele L. Fiala and Martin Schuring, Oxford University Press (2021).

I don't need to listen to. What am I going to tell you about them? If you missed a note and don't know that, you shouldn't be here. Work on your scales on your own, develop that privately." Of the etudes, he said, "You're never going to perform them. Why don't you just work on the orchestral repertoire, three percent of which is really difficult and just work it out?" He is right. You want to play *Le Tombeau de Couperin*? Play it every day, different ways and develop and perfect it. I would have to disagree with him to some extent. Three percent of the orchestral repertoire is digitally difficult true, but to have a residual facility is not a bad thing. Playing beautifully is another issue. I don't care if you're just playing one note.

Early Career

I was making a lot of money in Chicago before I moved to New York City. I was principal oboe of the Lyric Opera of Chicago. I was principal oboe of Grant Park, also in Chicago. And I had the principal oboe job of Florida Symphony in Orlando, Florida. I had a year-round season in those days, the late fifties, earning about the same as a major orchestra player per year. I left that because I got tired. For me, an orchestra job would not work in the end. I admire people who can. But for me, I have really enjoyed the variety of the career that I have developed.

After being successful in Chicago for about five years I thought, "What am I going to do?" I was twenty-five years old; I knew I wasn't going to get the Chicago Symphony. Ray Still had just come to the orchestra. I thought, "Go to New York." Having met Robert Bloom when he played with the Bach Aria Group in Chicago, I came to New York, called him and took some very important lessons, but wasn't doing much performing. Nobody knew me. My first year in New York I earned three hundred dollars. I had to sell my little VW Beetle. I ate Kraft macaroni and cheese for weeks because it was ten cents a box. I didn't have any concerts, so I decided, "I have to do a recital; I've got to do something." I put together a solo recital, and in those days, you could rent Carnegie Recital Hall for very little money, and borrowed money from some friends.

I thought so naively, "Let me introduce myself to the city by doing a solo recital." I did the recital at Carnegie Recital Hall, and the *New York Times* critic came and said, "Mr. Lucarelli is a very good player. Probably could play in a major orchestra, but the oboe is not a solo recital instrument." Never say no to me! That will only challenge me, thinking, "I'll show you that you're wrong." It's not the instrument that creates a recital—it's the performer, the character behind it, what they have to say. You can have a solo career on a harmonica.

That's when I started studying drama, painting, sculpting, and yoga, trying to figure out what the creative process is. What is the difference is between being an orchestral player and being a recitalist? Clearly there is a difference. It took me about three years. After three years, I did another recital at Carnegie Recital Hall and ironically the same critic came. Now he said in his review that this was an ideal recital. I thought, "Why aren't more Americans doing this in the United States?" There was my teacher Robert Bloom, Harry Shulman, Mitch Miller, and a couple others, but not many Americans playing solo recitals and recording. At the time, Lothar Koch was performing as a soloist, there was Pierlot, Goossens, and a couple of other Europeans, mostly French, doing solo concerts, but no Americans. There were not many recordings of and for American oboe players. I was the first wind player to get a grant from what was then the Rockefeller Fund for Music. That's how the second recital came about and was funded. I used the money from the box office to do a recording. That was the Britten recording, and it got really good reviews.

During this period, I became principal oboist with the Royal Ballet of London on its American tours and played with them for three years. We were at the Metropolitan Opera House rehearsals before going on tour, and the concertmaster, Guy Lumia, said to me as we were walking past Tully Hall, which was just opening: "I'm scheduled to play the first solo recital in Tully Hall and I have to cancel. I've just been accepted for management by Sol Hurok." Hurok was, of course, one of the most important concert managers in the United States. He managed very important careers; Janet Baker's career was one of the last he did. Hurok had taken Guy on and said to him, "I don't want you to play in New York. I want you to go out, do concerts and recitals and then we'll bring you into New York as a success." He was very clever and knew how to build a career. Guy said, "I'm stuck with this hall. I don't know what to do." I said, "I'll take it."

There I was—totally fearless, totally naive, and totally stupid. It was a big deal. I did the recital; it got a wonderful review, and it encouraged me. So, the next year, I had to make a statement about myself. The statement was, "I'm a soloist." It was just about that time that I started getting tired of playing in orchestras and doing the freelance scene. I scheduled three recitals at Tully Hall in one season and did them as theme concerts. One was called "The Romantic Oboe" and it included the Schumann Romances, the Loeffler Trio, and the Saint-Saëns Sonata. The second recital was called "The Oboe Now." It included commissioned works—all premieres—including the American premiere of the Berio *Sequenza*. The third recital was called "The Baroque Oboe." Five Baroque concerti with a string orchestra. It's a good idea to make a concert not only musically but also intellectually interesting as well. You should have reasons for every piece on it. I studied Baroque ornamentation from four different people specialized in French Baroque, German Baroque, Italian Baroque, and English. The program included a Bach and a Handel concerto, I forget what the French piece was, and then I even ended with the Cimarosa Concerto, which is sort of a twentieth-century take on Baroque concerti. The series got wonderful reviews. From that point on, I was known as a soloist. That's how it built. Then, even the Carnegie Hall manager contacted me and wanted me to do something at Carnegie.

A lot of it was done with borrowed money, but if you believe in yourself, you invest in yourself. And it came back. At one point, I would say in the early to mid-sixties, I was about thirty-five years old, and forty thousand dollars in debt. In those days that was a lot of money. But it worked out. And the most important part is that I had fun doing it.

A Solo Career

Subsequently there were a number of concerts in New York City as a soloist, including seven solo recitals at Tully Hall, plus that first solo recital at Tully Hall when it opened. There were theater events that were the fashion at that time. The concept was that we were trying to break down the centuries-old traditional conventions of concerts and create a new experience. The only caveat was that when I played it was to be completely traditional. In one of them, my entrance was in a basket through the ceiling of the hall. The entrance was spectacular: the hall got completely dark, and then all of a sudden a spotlight hit the ceiling, and I was on the ceiling, inside a basket that was being lowered slowly with me in it, playing "Pan" from Benjamin Britten's *Six Metamorphoses after Ovid*. The audience went nuts. John Herbert McDowell, who was a friend of Andy Warhol, was the director. There were a hundred actors onstage with me and all kinds of wild stuff going on.

One of the disappointments for me is that no one's followed me as a soloist yet—at least not in the United States. There are so many wonderful young players out there. I'm just stunned at the great level of playing and the quality of what's going on. There are about thirty professional orchestras in the United States, orchestras that pay a living wage. There are three oboes in an orchestra on average, which means that there are less than a hundred jobs. We probably graduate more than fifty players each year from major music schools. It's certainly close to that. When somebody gets one of those jobs, they don't leave it too easily. Maybe one or two openings come up each year. But we have this accumulation of something like fifty additional oboists each year. After that if people don't get a job they don't just disappear. They can get into teaching, do chamber music or they get a certificate, maybe an advanced degree. There's probably a pool of five hundred players available for these one or two jobs. Does that not break your heart? And these are really good players. Most of them could handle a major job without any problem.

I would love to see more young players building careers as solo and chamber players. What happened to me, so much of it was luck. What's wrong with using the word luck is it implies if it doesn't happen to you, then you're an unlucky person. I don't like that. If you want to define luck as nothing more than being in the right place at the right time and ready for the opportunity that comes to you, that's okay—you are taking advantage of opportunities. For a period in New York I was called "Lucky Lucarelli" because a lot of good things happened. Certainly, you can attract that. We attract negativity to ourselves or we attract positives. I like to see the possibilities for good things. My parents taught the only way you can grow and learn is if you put positives together. That's a big part of it. If I've been resented sometimes, it's because people see me having luck and putting good things together.

I used to be a jealous person, and was taught not to be. Richard Pearlman, who became the director of the opera program at Eastman School of Music, was an assistant to Franco Zeffirelli, the celebrated opera director. Dick and I were friends. What is that luck, meeting and becoming friends with somebody of that intelligence and stature and spirit? We were talking one time and I told him about the fact that I was jealous, and he said, "Why? Jealousy is nothing more than wanting what someone else has. If you want what they have, get up and go get it. Most people will not want to do the work and sacrifice that they've had to do in order to get what they've got. It's much easier to be jealous than to do the work." That changed my life. Anytime I thought I wanted something, I would say, "Do I really want it? What is it going to take for me to get there? How many hours of scales am I going to really have to play to do that?" Or, "Okay, if I want it, let's get to work. Whatever I have to do."

I've been blessed with a lot of energy. We were talking about what ties good players together. I wonder if that's part of it, the energy. I'm thinking about all the players I really knew. Think about Mack, Lifschey, Bloom, and Ray Still. It's energy and passion. They loved the instrument. If you as a player can put together the energy and the passion, there's no stopping you.

Musical Decision Making

Some people love to play Pasculli. Some people like to play Bach. Those have different challenges. I don't think one is more difficult than the other, and don't think one is better than the other. Everybody has to do what suits his or her personality. The fun is that over time it changes. When I was younger, I played different repertoire than when I was older. Everything changes. Tempi change; phrasing changes.

One of my favorite conversations was with a cellist who had a huge career in the 1930s. She was teaching at the Hartt School of Music while we were staying overnight in hotels, so every Monday night we would have dinner together. Her name was Raya Garbousova. Raya married Dr. Biss. Her grandson is Jonathan Biss, renowned violinist Miriam Fried's son. He's become a very well known pianist. Raya and I were having dinner one night, and we were talking about life and playing, and she was so philosophical. She was in her eighties, maybe late seventies. She said, "It's a funny thing. All my fast movements are getting slower, and my slow movements are getting faster. Now when I play fast stuff, I see more that I want to do in the phrases. It takes me a little more time to do it, so I have to slow them down. And the slow stuff, I don't need as much time to get it done. I can say it with more ease and quickly. All the tempi are becoming the same!" Isn't that fantastic?

It is critical to surround yourself with people who make you grow. I sought pianist collaborators who would grow my musicianship. It began for me with Herbert Rogers, who encouraged me in the beginning to play solo pieces. Then there was Martin Katz, who played recitals with Marilyn Horne. Marty taught me that I had to play in a way that made people feel I had something to say that was unique. Later I met Thomas Hrynkiv, with whom I did hundreds of concerts. Tom taught me to listen to the piano for the details—that the difference between really good playing and great playing was getting the details of intervals, rhythm, attitude, and everything else that goes into performing beautifully. Finally, there was Dolores Stevens, whose understanding of music has no boundaries. She not only understood the details as well as the larger scope of art. Dolores's understanding of music has profoundly affected everything in my life and I consider her a special gift. She made me understand form: how measure four related to measure one hundred and forty-five. I would be much diminished without having known and worked with all of these people.

One of the things that I don't like about recording is that people say, "That's the way he plays this piece." The truth of the matter is that's the way I played that piece on that day, that year. Strauss Concerto: I think my recording of it is too fast now. I've heard other recordings, well-known players, that I think are too slow and we talk about it and they say, "Yeah, mine's too slow, yours is too fast. We should put our two performances together and then we'd have it." It's fun to have that kind of attitude.

Recently, I've been teaching the Bach G-minor Sonata, BWV 1030b, the "Big One." I've heard the slow movement played very slowly, and I've heard it played very fast. I think it should move because it's a *sarabande* and it should have that sense of motion because it was originally a dance. The flute version is in B-minor, and the tempo marking in that second movement of the manuscript is Largo e dolce: Sarabande. That puts a special light on this piece. I'd say the Largo is to the half bar, not to the eighth. A lot of times the tempi have to do with the movement of the harmony, not necessarily with the voice leading. All these explanations to me are rationalizations so you can do what you want to do. I've often joked, "For fifty dollars I can find you a musicologist who can justify anything I want to do." Anyway, I teach it moving along. I have a student, Washington Barella, who recorded it. His recording of it is pretty slow. My students say, "I love Washington's recording; it's so beautiful and slow and gorgeous when he plays it." About two months ago Washington was here in town, and I had him teach some master classes; he gave a recital and I heard him play that piece. His slow movement is faster than mine now. You have an obligation as an artist to do what you believe. That's an important part of the whole process of what we do.

When you're doing solo work, there's much more responsibility on your shoulders to make decisions of that sort. The renowned principal flutist of the Philadelphia Orchestra William Kincaid once said, "The job of playing in an orchestra is making conductors' stupid demands sounds musical." [Laughter]

When you're doing solo repertoire, you have to start thinking about what it is you want to do and make your own stupid decisions sound musical. It doesn't mean that my Strauss was wrong because it was too fast. It was what I did at that time. In some sense when you're doing that recording, you're doing a document about yourself and everything you think of the piece. It may have been at that time I feared that people would think that I didn't have the chops to do this thing. "I'll play a little faster." It wasn't a conscious decision, but now looking back, that had to be somewhere in my thinking. My recording floats between 116 and 120. My real love tempo for that first movement is somewhere between 104 and 116. I do circular breathing, but I don't think that you have to circular breathe in Strauss. There are places to take legitimate breaths. I have a manuscript of the first two pages of the Strauss concerto and the slurs are different in the manuscript than in the printed version. There are places where there are logical breaths to be taken. You need to look at the manuscript. You need to understand the aesthetic context of the piece. For me, the Strauss oboe concerto is the real *Ein Heldenleben*, "A Hero's Life." There are even sections of the oboe concerto that remind me of *Heldenleben*, in the cello part. It goes back to *Rosenkavalier*. My image of that slow movement is that it's in her monologue of *Rosenkavalier*, when the Marschallin's husband has been cheating on her, and in that monologue the Marschallin sings in front of a mirror, and she's looking and wondering what's wrong with her, how she's changed, asking herself how could he look at another woman. That's the whole slow movement. It's about the internal. There's anger in it; there's self-pity. Every phrase transmits something that's important. You wonder even if at that point Strauss is looking back on his own life in some way, wondering if he has lost his power. When you perform you need to think about ideas like that. Otherwise, you're really just playing an etude. The concerto has been criticized for rambling and being without form. Maybe that's the charm of a concerto that was written toward the end of his life, that it is rambling full of reminiscences without form like a conversation of the old man he was. Let's give him a break!

Storylines in Interpretation

Even if a piece of art is abstract, it evokes some sort of emotional response, some sort of mystical response. There's a feeling there. It can make you angry or feel good. Even the most abstract Bach piece elicits something, and if it doesn't, you're boring the audience. As a soloist, if you don't make the audience laugh and cry, feel good and bad, there is no reason for them to leave their home and go to a live concert. That's what it's about. When you're playing in orchestra, there's some of that, for instance the way you play the solo in *Don Juan*. You can have an attitude in that and it is okay to be subjective. My take on that solo is that it is the seduction scene from *Romeo and Juliet*. Don Juan was the world's greatest seducer, so he goes [sings opening phrase]. He's almost pleading, being almost oily in his approach to wanting her. As an orchestral player it's a good idea to have notions like that. Go to your first rehearsal with your approach to this piece. A conductor may disagree with you and stop and say, "Can I have that be a little more aggressive?" Or, "Maybe a little bit more dolce." But at least you've given a conductor something to work with. I've had conductors who've done both. I once played a phrase in Tchaikovsky's *Swan Lake* and the conductor said, "Hum, I never thought of that." I also played with Stravinsky conducting. We did *Symphony of Psalms*. and I remember he stopped and said, "[Clucking sounds] Oboe: it's too musical." I knew exactly what he meant. He wanted it to be more pointillist and have angles, and I was doing what I jokingly call my macaronic, Italian-opera phrasing.

I played with Stravinsky several times, performed *Rake's Progress* with him conducting and did some recordings with him. Conductors of that sort aren't around much anymore. Once, halfway through a bottle of Scotch, Bloom turned to me and said, "I remember when a conductor was the best musician in the room." Naturally. Part of the problem is the job. It's changed. Fritz Reiner, when he was the conductor of the Chicago Symphony Orchestra, had in his contract that he did not have to go to fund-raising cocktail parties or dinners. He stayed home and studied the scores. Poor conductors, now they have to be public relations experts and fundraisers as well as great musicians. Therein lies a big issue for conducting now.

Great Performers

As an orchestral player, you can absolutely play several measures in the most wonderful, beautiful ways imaginable. The best of orchestra musicians do that and they all do it with their own personality. My definition of a great artist is somebody that does what they do better than anybody else. You have almost no right to judge, because there's a level of accomplishment in which that kind of judgment becomes superfluous. It's so individual. I don't like the concept of schools of playing because schools of playing deny the individual. Art is a celebration of the individual, so the concept of a school of playing is anti-art. I mean, Picasso doesn't paint like Miró or Degas. Who's right? Even if you go to the Picasso Museum in Paris, the range of what he did during his life is astonishing—starting with the Blue Period and evolving into Cubism. Was he ever right? Performers have to be like that. The great performers of stature are those who do what they do better than anybody else. It is unmistakable when they do it.

When we were kids, we used to sit around trying to distill what the well-known players did into one word. Ray Still was "dramatic." Marc Lifschey was "liquid," a kind of fluidity in his playing. Harold Gomberg was "color." If you listen to those Mahler recordings with Bernstein, you hear it. Bloom was "poetic." When Bloom is playing you feel like he's talking to you, he's changing your life. None of these artists are right or wrong, but they do what they do. Nobody could do what Marc Lifschey did. John Mack, he was so good, so right all the time, beyond criticism. John was a good friend. At that point, how can you prefer one or the other? It's not fair. You're limiting your own ability to enjoy life and music. Gordon Hunt is one of my favorite players. He emits a joy of music and love of the oboe. There are so many European players who I just love, too numerous to mention here. There are very few major players that I would pull back from. It's a mistake. We limit our own experience by doing that. That's a pity.

On Studying Drama

Studying drama made me much more aware of the notion that an audience was out there and that I had to project what I was feeling about the music in here—I had to move that across the stage and out into the hall. How to do that is very mental as well as spiritual—it's internal. I've seen great actors live on Broadway, it's wonderful because you're there watching it happen and molecules are moving in the room. I'll never forget Geraldine Page in *Three Sisters*. In the first ten minutes of the first act, she was sitting onstage with her back to the audience. And I swear you heard nothing onstage, all you could see was her back. She was so powerful. She projected so much energy that I don't remember anything about the first ten minutes of talk. She was reading a book and she turned a page, and she turned another one, and eventually she said, "Oh my God, am I bored!" And the whole audience went *gasp*! That is what you have to learn how to do if you're going to do recitals.

Bloom used to talk about that in phrasing, "Don't give it too easy," or if you do, it's something you do because you want to do it. Let them wait. He said, "Take the time to send the very best." If you do something that you want to be beautiful, it's done with care. How you do it, how you touch the phrase, it has to be what you're trying to project to the audience. That's very important. There were certain technical things that I learned from being onstage. I had just recorded the Benjamin Britten *Six Metamorphoses after Ovid* and after it was edited—it was one of my very first solo records—I listened to it and hated it. It was technically really good oboe playing, but it was so boring. I couldn't issue it—just couldn't do it. That's why I started studying acting. My acting coach actually coached me for six months on that piece before I went back and recorded it a second time. He questioned everything I was doing, like if I did a subito piano, he'd say, "Well, why are you doing that? I don't understand the context of what you've just done. Why is that forte there? I need you to explain that dynamic to me in the way you play." He said to me, "You can't just go out and buy a bunch of fortes and pianos at a dime store and then paste them on the music. They have to be internal. They have to be indigenous. There's got to be some reason for them." He came to concerts and criticized everything I was doing onstage, like where I was walking and where I was standing. I went to hear a bunch of recitals and watched so many great instrumentalists and singers, how they projected themselves and what they did. One of the most memorable concepts for me was before becoming a professional musician and I didn't quite understand the depth until later—I was ushering at Orchestra Hall in Chicago and was about nineteen years old. I remember getting to the hall early; Elisabeth Schwarzkopf was the singer and she was singing Mahler songs. She was onstage a half-hour before the concert with a makeup kit and a mirror and she's applying her makeup onstage, in the stage lights. At the time, I remember thinking, "How superficial. I'm so disappointed in her." That she would care that much about her external presentation, but she knew exactly how she wanted to look to that audience. Is a diamond ring any different if I present it to you in a brown paper bag or a Tiffany's box? Of course it is! Presentation is important. You have to understand how you want to present your performance. It's not to say that one is better than the other. I've played concerts in Levi's and funky clothes and my first recital in Carnegie Hall, in the big hall, was with a rock band—electric oboe with a wah-wah pedal. It was my group called *Musimorphoses,* about a year and a half after the Beatles had quit and a review came out that said we were the best band since the Beatles. This concert was 250 years of western music, and we started with the Renaissance and ended with a heavy metal version of Tchaikovsky Fourth Symphony, the last movement. This is one of the many sins of my youth. [Laughter] Crazy. But we did it.

On Visual Arts and Music

When I was painting, I studied with Lucia Tallarico who was a student of Hans Hofmann. He developed what was known as the American School of Abstract Expression. What is music? Abstract expression. Same thing. So, I first started painting. She said, "You're not using color. You're drawing; you're using paints to draw lines instead of using color to create depth and perception." Does that open an ear? I found I had the same problem as a painter. The observation was just so on the mark. It took me about three years, working with her. I took lessons every week and finally began to create something that was interesting. It's fascinating to me that other good oboe players have been painters. Marc Lifschey, really good stuff. Harold Gomberg was also a painter. He had one-man shows in New York. It is well known that cross-pollination of art disciplines gives more depth to an artist.

The other medium was sculpting. My teacher, Peter Nicholson, put a rock on the table and he said, "I want you to sculpt." He said, "What you're looking for is in that rock. Take away what doesn't belong." How beautifully similar to playing a phrase that is. Don't impose yourself but try to find what's in the music. Go from the inside. That became an important part of my concept of performing music. As a soloist, you have to be aware of the form of the piece, not playing only four bars. Even when you're playing four bars in a symphony, you might play those four bars in the exposition and ask how is it going to be different in the recapitulation after the development? And why? There's so much to think about. It's not just playing the oboe. Bloom used to joke about some players, saying, "That's a good oboe-blower." I've heard some beautiful oboe-blowers who knock me out. In fact, sometimes I wish I could have had some of their phrases. It just doesn't have the big picture. You only have a hundred percent to focus, and if you spend ninety-eight percent of it on blowing the oboe, there ain't much left for the audience.

Advice

I keep saying to my students, "Don't worry about getting the orchestra job." Try to get the orchestra job, to take on the challenge, but if it doesn't come, look at other possibilities. You can teach. You can build a multifaceted career. Mine was one. I taught the whole time. I was at the Hartt School of Music for forty-seven years during the whole period. I jokingly said, "How do they put up with me?" Because I would go on tour and play eighteen concerts in one month. They put up with that. Part of it was they wanted to have somebody out there from their university who was doing things. Because I love to teach, I never cheated a student out of one lesson.

The best things that happened to me were accidents: the John Corigliano Oboe Concerto, for example, was a turning point for me. A friend of mine was working with the New York State Council on the Arts. He was working in New York City and they had just come up with a commissioning program to give young artists funds so that they could commission a new work. He called me and said, "Would you like to commission an oboe concerto?" What's the chance of that happening? It's because I was out there, doing things as a soloist, and they were looking for something. "Let's do wind instruments. Let's call Bert, he's out there doing stuff." They gave me ten thousand dollars to commission a concerto. I got John Corigliano to do it, and it was a real stroke of luck, the first major work that he had written for a soloist; as a matter of fact, I have a photocopy of the manuscript, which he autographed, writing, "Thanks for starting it all for me."

And that's even an accident. How did I have the sense to choose someone that had that potential and that possibility? I don't know. I've commissioned pieces that have sadly never gotten played again. Malcolm Gladwell wrote in his books *The Tipping Point* and *Blink* about how in a blink, you pick up what's going to happen. It's about what you see without really seeing and what you see subconsciously that makes you realize what's going to happen. John had been around great music making all of his life. His concerto would be magnificent. I didn't think about that, but somewhere, it must have programmed itself in my decision. I'm suspicious of everything I do!

"Puffing"

The Hartt School said, "We've got some money left over. We need some master classes." So I invited three prominent oboe players. John Mack, Ray Still, and Robert Bloom came to do master classes in one semester. After it was over, students came to me and said, "Oh, Mr. Lucarelli, we're so confused. We don't know what to think and do. Why don't you do a master class for us and we can talk to you about it?" So we did the class. First thing that struck me was that they only saw all the differences between these great players. I saw what was the same. It's what I mentioned to you earlier: energy, commitment, and passion. That's what the three of these great musicians had. They're totally different personalities as performers. I would love to be a fly on the wall watching Ray Still take a lesson from John Mack, and vice versa. It would be total war and so much fun.

Let me dive into a bit of controversy here. In the middle of class, one of the students said to me, "How come you don't teach us to puff our cheeks?" I said, "What are you talking about?" I've been taught to never puff my cheeks when playing the oboe. He said, "Well, they all puff their cheeks when they play and so do you." I took an oboe and looking into a mirror I was shocked, there it was. I said, "I don't know what that's about." But obviously if I'm doing it and they're all doing it, it can't be that wrong. So, let's try to figure out what's happening. I love teaching this way, more of a dialogue. I enjoy my students challenging me. So I said, "Well, first of all, if we are all doing it, I've got to figure out how it is that they got me to do puff without telling me to do it." I studied with two of those people, but I never studied with Mack. I played second oboe to him when I was nineteen so we remained lifelong friends. Anyway, I started thinking, "How am I doing this? How was it induced?" Ray Still said to me, "You have to play like you have a totally relaxed face. Relax your facial muscles. Drop your jaw." Well, if you drop your jaw and you relax your facial muscles totally and then you blow, there's no way to stop the puffing from happening.

I played second oboe to Bloom for twelve years in the Bach Aria Group. Once, just before we went onstage, he said, "I know I'm playing right whenever I feel [whispered] 'puh-puh-puh-puh.'" And I'm walking onstage, thinking, "What's that mean? (puh-puh-puh)" That's how it was induced, I'm sure. Then I had to figure out why was it important? What is it doing? I started asking flute players. Julius Baker [Julius Baker, former principal flute of the New York Philharmonic] did it all the time. Flute players are all telling me what it does is it keeps the air at the front of your mouth. If you do that, you cannot close your throat.

I'm not talking about Louis Armstrong. It is possible to do too much. I had one student that went over the edge. The result is that the sound is too voluptuous, it's so rich and warm and deep, and unusable. It's just gorgeous but you can't phrase with it. It's stuck in that place. If you're going to have any palette of color, you can't just be overextended. It has to be the right amount. When it's right, it should not vary while you're playing. It should not change because it's the fuel going through the reed. You don't reduce the size or the flame will die. The pressure is always there. How you change the sound is actually more with your embouchure and rest of your oral cavity, but the air has to be there all the time, at the front of your mouth. Bloom used to say, "Focus the air on the tip of the reed." Singers talk about focusing at the gum-line of their upper front teeth, or in the "ng." All of these concepts are in the snout. It all has to work at the front of the mouth. That's the thought in it; the puff keeps the air at the front of the mouth. The rest of the body will then fall away without tension. I do Alexander technique so I know this cannot be wrong!

One morning I was teaching in New York, at my studio, and a student was playing and the phone rings. Julie Baker who I mentioned earlier called. "Hey Bert, I just heard your Strauss on the radio. It's the best one out of all of them." I said, "Aw, thanks Julie. It's so funny, I was just talking to a student about you because I was talking to them about puffing cheeks a *little* bit and I told them, even Julie Baker does that." He said, "Don't tell them that," like it's supposed to be a secret! [Laughter] Like you shouldn't do it. I said, "But why, Julie? It's so good." He said, "Yes, of course, you can't play if you don't do that." I said, "I do it on the left side more than right, I think because I'm right-handed and my left side is weaker." "No, no," he said, "I do it on the right; I'm right-handed." He even knew on what side of the mouth he was doing it and he wouldn't tell people.

As I mentioned earlier, Washington Barella was a wonderful student of mine. He objected. He couldn't deal with the puffing. Somebody had told him when he was young that you should never puff your cheeks and he just couldn't stand the idea. So, to get around it, he developed another concept that is very similar, which was "to fill your jowls with air." Well, have you ever looked up the definition of the word "jowls"? There's no defini-tion for it; really, it's just an area. It's in there [indicates lower cheeks]. I've seen some wind players puff up here [upper cheeks]. Don't do it. First of all, the danger is that you will get air around your embouchure when you do it. Big mistake. The sound will tend to be a little shallow if you do it up there. You want to do it around your lower molars. It's just what you think of Bloom doing, and Still with the "totally relaxed face." It gives the sound much more depth and warmth.

Raising the Back of the Tongue

Every instrument has its own oral-pharyngeal format. First of all, we only have two octaves. The third upper octave doesn't exist in my book. Hans Moennig [most respected repairman in Philadelphia during the time of Tabuteau] once said to me, "You shouldn't play above a high D. Bach did a lot with two octaves." You can get those notes, but to me, that doesn't sound like the oboe anymore. The back of the tongue is part of that ma-trix. The low D works better with the back of the tongue up. I use that as an exercise—to have my students play octave D♮s by raising the back of the tongue. When you find the octave D♮, you back off from that just a little, so that just the bottom D is playing in the most focused way you can imagine, and that's the format for your tongue for the entire instrument.

I studied voice with a woman who taught singers at the Metropolitan Opera who were losing their high register. She claimed the reason they were losing their high register was that they tried to get too big and opened with the bottom of their sound too much, so the high register got lost. It's a triangle. If I open the triangle at the bottom too much, the bottom comes out and the high register gets lost. If I want the high register to come, you must narrow the bottom. She used to say, "Do it upside down. Think of the bottom narrow this way." She even used to have singers sing music up-side down on the stand, so that the high notes would look like they're low notes. You've got to get focused because if you get the bottom too wide, you get a boomy sound and then what are you going to do in the middle and upper registers? It sounds small and out of tune. The worst case of that is the English horn, where that whole left-hand octave sounds like it's wheezing and the low register sounds really kind of tubby, big, and macho.

D'amore is even worse. Bloom used to say, "D'amore doesn't come in a case. It comes in a cage."

Vibrato

I used to joke that vibrato was like drugs and sex; no one ever talked about it. Vibrato was the forbidden subject. But string players talk about it all the time. Singers talk about it. Why shouldn't we? The reason we don't is because nobody really knows where vibrato comes from. It is said that when asked about where the vibrato comes from, Tabuteau replied, "When you blow right, the vibrato will be there." I had to think about it a bit. First of all what is vibrato? What are the components of it? It's an oscillation of the intensity. Maybe pitch is part of it. Carl Seashore talks about vibrato in his book *The Psychology of Music*. Fabulous book. He's a very famous acoustician. He broke music down into four main characteristics: pitch, rhythm, dynamics, and color. He claimed he could measure that at any age, three, four years old, even, and tell you what instrument you should play. If you didn't have a good pitch ear, you should play piano and hire a piano tuner. He found that most musicians were strong in two of those areas and weak in two. He has a chapter about vibrato in the book. It gets a little technical at times, but mostly it's for the layperson. He charts the speed, pitch width, and intensity level of the vibrato of famous singers. Speed is obvious. You can hear that. Even width is pretty obvious. Intensity maybe gets a little sketchy. The other one I attribute to it is placement. Is it below the note? Is it in the middle of the note or is it above the note? That's hard to hear and even harder to figure out how you do it.

You should practice doing all three of those: speed and width and placement. The normal vibrato according to Seashore was somewhere around six [per second]. He lists about twenty singers and their various speed and intensity levels, during the *bel canto* period—Caruso and Galli-Curci. The speed and width of vibrato can be also related to personality and fashion. In the 1930s it was faster than now. I found that the idea of practicing six oscillations per second isn't too good, because I don't want to get a mechanical concept in my ear. So I'll do four. It's the fastest speed I'll practice. Four is like the speed of an airplane going down a runway. When four gets really comfortable, all you have to think is faster and it goes. When it hits four, it'll take off. The great trombonist, John Swallow, when asked where he got his vibrato used to say, "I get it in my ear."

In an aesthetic sense, in some pieces you want the vibrato to be slower than that. The last note of the Poulenc Sonata, that E♭, it's very sad. He's exhausted from losing his best friend, Prokofiev. Vibrato has to vary. It is another tool, another expressive device. It mirrors what you feel about the aesthetics of the music. What makes the oboe so beautiful is that the sound erupts from your soul. It can touch people in a way that you can't with any other instrument.

Character of the Oboe

In Hollywood, when there's a moment that's very touching and very moving, you'll always hear an oboe. The oboe goes right through your breastbone into your heart. That's its real strength. It doesn't play high notes so beautifully; it doesn't play fast. Once when listening to a student play really fast, Bloom said to me, "Never have so many notes said so little." There was a poster in a drugstore about a woman's cologne that I would love to get a copy of to hang on my wall. The poster read, "Its strength is in its gentleness." That's the oboe! What I love about Dick Woodhams's playing is that it's magical. He's so gentle; he draws you in. Bloom said once, "Projection is beauty." Half of projection is trying to get the audience to want to hear you. Not loud and big. This concept of projection that's going on right now in the world of music playing destroys the sound and consequently destroys the instrument. Everybody's trying to get a bigger sound. If you've ever been in the hall where the Beethoven "Eroica" was premiered, you will see that the stage cannot have held more than twenty-eight players. Once you get the winds, you've got about fourteen string players left. Today's orchestra has twenty firsts, twenty seconds, and no conductor has the courage to ask them to play softly. I don't think there's anything wrong with having twenty first violins, but they have to be able to play softly. There are very few things in life more beautiful than twenty players playing really softly. They can do it, but are rarely asked to do it. So you've got everybody screaming at the poor little oboe trying to get that solo from the "Eroica" out. We're going up the wrong tree.

As a soloist you don't have to worry about projecting so much. First of all, you're standing in front of the stage. Your sound is bouncing off the floor into the hall. If you played the Strauss Concerto sitting in the middle of the orchestra, you'd have to play completely differently because there are people around you with clothes and music stands. When you're standing in front, you can project with a small beautiful sound. One of the great oboe repairmen, Carlos Coelho, heard me perform once and he said, "It's amazing. No matter how softly you play, I always hear you." That has to do with the resonance and the way you're dealing with it. It's not just volume.

It has to be beautiful. It's what we do. There's not an instrument that could be more beautiful than the oboe. It has been a privilege for me to be an oboist because it has given me the unique opportunity to express the joy and love I feel for people through music.

19

Frank Rosenwein

Frank Rosenwein joined the Cleveland Orchestra as principal oboe at the beginning of the 2005–2006 season. Since 2006, Rosenwein has been head of the oboe department at the Cleveland Institute of Music. He also teaches at the Kent/Blossom Music Festival. Born in Evanston, Illinois, Rosenwein holds a bachelor of music degree from the Cleveland Institute of Music, where he studied with former Cleveland Orchestra principal oboe John Mack, and a master of music degree from the Juilliard School. Prior to coming to Cleveland, he served as principal oboe (2002–2005) of the San Diego Symphony and San Diego Opera. This interview was conducted in May 2009 by Michele Fiala in Rosenwein's Cleveland apartment.

Note from Michele Fiala: *I arrived for the interview just as Rosenwein was playing a Yusef Lateef video. He was so excited to play me a section in which Lateef played the oboe. "It's fantastic," he said. "He plays the oboe like no one else. He can pitch bend and do stuff like you've never heard before. You recognize it as an oboe, but it's like nothing you've heard before." His enthusiasm was contagious.*

Early Career

I started music when I was about five on the piano. My parents are very musical people; my dad plays flute, my mom plays viola and at the time my mom was playing piano, so I gravitated toward that. When I was nine or ten, I took up the clarinet and around ten or eleven I took up oboe and played it in the school band. We had a family friend who I subsequently studied with, Bob Morgan, who's a fabulous teacher and so I was exposed to oboe and I thought it was great and I wanted to do it.

Great Oboists on Music and Musicianship. Michele L. Fiala and Martin Schuring, Oxford University Press (2021).
© Oxford University Press. DOI: 10.1093/oso/9780190915094.001.0001.

I studied with Bob Morgan from the time that I started until the time that I left to come to the Cleveland Institute. I was lucky that I was able to start with someone who was equally as skilled with the rudimentary aspect as well as the higher ideals that I was trying to grow into. I studied with him for probably seven years. I took lessons with various people all over the place, spent summers at Interlochen, but Bob was the main influence on me as a young oboist and he had a truly profound effect on the way that I play now. The feeling of freedom in the sound, that there's an ease to it, that the blowing process is not constrictive, that there's a vibrancy about the tone, those are some of the most influential, important things that I got from him. Other aspects of phrasing, of musicality, he was really good with those aspects. With phrasing, like in a Baroque passage, the first three sixteenth notes are one thing and then the fourth sixteenth links to the next thing—he introduced me to that idea and that's a really important concept. In a more general sense he was able to get me off of the page and that's a super important thing that sometimes gets lost.

When I was a sophomore or junior in high school, I decided that music was what I wanted to do, and oboe. I gave it my all. I think it can work to hedge one's bets and go to a place and do a double major, but I think it also can work to put your eggs in one basket and say, "I'm doing this and if it doesn't work out, there's always law school I suppose." I really was committed and can't think of anything else that I would ever want to do, so I came to the Institute and once you're in that kind of environment, the end goal is clearly to become a viable professional, and to make a mark in the world, musically.

Going to summer festivals was important to me in that regard. Those are places that can really further one's career with regards to repertoire, with regards to being a lot of places. You're going through rep really quickly. That's the only thing you're doing; you're not taking any classes or anything like that. But also there's a circle that you meet of people you become friends with and you see at other festivals and then you ultimately become intertwined with those people in real life, when you get out of those situations. So making those connections at summer festivals actually is a super important aspect of coming along, musically. And then certainly taking oodles and oodles of auditions.

Auditions

I don't necessarily recommend taking auditions as soon as one can. Obviously, we're always auditioning. We're auditioning for youth orchestra or auditioning

for summer festivals or auditioning for whatever, but when it comes to a professional orchestras and professional gigs, as a freshman, as a sophomore in
college, one should focus on those aspects of music that are the most important. Those translate to excerpts; those translate to the kind of skills that you
need to be able to play a great audition. But oftentimes people get either burnt
out or ossified with the excerpts. You start on the excerpts so early—playing
Tombeau [de Couperin] for twelve years—it's boring! It's an exercise that you're
trying to perfect. I have some remedies for that lethargy, but I think it's maybe
not necessary to begin the audition process too early. Nevertheless, when you
do start on the audition process, that definitely propels you forward. Every
time you prepare, those weeks before the audition, the prep time, the mental
crises, the coalescing of various ideas about these excerpts and about your
playing and how you want to present yourself—all that is at such a fevered
pitch as the audition comes around and that steps you up, and then you play
the audition and you want to turn that into the best experience that it can be.
Really the preparation is what elevates your game. You take thirty auditions,
you've elevated to a certain level. I took tons and tons of auditions. I was lucky
enough to land San Diego out of grad school. Started as principal oboe in San
Diego in the fall after I graduated. That was complete luck but it was so happy.
Winning a job is great, but actually going about the job is an entirely different
subject and a different thing and the playing of a job is what ultimately propels
you. You have to be at a certain level to be able to get a job, but when you get a
job, that's when you can really start to advance in a way. You're not in the mode
anymore of necessarily needing to satisfy a committee's opinion of you. That's
a different skill, almost, than coming into your own in the orchestra. You've
been listening to oboists for years and years, on CDs and records or whatever,
and you have this ideal in your head of how you want to sound, how you want
to project yourself, and you're able to work towards that goal. It's a little bit of
a Catch-22, but somehow the process of interacting with your colleagues, of
trying to picture your sound in the hall, picturing your ideal sound, that furthered my career more than anything. That's sort of ironic, because that's the
career. The career forwards the career.

I still took a bunch of auditions when I was in San Diego. I was again lucky
enough to win the Cleveland audition. That also propelled me. I listened
to some things that I did in 2005, when I started, and I'm embarrassed because that's not how I play now. I feel totally a different person from who
I was when I started. Progressing in the job has really furthered my musical
understandings.

Joining the Cleveland Orchestra

Luckily, going to the Institute for my undergraduate, I knew most of these guys. I coached with them; I listened to them every week. I had lessons with them. I studied with the teacher who you could say imprinted a certain way of doing things in the orchestra. So I felt very comfortable coming into the situation, knowing what will work. That said, clearly these people have had a profound, profound influence on me. The issue of what I was talking about earlier, thinking about how you project in the hall and how your sound wants to develop, that's super important. In a solo context that's wonderful, but I prize the ensemble playing, knowing when you're a principal oboe, when you're a second flute, when you're a third clarinet. These things are prized more highly than "how was my sound on that solo?" or "did I really do an interesting whatever in this passage?" It's those aspects: to what extent are you dealing with a color aspect with the flute, is there sort of a washier color that you're using with the flute? Josh, the principal flute, is just a fantastic and amazing musician, and hearing him and how he interacts with the ensemble, that's been a profound influence. He has a very mellow but intense and vibrant quality. That maybe defines the wind section. Mellow but vibrant and projected. Those aspects of weaving oneself in and out of the texture is something that the orchestra does extremely well and that's been a great benefit to me and an amazing continual discovery.

Avoiding Excerpt Burnout

You don't want to have these things be so extracted that they become their own thing. An excerpt is an organic part of a composition. It was never meant to be its own entity. So you have to get back to the music; you have to get back to a) why you love to play music, b) why you love this piece. We play *Tombeau* over and over again, but actually it's an amazing, beautiful piece, so if you get back into that by listening to different recordings, and you can get the piano recordings of *Tombeau* and that's really interesting to see how the piano plays it. We have these preconceived notions of how difficult it is and what we need to do to overcome certain things, and the piano just makes it sound like it's nothing. Listen to your favorite recordings and play along with the recordings, so you're internalizing the surroundings. When you're playing it, either practicing it or in the actual audition, you have your imaginary friends around you playing with you. That really helps, making sure that you're cognizant of how much you love to do this, how much you love to play music. And it's music. It's beautiful music.

Inspirations

I recommend listening to singers. I studied with Elaine Douvas in New York. Anyone that comes from that opera background has been either unconsciously or consciously influenced by the ease of the voice, the legato of the voice, the fluidity of the voice, the golden roundness of the voice. We're always taught, telling people or thinking about how to make our instrument sound more vocal. I recommend anyone from Callas to Pavarotti in the sixties and seventies. You listen to Pavarotti, it's the most beautiful thing you've ever heard. There's amazing stuff on YouTube actually. Caruso on YouTube—and the recordings are decent, from 1904. It's fabulous, not only to listen to it and say, "Okay, that was beautiful," but to say, "What are the aspects that make it so beautiful?" And to mimic that.

When a singer leaps up through an octave, there's something so filled in about those leaps. It's never "Ah—Ah!" As instrumentalists we can flick a key and boom! You have an octave. But if we're really influenced by singing, we fill that in. And we take a little bit off the top so it doesn't go "ah . . . AH!" It's almost natural instincts of a singer to do certain things that you have to be careful to think about. A singer doesn't have any keys to put down. A singer has diction, so that's in a way their equivalent to these little keys, but the greatest singers are able to make you feel like this line is going on forever, even as they're very careful about elucidating the text and making you hear each word and think about the meaning of these words. So there's this overall concept of absolute melody, where even if you dip down, you never interrupt the line. But then, within that, there are all these details about colorations and certain notes, about the forcefulness of the consonants. That's an ideal for us to aspire to, the articulations that we have—slur two, tongue two—how to make that interesting in a textural context but without making those little details too big. Those are ways singing or listening to singing can help. We're not all great singers; I know I'm not. But if I'm stuck with something in a passage and I really try to sing it in the most natural and musical and beautiful way, if I can get that ease and then I've got something.

Teaching Phrase Shaping

You have to start with an overall and overarching sense of what you're trying to do and then from there come in with the details. I try to impart the importance of character, of mood, and then from there thinking about how can we best give this line direction. Within that, what are the various harmonic components leading to here? Coming away from here? What are the various melodic aspects? It's not just directed wholly toward one spot, it goes to some spot and then develops into the next spot and that next spot is probably the more important spot and then it comes away. So, there's an element of analyzing where in this line is the most important point. Most music, there's a degree of tension and release. We move towards something, we come away from it and so, how to best illustrate that in a given melody? We don't play harmonies, really. We're just one-line creatures, so we have to really ensure that within that line we have all the kinds of delicate features that we can possibly have to make it as interesting as possible.

Breathing and Support

With wind instruments it's difficult to actually say what's happening because it's so internal. One does have to rely on analogies and metaphors to get at the essence of whatever it is that you're trying to explain. With breathing I try to be as simple and direct as possible. I ensure that people are taking good breaths, meaning that the chest is not rising, or the shoulders rising as they breathe, that it's the stomach, as it were, and the back that's expanding. I make sure that students are breathing in that manner, that they're feeling it from the—I don't know if it's the diaphragm—let's just say stomach, and your chest stays where it is.

Support and blowing, I think is an important concept people keep as separate. People start equating support with blowing. So you say, "Really support that," and they'll blow harder. But the support is that great breath, taking all the air to the lungs that you want. Those who have that actually don't blow so hard. I'll have to make sure that people are separating this idea with taking in the good breath with releasing it in a controlled and rationed manner. That the air isn't slipping out, that it's slow moving. And that creates, certainly, a much better legato. That can help with people who are having trouble in the high register, having the high register ring and have breadth. If we're forcing, if we're really pushing with the air, it can be tinny in the upper register; it can blow over the tone so that the tone is too "uppy." I'm always trying to conceive of the tone as down into the note. I want to have a tone that sits as low in the sound as possible, with a reed that's up to pitch. So, we're low in the tone; we're not flat but we're low in the tone, and to do that, you can't blow super hard. You have to release this air in a controlled manner. When it comes to articulation, people get tense, they get anxious when they see lot of articulation and as a consequence, they blow hard. "Oh, it's a staccato, I have to blow harder." But if you're supported enough, if you just let the air flow from you, from this nice balloon of support, you don't actually have to blow hard. You don't want to blow hard when you're articulating. It makes you less able to articulate quickly and it can make it heavier and peckier. Sometimes that's okay, but most of the time we're trying to create an articulation that's bouncy and flowy and leading somewhere.

Warming Up

I'm not a big fan of an all-encompassing warm-up that one plays all the time. That can work for some people, but more often than not, when people have their warm-up that they do that's fifteen minutes or half an hour or an hour long, it quickly becomes routinized; it quickly becomes an exercise and starts relating less and less to actual musical production. I want my warm-up to be as connected to a musical situation as possible. So I like to listen to myself, I like to listen to my body, listen to my lips, to see, on a given day, how am I feeling, what kinds of things are important to me to work on this month: "I'm going to make this project a month-long project of X." Listening to yourself and what you need any given moment for your warm up is helpful. That means that I'm not necessarily playing long tones for every warm-up session. With that said, one can do many varied things within a similar warm-up. If you're used to doing long tones, if you're used to taking the note, starting it softly, expanding it out and coming back, you can switch that up by doing things like starting the note, expanding it out, and then at the peak, changing notes, and then coming back. Doing that changes the dynamic of it because you have to think about the connection between one note and another. The simplest things are the best things to work on in a warm-up. Getting from one note to the next is a much harder task than it would seem to be.

Often, if you're going from a two-finger C to a D, where you have all the fingers down, we're dealing with a mechanical aspect of putting down four fingers and getting to a half hole. There's a mechanical, physical aspect to going from note to the next; it's not as simple as it might be. There's the issue, if we're using vibrato, of carrying the vibrato through the C into the D—again, not necessarily an easy task. There's a tonal aspect and a pitch aspect, too. Often our Cs are maybe slightly lower, so we have to deal with a pitch issue. The tone of the C is more strident than the tone of the D, generally. We try to make reeds that minimize that, but we have all of these aspects to deal with that are outside of simply the issue of the long tone. Trying to get from that C to that D can be a trying task, and the context of also thinking about how you're attacking, the beauty of the attack, the dolce quality, the gentleness of that initial attack, that's important. So you're thinking about that, you're thinking about how your vibrato develops through the C, you're thinking about the tone of the C; you want to keep open and beautiful and deep, even as you're crescendoing. And then when you get to that D, you don't want to flinch; a lot of people go from the C and there's a glitch or something in there, whether that's the mechanical aspect, that's something in the throat, so you're working on that, and you're working on diminuendoing with those same ideals, so that the diminuendo doesn't die away too soon, that you're able to create this beautiful arch downward towards the piano, that the vibrato stays full throughout, that when you end you have this nice, lovely taper. There are so many aspects that one is working on within a long tone, that just adding one extra element to it, say, going to another note, can be a totally different experience than what you're used to.

That's what I mean in terms of listening to yourself and feeling what is it that you really, really need to work on. That's just an example, but it's good to put into one's warm-up, these kinds of slow, very methodical and very intense sorts of little exercises. It's also good to have some aspects more just general playing, scales in thirds are good, regular scales, in different patterns. But you want to mix it up. If you always go [scale through the ninth and down in duple], okay, great. But if you're always doing that day after day, then that becomes something of a routine. Then you mix it up [sings scale through ninth and down, then scale from degree two to tenth and down], so you add different aspects to that scale. You can add articulations and you can stop on certain notes. Just make sure that the tone of the C is as full when you're on your way up as when you're coming back down, so you're working on the things that are important to you and you're not just going rotely and routinely through whatever it is. To that end, I definitely recommend that people not be distracted when they're warming up. A lot of people like to say, "Oh, I turn on the TV, and I go through my scales," and that's really the wrong approach. Your most intense listening and feeling and tactile experience should be in that warm-up.

The other thing about warm-ups is that, when you're stuck, when you have a hard passage, I encourage students to make up their own etudes or their own exercises based on problems that they're experiencing in a given piece of music. If you're having problems, for example, with downward slurs, which often want to crack on the bottom, they want to come out too loud. There's no arch in the slur, just sounds like you went from one note to the next. We can talk about what it is that you have to do to get from to this note and then to drop to the lower note, but if you can come up with an exercise that you can work on in your warm-up, then that will greatly benefit you. So you come up with an exercise that uses broken arpeggios [sings broken arpeggios, with portato between notes]. It's up to you to determine what the best intervals are to work on, if you need help in the lower register versus the upper register, if there's a particular note that always wants to crack, and where does it crack? Does it crack on the top or on the bottom? Making up one's own exercises is important and creative way of getting off the page and focusing very carefully on just one aspect.

Technical Development

A lot of people have a tendency to play through things too much. We need to slow down more and not put off to tomorrow what we can get done today. Sometimes it works to say, "Okay, I've done what I can do today and to-morrow it'll probably get better because it'll somehow get into my muscles and then I'll work on it tomorrow." But we often overlook the most salient features of the passage that are giving us the difficulty. Try to find the note or the couple notes that are the actual issue. Or maybe it's just difficult to get from that octave key to get back down, so you focus, because initially we think, "This sounds bad." "This passage is sloppy." If you just work on it slowly, that's good. We want to work on things slowly, but if you haven't iden-tified specifically what it is that's tripping you up, it's going to be inefficient. I'm always looking for efficiency, with practicing, with reeds, with time man-agement. In the least amount of time we can, we want to get done the most.

So identify the key characteristics that are giving you the most trouble and then turn that into an etude or really work that with different rhythms. That is probably the most important aspect.

We have a tendency, when we get into a technical difficulty, of trying to work out a technical way of dealing with it. "I'm going to move my finger faster," or "I need to keep that finger closer," or whatever. Oftentimes we can get out of a tricky technical situation by thinking of it in a musical way. If this passage is really difficult for you, maybe it would get easier if you phrased it in this particular manner. Maybe it would be easier if you played it with real, heartfelt emotion. Sometimes we get into a technical passage and we get scared and we start playing mousy or without expression, and that's actually hindering our technical abilities. We play it like it's the most beautiful thing in the world, wow, that helps. That's important to me, to make sure that it's musically sound.

Vibrato

My teacher was a proponent of a constant but beautifying vibrato. Sometimes that can result in this annoying, persistent vibrato, but that's not really the idea. The idea is really more that you want every note as beautiful as it could possibly be. I love that concept, but I often find that we can use vibrato as a sort of an ornament, as a beautifying element, but that there are other ways of beautifying notes and that some notes don't need to be as beautified as others within a given line. I encourage people to make the vibrato as varied as any other component that we're dealing with. Much of the time we do want there to be a hovering of vibrato, which either intensifies or diminishes in intensity depending on the context. But oftentimes we can make more tension if we lose the vibrato and think about epic legato. That then results, when we get to the place where we want to go, in a kind of a blossoming which then can be enhanced by vibrato. You don't want to think of vibrato as a monolithic entity that's always ongoing, but you don't want to think of it as on and off, either. It's an expressive tool and you have to pay attention to it. A lot of people play vibrato on this note, and then not, and then vibrato on this note and then not; it's off and on and off and on. That's not what we're talking about. But if it provides an expressive result, then that's more valid.

When it comes to producing it, I've heard lovely vibratos that are "diaphragm vibrato" and I've heard lovely vibratos that are "throat vibratos" and I do a throat vibrato, but I don't think it's necessarily the only way. What you don't want in terms of vibrato is to have it constantly the same, so if you're using diaphragm vibrato you have to be able to make sure that you're able to get it fast enough when you need to have it be fast enough, and when you're using throat vibrato you need to make sure that it can be wide enough when you need it to be wide, that it's not always wiry and beat-y.

Teaching

It has a tremendous impact on one's playing. The articulation of one's principles is something that you really have to do some soul-searching in terms of what's important to you, in music, in general, in oboe with this particular piece, these elements that we don't necessarily have to think about when we're just performers, but when we're teaching we have to understand what it is about music that we find really important and then we have to articulate that in a way that's going to have some impact. So there's a lot of searching of one's own banks of experience and of one's desires for what they want with music and an overall sense. Why are we doing this? In general and also on a very specific level with, in this piece, what are the important elements? That helps tremendously with staying on track and growing at the same time. Teaching helps you to expand yourself; you're always thinking of new ways of looking at things. A student comes in and plays something and you say, "Oh, right, that's an interesting way of looking at that." But also a student comes in and says, "I don't get this. What's going on with this passage?" "Hmm, let me think about it." And then you come up with, "Well, I think that this really is the most sound way of doing this." But then you have to be careful that that doesn't become the end-all. There's no endpoint; we have this knowledge but we're constantly learning and we have to keep our minds open to new possibilities, and that's a danger of being a teacher, actually, is to get too dogmatic, is to get too self-centered or thinking that you have all the answers and not being open to saying, "Hmm, I'm kind of stumped by that too, let me go figure it out." And then you figure it out, and you say in the back of your mind that it's not immutable. For now that's a good solution, but maybe down the road there'll be a better solution. You're always aiming toward the Platonic ideal, but realizing that you'll never come up with it yourself.

Keeping a Job

Once you get into the orchestra then that's an entirely different experience and one that requires different skills than you've been working on to get the job. There's the process of auditioning and that's its own animal with its own skill set. There can be a tendency with auditioning to position your playing in such a way that it appeals to the most people at the time. Oftentimes the committee is made up of not oboists but of the principal percussion player, a trombonist, who knows where these committees come from, and you have to appeal to people of all stripes and that can cause you to become a little more remote from real music-making. That process has a tendency to whitewash people a little bit, and so you have to make sure that you're a real voice, at least as a principal player. It's different in some respects when you're not principal, but you have to maintain a real point of view, musically, so when you do end up in the job that you have something to say.

Getting a job and keeping a job once you get it is about 90 percent who you are as a person and about 10 percent how you play. People hired you so they're pretty confident as to your playing. You have to make sure that it's great, but if your playing's great and your personality is weird, it's going to be hard. People can live with certain things in people's playing that they don't maybe like that much: "When he gets loud it sounds a little crass, but okay, whatever." But if someone's going to sit next to you for thirty years, they want you to be a great person that they can count on and that they like, that they're not threatened by, but that they can't totally overpower. There's a really in-depth sociological aspect to assuming a role within the orchestra, especially in the winds and if you're principal oboe especially, because there's a sense in some orchestras that the principal oboe is a leader and there's a sense in some orchestras that it's not so much of a leader. There's resentments from various quarters about your supposed power. The best thing that you can do is to play great, let your playing speak for itself, assume a role of real responsibility, especially for your own parts, never come in unprepared, always have listened to things beforehand, and have the confidence of believing in your own playing while being open to suggestions.

When talking with colleagues, be as demure—I don't want self-effacing—but be as non-threatening as possible. If your flute player sitting next to you is playing really out of tune, you have to come up with a way of saying, "Can we just try those Es? I'm feeling a little bit weird." There's something that you have to cultivate, and it's not to say that you shouldn't say something. You should say something; you should talk about those Es if they're out. That's your responsibility musically. But you have to figure out a way to have it be as collegial as possible. That's a super-important thing that people, in school and elsewhere, never talk about. That's really important: the balance between collegiality and being open to people's suggestions and the firmness with which you have to believe in your own convictions.

20

Grover Schiltz

Grover Schiltz was one of the Chicago Symphony Orchestra's longest-serving members, from 1959 until his retirement in 2005. He played assistant principal oboe until 1964 and served as principal English horn from 1964 to 2005. He also taught oboe and Baroque performance practice at Northwestern University, the University of Illinois at Chicago, and Roosevelt University. This interview was conducted by Michele Fiala at Schiltz's home in Lake Forest, Illinois, in May 2009. Schiltz died in 2012.

On Warming Up and Technique

When I was studying and when I was first getting started I tried to keep a regular routine each day for scales, scales in thirds, and technical studies. Using the Barret Sixteen Grand Studies, I would pick an etude each week and work on it for a week and then go to the next etude and then come back and clean it up. It's for a good reason that when Tabuteau had students go through the Ferling, they would actually do them in transposition when they finished them up. What it amounts to is just a question of analyzing your technique and making sure that nothing is slipping; if you feel articulations or finger intervals are getting a little sloppy, then find some etudes that concentrate on those particular aspects and work with them more than anything.

But always practice scales and scales in articulation. I teach my students, "Don't ever settle for two slurred and two tongued." Because that's only one of a dozen different articulations—three plus one, one plus three, two tongued and two slurred, and others—so that you never get into a rut. It seems to help them to develop finger and tongue independence and complete coordination between the two.

I teach at two universities, at Northwestern and at Roosevelt, and I find most kids coming from high school are pretty deficient at scales. Most of

Great Oboists on Music and Musicianship. Michele L. Fiala and Martin Schuring, Oxford University Press (2021). © Oxford University Press. DOI: 10.1093/oso/9780190915094.001.0001.

them have got absolutely no systematic approach and most of them think the oboe ends at D. E and F are strangers to a lot of them. So, we take apart the scales and spend a lot of time, two notes rocking back and forth, then three, then four, and I try to devise studies for them and show them how to make exercises for themselves so that in their practice room by themselves, they don't feel lost. They know how to systematize their practice in order to get the greatest amount of benefit. I tell them right off the bat, "Look, I'm with you one hour a week and I can't trail you around and be on your shoulder every minute of every practice session. What I have to do is teach you to teach yourself."

When you play with the Chicago Symphony, you keep so busy playing all the time that mostly the practicing you do is like housework. If you have time for anything, you usually do scales and arpeggios, maybe go through some of the difficult material that's upcoming, and if you see you have a little bit of a problem technically, you analyze what the problem is and work at that. When you do over 200 concerts a year and teach in addition and maybe even do a little freelance playing—recording, chamber music—the time for systematic warm-up routines gets pretty small. It's mostly devoted to reeds, especially when you're traveling. One day you may be in Los Angeles and it's 80 degrees, the next day you may be up in Denver with a totally different kind of acoustics, totally different temperature, totally different altitude, and you have to find something that works. When you're on tour, it's just a matter of survival.

On Breathing and Breath Control

Most students don't support the sound when they first come to the university. They don't support the air well enough and don't realize how much intensity of air is necessary to make a resonant sound that projects. Most of them just play to the reed instead of through the reed and through the oboe. What you have to do is to play all the way down to the bell and not just to the note itself.

When I was first studying, my teacher said, "Look. It's like trying to blow out a candle across the room. You can't do it by going 'Ha'. It has to be 'pfft,' a really fast moving, compact, and fully supported stream of air." That's the only way that you can get a resonant sound and a sound that projects. It's very important that the stream of air be absolutely steady so that you're not favoring every single note, playing one- and two-note phrases. When you're playing a phrase, the sound may get full or less full, but you still have to have a connection between the notes. It's almost as though what you do between the notes is more important than the note itself. Don't play like a string of beads, or a string of pearls, where each one is separate from the other. Make it like a cable—it may get narrower or wider, but there's still that strong connection between the notes, so that there is no gap in the intensity. Sometimes in a master class, I will take just one disparate thing like the idea of going on a five-note climax from a C to a G and then back to a C and hearing that perfect connection between the notes. There is no bulging and you get a feeling of conicity. The crescendo doesn't go note-note-note, but goes through all the notes, up to the climax and then back down. I don't want a feeling of pressing into each note with the air. One of the excerpts that is most revealing is the slow movement of Tchaikovsky's Fourth Symphony. When you can play that beautifully, legato, without inflecting and without losing the intensity of the air, then you've got your air pretty well under control.

On Vibrato and Its Control

I divorce vibrato production from air production. I don't want to use the same muscles that are used to expel air to make vibrato. I want it to be two systems. I know there has been a controversy in the past between the throat vibrato and the diaphragmatic vibrato, which is a misnomer of course. There is no such thing as "*a* vibrato"; there are many different vibratos. There are strong, weak, fast, slow, crescendoing, diminuendoing, intensifying, and dropping away. I don't feel that you can exercise that kind of subtlety with your vibrato by using a diaphragmatic vibrato because there's a limit on the speed that can be produced in the first place and you can never produce sforzandos, for example—the short, sharp, stress accent—when you're using diaphragmatic vibrato.

The first thing you have to do if you've got a bad vibrato is get rid of it. I use long tones, without any color on the sound, to try to make this perfectly conical crescendo from one to ten and then back to one. I always encourage students to think about what it would look like if it were being drawn on a graph. Is it going to be a snake trail or is it going to be a perfect conicity up and down? Once you achieve that, once you're able to control that, then you can start to color the sound with the vibrato without distorting or without changing that conicity—without changing that feeling of being in control of the airstream, separately from the vibrato.

I sometimes have them take a C major scale and vibrate the first note, the third note, the fifth note, the seventh note—so that you have stress-release, stress-release—that tells me whether or not they've got control with their vibrato.

The amount of resistance in the reed colors to a great extent what you're doing with your vibrato. A really heavy reed is going to produce a slower vibrato because it's going to take more intensity of air to produce the nodes involved in the vibrato. If you use a light, easy reed, it's awfully easy to just make sort of an antinode vibrato and you get this "eeeeee," a little quiver of sound. Usually you can slow it down by adding a little resistance to the reed.

My first major teacher was Bob Mayer, who was the English horn player with the Chicago Symphony when I was in high school—I grew up in the suburbs here. He had studied with a Frenchman who played principal in the Minneapolis Symphony. His name was Alexandre Duvoir. Bob played old-school French, short-scrape oboe reeds. As a result, he played with this tight, fast vibrato that you heard on recordings from many French oboists at that time. If you listen to the recording that Geoffrey Burgess made called *The First Fifty Years*, you hear some of that. You also hear no vibrato at all in many players because the concept of controlled vibrato in oboe playing is almost within my generation. When you consider the first people who really worked hard at controlling and using vibrato as an expressive device, it's Tabuteau, Léon Goossens, and Jaap Stotijn. There were a number of people who, when vibrato started to be used in orchestral playing, weren't sure how to do it. When I was a student, I used to hear some wide ranges of vibrato. The English horn player for the Boston Symphony, Louis Speyer, he was the absolute epitome of nanny goat. He had studied at the Paris Conservatory and, boy, it really showed. He had a tight, fast vibrato—students would make fun of it, basically behind his back—but he was a very good player from the standpoint of technique and consistency. We're a long way away from the days when half the orchestras had imports. When I first started studying, the Cincinnati oboe section was all Frenchmen: Marcel Dandois and the Andraud brothers.

On English horn, most of the solos tend to be lyrical. You play low and slow and then you go. You have to develop a lyrical style—*Roman Carnival*, *New World*, Debussy *Nocturnes*—and yet on the other hand you have to get snotty once in a while with *Pines of Rome*. But it's usually pretty mournful. *Swan of Tuonela*, *Tristan*; yet, within *Tristan* you have to have that range of intensity where you start out at one range and then as you accelerando you make the center section much more involved and emotional; you have to indicate that with your vibrato as well as with the speed at which you play. Those things, they're both important, but lyricism is especially important, in that 90 percent of the solos you play are going to be that lyrical kind of thing.

On Reeds

Perfection: that's what we all look for. You want articulation; you want control, tone quality; you want projection, and you want comfort. All these things have to be considered and a well-balanced reed has as many of those things as you could put in one package. Unless you're comfortable, it's not going to sound comfortable. And that means finding the right tip opening for whatever it is that you have to do. Elaine Douvas once made the remark that you want to play a tip opening that is only as big as necessary. If you have to work with a tip opening that's too big, you're going to suffer, because partway through a solo passage you feel like you're starting to get tired and it pulls in your expressiveness; it means you're just trying to survive until the end of the solo. And it communicates; you can hear that.

This is one of the big problems in modern playing. When you're doing a Baroque sonata, Baroque music doesn't take into account the kind of playing we do as orchestral players. The Baroque oboe reed is a much, much different reed. It's much more closed, it's much freer, and you have to have an entirely different approach to the instrument because you have these long, extended passages to play with no place to rest your embouchure and regroup your forces. If you're going to play Baroque oboe, you have to approach the reed in a wholly different way. I play Baroque oboe as well as modern, but I try to keep the two separate from the standpoint of equipment. If I play in the Chicago Symphony I'm not going to play the same reed I play for a Baroque group.

There are some people who manage to go back and forth and have done so pretty well. Jim Caldwell played terrific Baroque oboe as well as modern oboe. Alex Klein plays Baroque oboe and also a number of European players like Jürg Schäftlein, who was principal oboist in the Vienna Symphony as well as Concentus Musicus. You have to think about what kind of repertoire you're going to play.

What makes auditions difficult is the fact that you are playing all the most difficult stuff in the repertoire within ten minutes and that means a bionic reed. It means a reed that has to be so good that it can just do everything and to your satisfaction. For all-purpose playing, comfort is an important thing. Also, you want a reed that's focused enough so your sound quality is what you want it to be all the way through the dynamic range. You don't want a reed that spreads when you go above a certain dynamic level. It has to have focus, and the same kind of focus, at every dynamic. You have to have a reed that articulates well throughout all the registers because when you're playing an audition—*Scala di Seta* followed by *Tombeau de Couperin*— flexibility and ease of technique and articulation all over the instrument are absolutely important. Sometimes, when you're playing a concert, you have to switch reeds between pieces. The reed that plays *Tombeau* beautifully may not play the Shostakovich 1st very well. When you're in an orchestra you have that luxury. When you're playing an audition, you have that bionic situation where you really have to find a reed that does it all and does it all beautifully. Good luck.

On Auditions

You have to know your material so well that if I were to wake you up at two in the morning and hand you an oboe and say, "Play me the Brahms Violin Concerto," you could. Too many students are not aware of how exacting an audition has to be. The level of the graduates of the best conservatories— Juilliard, Curtis, Eastman, Oberlin, and more—means that everybody is going to be playing with a pretty good tone, everybody's going to be playing the articulations, everybody's going to have listened to the recordings and play the proper tempo, right articulations. Now what's going to make you special? You have to do all those things and more, which means that in addition to technical perfection, you have something special to say. This is something that is hard to transmit. After all, there's a lot of wine made in the world, but there's only one Château Lafite or one Corton Charlemagne and in that sea of good wines, what makes this one special? Maybe it's extra care. It's some sort of special understanding that goes beyond just playing the notes or just putting wine into a barrel. You have to teach your students that every note is important, that every note has a function and that every note should have its place in the ideal phrase. And you must try to discover what is in this excerpt that makes it different from that excerpt? Can I play this in such a way that it makes it unique? You don't play Brahms like Mozart, you don't play Mozart like Schoenberg. You have to prepare yourself so that you can shift gears rapidly, so that when you go from the Brahms Violin Concerto to *Le Tombeau de Couperin* that you're ready to make the change and think in a different mode right away, so that each excerpt has its own special and unique character. A Brahms symphony calls for a weight of sound and a massiveness of sound that *La Valse* doesn't. Try to find out from listening to great recordings, through working with good teaching, exactly what you can do to make every solo unique, and that means controlling vibrato, controlling tone color, listening to the weights and the balances of the notes so that you hear how the phrase is made and can project it.

On English Horn vs. Oboe

The English horn is not just a big oboe. You have to approach it somewhat differently. It has different problems. One of the big problems with English horn is developing a full enough sound in the upper register; it's difficult to get it to project. The alto voice has more problems cutting through the orchestra. Some students try to make up for it by making a very thick or very heavy reed and blowing really hard. That kills off nuances, so you have to find a reed that's balanced in such a way that the sound rings and has stability but still lets you make some nuances. Many of the English horn solos are quite long. If you're going to play the Shostakovich 8th Symphony you had better be ready. It's a very long solo, it's over three minutes, and there's just no rest in it; it's like a big cadenza. You want a reed that's almost stable enough that if you abuse it, it still produces a pretty good sound. A reed that's too loose means that the minute you start to tire, you lose the best control of it.

Picking the proper bocal is very important. English horn has that extra problem with bocals. We have more choices now than we ever did as far as having good bocals. When I was a student, one of the biggest problems of all was a dropping third space C on diminuendo. I think an awful lot of English horns got sold to students because they weren't suitable for a professional, and yet it may have been the bocal rather than the body of the instrument itself. Now there are a number of other people who make good bocals. It's almost like flute head joint makers; it's a whole separate industry itself now. Almost nobody plays the same flute body and head joint. When they find a body they like, they go shopping for a head joint. The trouble with bocals is that, even though they're supposedly standard, no two of them are exactly alike.

On Tone Production

In the first place, you need good posture. You can't dedicate the thoracic muscles to producing a good airstream and good support if you're leaning. If you're out of balance, you're using part of the musculature just to support yourself in that position. I try to feel as though I'm stacked like a pyramid, so that I'm never really off balance. Different teachers teach it different ways. Some will teach, "Feel as though you're hanging by a cord from the top of your head," so that everything is in alignment, everything is in balance. I try to feel as though I'm never forcing it, not squeezing out the air. Instead it should feel, as with good singing, there's no constriction. You want all the musculature to be working steadily towards a point of rest. You are expanding and contracting but you never feel as though you're pushing beyond what's in the air, what's in the lungs. The oboe has such a tremendously small flow rate, you have to think about getting rid of bad air. Too many times, students will keep inhaling, "hu, hu, hu!" and you end up swelled up like a frog and where is all that bad air going to go? Sometimes you have to teach them to deliberately exhale and play on what the residue is. Again, without pressing, without forcing. Sometimes I'll just [exhales], go to a resting point like that and then play a solo and go on for eight or ten bars. Try to maintain the same lyric quality and the same kind of control that you had with a full breath, so that you don't revert to squeezing and pressing.

Many times, students get their shoulders up and then squeeze and what they do is choke off their neck. So shoulders down, arms away from the body, with a relaxed posture, head slightly up and forward, so that you're not pressing your chin. All these things are important to maintain a good air flow. Sometimes when you tighten up, what you're doing is shutting off blood flow through the carotid artery up to your brain and I've had students almost black out because they're just squeezing the blood supply off. By keeping your head up and feeling as though you're not burying your chin into your neck, you're going to have much, much better results.

On Preparation

It's a combination of technique and analysis to get a piece under control quickly. First you try to find out what the piece is about or what it means. Think about the parameters of the piece, take it apart from the standpoint of tempi, keys, and key relationships, and then try to isolate aspects of it. Okay, this is going to be lyrical. Think about what registers it's in, how extended it is, and start working on it from that standpoint. With lyrical material you almost have to wait until you have it in the orchestra or in the ensemble before you make decisions about where to project, where not. If possible, you get the score and study it and see how you relate to the other instruments and how your part fits. If it's technical, take it apart and see—what's the range? What are the technical problems? Then, start to think about analyzing to find patterns, find things that allow you to almost throw away the written music so that you know it well enough that you can almost play it from memory. It's too late to read when you get into a performance; you have to just know it. That means you've gone beyond the conscious, from the page to the instrument.

It has to go beyond an intellectual thing and become part of you. Find patterns, make sure you get your fingering patterns learned, and do the same patterns all the time so that when it comes concert time you know where the fingers are going to go. If you have a good general overall technique, then it becomes easier. It's difficult to explain to students how important a good strong technique is. Unless their technique is secure, they're never going to be able to forget it and just play the music.

As Gillet said in his study guide to the Gillet studies, if you do it right, three hours a day of practice should be enough. He spends an hour a day on scales, arpeggios, all that technical material, the second hour is on technical studies, and the third hour is for orchestral excerpts, concertos, and that sort of thing. If your day doesn't call for three hours, take what you have and divide that into three and that way you're building a technique *and* a soloistic kind of style. Don't divorce one from the other—when you play a scale, you try to play it as beautifully as you can. Don't just think about the notes; think about the articulations, think about the dynamics, think about the tone color. All these things are important because, after all, almost everything in music is made up of scales or intervals and if you can play a beautiful scale, you should be able to play the passage beautifully too.

Memorization is important. Good performance depends on playing a piece almost from memory. The music is just there to act as a reminder. If you dropped the music and you would have to stop, then you don't know the piece well enough.

With contemporary music it's harder. There's less in the way of patterns. You have to learn it by brute force. You have to be ready to take in groups of notes. Start with small groups and add groups of two, groups of four, groups of eight, until you really feel like the whole thing is yours. You have to work hard to get the extra technique that you need to do some of this extraordinary material, with multiphonics, with quartertones, with all the other contemporary effects. It's a harder life than when I was a student.

On Talent and Teaching

I can only admire somebody like Boulez or Barenboim who can do the things they do from memory. For example, Barenboim has twenty-seven Mozart piano concertos from memory, all of Beethoven, all of Brahms, and it just goes on and on and on. Then there are all the operas that he does from memory, standard repertoire, Mahler symphonies, Brahms symphonies, Beethoven, it's all in his head. And he knows it all. It's not as though he's faking.

There's a certain thing that's called talent, and it can be frustrating when you give your students as much instruction as you possibly can and with some it works and with some it doesn't. It's an ineffable thing—the ability to be able to take in all these things, put them together, and make them work. There are a lot of professional basketball players, but there's only one Michael Jordan. You feel lucky when you get good students. It's been said that there are not great teachers; there are great students. When Tabuteau had the pick of the country, throughout his teaching career at Curtis, he'd pick one player a year and give them a free ride. Why shouldn't he get the very, very most talented? Even at that, you read Laila Storch's book and see the list of those who went through Curtis—there are some people who never became professionals and never became noticeable names among the oboe world. Talent has a lot to do with it, but you also have to take into account the degree of really hard work and discipline that a student can put in. If somebody's a late starter and they show promise, should this person be discouraged? Or if this is a person who's played for a long time and is lazy, can you jog them to the point where they'll work? As a teacher, it is hard to play God and determine who is going to go on and who isn't. I once played for de Lancie when I was a student and he said, "You're winning the notes." I wasn't sure what he meant at the time; then he played for me and I understood. He said, "Give up the oboe, get a subscription to a good concert series. You'll learn, you'll get to hear a lot of good concert music." And of course, I said to myself, "John, you're not going to defeat me; I'm going to go ahead and get her done," and I did.

Early Career

I had this old-style French, short-scrape teacher through high school. Then I studied at the University of Michigan, worked with the English horn player from the Detroit Symphony. His name was Lare Wardrop. Lare himself was totally undisciplined and not a very good teacher. He could make reeds well enough to play, but he made them in a very unorthodox style and he couldn't fix student reeds. So I became self-reliant very quickly. Whenever a visiting orchestra came to town, I would buy a lesson with one of the players whom I admired. When the Cleveland Orchestra came to town, I would try to get a lesson with Marc Lifschey. In the Boston Symphony, Jack Holmes was there; Ralph Gomberg came in. And we'd have transfer students from other schools. If somebody came in from Eastman, well what does Sprenkle do in this case, in that case? It was kind of homemade for a while.

When I got into the service right after college, I went for six months to the Army Band's School of Music in Washington, DC. Manly Sanders, who had studied with John Minsker, was the oboe instructor there, and I also got acquainted with Earnie Harrison and did some study with Earnie. I also went up to Philadelphia and studied with Tabuteau for a short time. After I got out of the service, I came to Chicago and played in the Civic Orchestra of Chicago and studied with Ray Still for a year.

All of these teachers had something to say to help me; if you're perceptive, you pick up the things that you want and need. I felt fortunate that my first years were with a strong technical disciplinarian so that I didn't have to think too much about technique. I could concentrate on reed making; I could concentrate on phrasing, on other concepts that round you out and make a better player of you. My high school teacher, Bob Mayer, was a disciplinarian. Every week, two major, two minor scales, both diatonically and in thirds, and if you didn't get anything more than that done, you didn't get anything more than that done. You didn't get to play your Barret, you didn't get to play your Ferling, you played scales for the half hour. And it pays off. If you get sick enough of the scales and you want to play the music, you learn the scales so that you can get to the music.

On Artists Who Inspire Him

If you're listening to a flutist, you listen to players like Mathieu Dufour who's our principal flutist, or Emmanuel Pahud who is again a wonderful, wonderful flutist. Among bassoonists, I admire players like David McGill, who is our first bassoonist here, Arthur Weisberg, Sol Schoenbach. When I first joined the orchestra, Leonard Sharrow was our principal bassoonist. Marvelous bassoon player. These people all had a very sensitive kind of approach to phrasing and wonderful vibrato control. And violinists, players like Pinchas Zukerman, Gil Shaham—again, players who have a tremendous sense of color.

Cecilia Bartoli is a wonderful singer as well as Anne Sofie von Otter, Thomas Quasthoff, Dietrich Fischer-Dieskau. All players and singers who had marvelous communicating ability, with a wonderful sense of phrasing and a great sense of color. Somebody like Gil Shaham, you could almost put words to what he's doing and he shapes each note so beautifully and finds exactly the proper color for it.

On Teaching Musicianship

You have to find a function for each note and how to make a design that the composer had in mind when he made the phrase. The Barret *Oboe Method* is a good way of teaching phrasing. It may not be great music, but it has phrases in it that have the elements that you need in order to play Brahms well, and play Schubert or Schumann well. He tries to teach you something in every one of these Forty Progressive Melodies and you have to find what it is in this particular melody that shows you something that you didn't do before, or something that you have to be careful about. Often, he'll make a phrase in one articulation and then in a different articulation. Don't learn to play by ear; read what's on the page.

In the second of the Progressive Melodies, it's entirely falling phrases: "Mi, do, sol, do, mi, mi, re, do." What he's teaching you is take the intensity out of a phrase or out of a passage. The intensity is highest at the beginning of the phrase; you don't grow that opening E because it would give you an entirely different feeling from what he intended. It makes a great difference whether you're going to grow a note, whether you're going to hold a note steady, or whether you're going to diminish the note. You learn to play through the phrase and determine what the phrase is trying to do and what it will tell you to do, eventually. You go phrase by phrase. How does this phrase fit with the others? Is it repeating at a lower level or at a higher level? Are you going toward intensity, are you going away from intensity? How does this phrase fit into the design of the whole piece? Learn to take small elements, make them fit into bigger elements and into the whole of composition; then it gives you more interest for your audience. The worst thing you can do is bore your audience. As Arnold Jacobs, our former tuba player, said, "You've got to tell a story. It might be a lie, but at least it's a story."

On Baroque Ornamentation

When students get more intensely involved in Baroque music, they have to learn how to ornament. What constitutes ornamentation? What's good; what's not good? After you teach them the elements—the various kinds of ornaments—they have to put them to work, and they also start to study some treatises on early music: Quantz, Hotteterre, people like that. Quantz gives you a three-note phrase, "Do, re, mi," and then shows you twenty-five ways to ornament it and this helps a great deal in offering you the tools. But now you have to put these different ornaments together in a satisfactory package so that you aren't redundant in the kinds of ornaments that you use, and that you put them together in such a way that it's continually pleasing to the ear. That's what Quantz says: you should continually refresh the ear.

Students should begin by listening to different recordings and comparing. See how this player does it, see how that player does it. What ornaments do they use in what places? Do you like this, do you like that? Do you not like this, do you not like that? Learn to copy so that you at least have some ornamentation, preferably from a player whom you most admire. Many of the ornaments that I use for the Handel G Minor Concerto are ornaments that I picked up from Jürg Schäftlein who performed it with Concentus Musicus. And, you know, when you care enough to steal from the very best.

When you've learned by rote this series of ornaments, you think, "I'll substitute that in this place. I like this better than I like that. This is what I personally feel. I like a dotted rhythm here instead of a smooth eighth-note rhythm." All of that is fine. What I also do is try to get students to use qualified editions. Too many of them show up playing Handel sonatas from fifty-year-old editions that have been heavily edited. As you know, Handel didn't write with crescendo-diminuendos. You have this tremendous freedom in Baroque music to articulate as you like, to ornament as you like. Even up through Mozart, there's no agreement as to which edition of the Mozart Concerto is the authentic or the original edition, because there isn't any! I once asked Dick Woodhams what edition of the Mozart Concert he used. He said, "Mine."

Changes in American Playing Style

You can see it even within the graduates from Curtis. Those from the earliest years—Arno Mariotti, Bloom, Angelucci—they were much different in style and tone quality from Harold and Ralph Gomberg, from Lifschey, so I think the playing evolved a great deal over those years. Even Tabuteau's playing—compare his playing from the late twenties to what he was doing, say, in the late forties and early fifties. His vibrato slowed considerably, his tone darkened, so these things have all evolved in our lifetime, practically. We have a more recognizably American style of oboe playing than what we did when I first started out: Fernand Gillet was still playing first oboe in Boston, Duvoir was still playing first oboe in Minneapolis, de Busscher was still playing first oboe in Los Angeles, Bruno Labate was first oboe in the New York Philharmonic, and Paolo Renzi played first oboe in the NBC. These were all foreign players, some French, some Italian. A really recognizable American school didn't arise until probably the late thirties and early forties when the Tabuteau students started going out and being more influential and turning out their own students.

Now we're getting more alike to our European counterparts. I remember talking to Danny Barenboim about this and he said, "It used to be that I turned on a radio and within twenty bars I knew it was the Berlin Philharmonic. Not anymore." When I started out, you'd hear the New York Philharmonic on a Sunday afternoon, and you knew it was Harold Gomberg. You'd hear the NBC on Saturday night, you knew it was Paolo Renzi. You heard the Philadelphia Orchestra, you knew it was Tabuteau. But a lot of these differences have passed away. Almost everybody who's got a job now is either from Curtis or Juilliard. So they either sound like Elaine Douvas or they sound like Dick Woodhams. And sometimes it's difficult to tell one from the other. In a way it's good and in a way it's not so good. We've lost the sense of individuality where you turn on a program and, oh, that's Lifschey, or that's

Ray Still. We've gained some things; we've lost some things. After all, Eugene [Izotov] doesn't play like a Russian.

Reminiscence

There are certainly standout concerts, like doing the Shostakovich Eighth Symphony with Rostropovich, who knew Shostakovich and who worked with him. When you get this guy coming up, bringing you to the front of the stage and kissing you, it's pretty special. And doing *Tristan* in New York in concert version. We did it in Chicago and I was up in the organ loft, out of sight, doing the offstage solo. But for Carnegie Hall, they put me in a box over to the side because there's no backstage at Carnegie. It came time for it and all of a sudden the house lights go out and there's a pink spotlight on me! I didn't expect it, so I was somewhat taken aback, but it came off very well and I was very happy with it. It's one of those moments that stays with you for a long time.

Advice for Young Musicians

Listen, listen, listen. Listen to recordings, listen to concerts. Learn to be analytical; learn to be able to dissect a player's playing so that you can find the things that you like, the things that you don't like, the things that you need to make your own playing better. Be an omnivore. Devour the instrument, devour everything you can learn. Go online; there's material available online. It's a constant learning process and the more you know about it, the better player it's going to make you. Make sure to have the curiosity that is necessary to really, really immerse yourself in the instrument. Learn about different kinds of instruments. Get the IDRS [International Double Reed Society] journal; read it, memorize it. Go to the library. There are copies of *Woodwind World* and other publications that go all the way back to the fifties. Read them; see what kind of information you can get out of them. The more you know, the better player you're going to be. You've got to work at it; it's not a part-time profession. You have to be into it all the way. You can't work at it twenty minutes a day and be a great player. You have to be convincing technically, musically, aesthetically, intellectually—it all has to be in the package. That's what makes a great player.

21

Allan Vogel

Allan Vogel received a doctorate in music performance from Yale University. In 2016, he retired as principal oboist of the Los Angeles Chamber Orchestra, a position he held from 1974, having joined the ensemble in 1972. Vogel has appeared as soloist with orchestras throughout the country and has been featured at the Chamber Music Northwest, Marlboro, Santa Fe, Aspen, Mostly Mozart, Summerfest, Sarasota, and Oregon Bach festivals. He is on the faculty of University of Southern California and California Institute of the Arts and previously taught at the Colburn School. This interview was conducted by Michele Fiala in the garden of Vogel's home in Santa Clarita, California, in May 2011 and was updated in May 2019.

On Early Career

When I was about twelve years old, my brother was in high school and he was experimenting with different instruments. He ended up being a professional jazz bass player, but at the time he was trying the oboe. There was a radio program on and they said, "This is what the oboe sounds like." My mom said, "Come over and listen to what Stanley's playing," and it was the solo from *Swan Lake*. That, definitely, was the seed. I heard it and I'll always remember that moment; that was the actual seed of it. I had started on the piano and I studied with the neighborhood teacher. I was never particularly talented piano player even though I still try Bach's *Well-Tempered Clavier* every day. Just at that point, my parents had bought me with their last money a new piano, so I kept this desire to play the oboe to myself for a while. I wanted to play the oboe for about three years before I played it, from about twelve to fifteen. That was the germ of it, just hearing *Swan Lake*. I had a conversation with Liang Wang, how it was exactly the same piece that he heard that made him want to play oboe.

Great Oboists on Music and Musicianship. Michele L. Fiala and Martin Schuring, Oxford University Press (2021). © Oxford University Press. DOI: 10.1093/oso/9780190915094.001.0001.

I went to this great high school in New York called High School of Music and Art; now it's called La Guardia High School. I got in there as a pianist. It was an incredible musical atmosphere. There were like six orchestras. There was a great oboist, a fifteen-year-old by the name of Basil Reeve, who became principal in Minneapolis, and he became my hero. There was oboe all around me, music all around me. I remember walking into the orchestra once and they were playing [Bach's] Cantata 140 and there were three oboes in it. I had a pent-up desire to play. Because I started at fifteen, I didn't really know I was going to become a musician. I was kind of a beginner when people were auditioning for colleges. Also, my brother was a jazz bass player and kind of a rebel and there was turmoil in the household, so I associated musicians with being disreputable. I was probably right. [Laughter] I was right! I was a voice major there because at Music and Art you had to say if you wanted to be instrumental or voice, but if you said instrumental, the faculty would pick the instrument for you. And somebody walked by with a tuba, so I said, "Voice!" I studied singing but I became more and more obsessed with the oboe before I played it. Finally, when I hit sophomore year, I started playing it.

I studied with Tony Maly [Anton N. Maly], in New York, and he played second to Robert Bloom in Radio City Music Hall. I came full circle in a way. I studied with an American teacher. My second teacher was Josef Marx, Basil's teacher, and he was very classic. He said, "Don't sound like everybody else. Be yourself." So very early, I was getting an independent streak.

I remember from Maly's lessons, going down to this studio, New York, it was 48th Street. As I would walk down this long hall, I'd always hear him playing with the most beautiful tone. By the time I got down the hall to the studio, I was really inspired. It was after high school was out, maybe 4:30, and he'd say, "Go down and get me a roast beef sandwich and I'll make you a reed." I'd run down and get his sandwich and then he'd smoke a cigar, eat the sandwich, make a reed and by the end of the lesson—I'm a vegetarian now—but at the time, boy these reeds tasted good! I remember trying to smoke a cigar at fifteen. I wasn't too successful with that! But he was great. I had great training, great teachers. He once told me a story: "I just came back from a recording session. We did Royal Fireworks Music of Handel and twenty-four of the best New York freelancers were there. Everyone was noodling like crazy, and the only one who was playing slowly was Bloom." That was the first time I'd ever heard the name Bloom mentioned.

On the Relationship of Singing to Instrumental Playing

The LA Chamber Orchestra is the orchestra that I played in my whole career, and it was the original pit orchestra when the Los Angeles Opera Company first began. I've always found that the tone production in singing is very similar to tone production in wind playing, especially the whole breathing aspect. They're even more sophisticated about what goes on in the lips and mouth and throat than we are because our reed distracts from all those things. But there are a lot of similarities. When you hear sopranos, you hear all of this drama in the opera, and that makes you want to be expressive. Right now, I'm extremely interested in Bach, who also wrote a lot of arias. That's my main passion other than oboe. I'm constantly hearing arias combining oboe playing with singing and that is very inspiring and instructive.

Singing is good for learning things and memorizing music. People take ear training in school, but then when they're out of school there's no more ear training unless they do it themselves. Since I was an English major, I never had enough ear training, so I've been doing my own ear training. Basically I try to sing what I am playing. Sometimes it's impossible, such as with atonal music. But, if I'm trying to memorize the Strauss Concerto, fingering it and singing it at the same time is a very good way to practice.

An Unexpected Career Path

I went to Harvard as an English major and actually finished my degree, but I was always meant to be an oboe player, even though I started late and avoided it as long as I could. I didn't know I was going to be a professional oboe player until I was about twenty. But I was always practicing from day one as if I were going to be. It was always a natural process. In my senior year, two big things happened. I studied with Fernand Gillet. I'd been studying with Jean de Vergie, who had been second oboe player in the Boston Symphony, but then he retired. I was looking around for another teacher and someone told me that Mr. Gillet was still alive. As soon as I started taking lessons with him, immediately it made me want to be an oboe player. Not so much for musical reasons, but it was his whole attitude about how to practice and the technique of practicing that inspired me. He was a very spry eighty-three and he lived to ninety-seven. He said, "I'm here not to teach you how to play, but how to practice." Meanwhile, my English literature studies were bogging down. And, to be honest, I haven't read that much since I graduated, except things about the oboe, Bach, and Buddhism. The second thing was that there was a concerto competition at Harvard and I co-won it with the great pianist Robert Levin, who is a genius. Then I knew for sure, even though I had always known, deep down.

Combining National Schools

From college I had a chance to go to Berlin and study with Lothar Koch, who was an oboist I had fallen in love with in high school, along with the sound of the Berlin Philharmonic. I'd never heard anything like that before. I was lucky enough to win a Fulbright and I studied with Herr Koch for two years. Then I came back to America and began three years studying with Robert Bloom.

For my doctoral degree, I wrote an article called "French, German, and American Oboe Playing," which was published in the IDRS [International Double Reed Society] journal. But actually, the important thing to remember is that I didn't study with three schools of oboe; I studied with three individuals: Koch, Gillet, and Bloom. If I'd studied with a different German, a different Frenchman, and a different American, it wouldn't have been the same experience. Fernand Gillet was so great and an inheritor of such a great technical tradition from Georges Gillet, his uncle. And Koch was just who he was, a total genius who could play the Strauss Concerto from memory and also the piano part of the Strauss Concerto from memory. One amusing thing—in the IDRS journal many years ago and someone was writing an article about Koch and it said he was one of the greatest musicians of the last hundred and fifty years. They just couldn't say a hundred, right? They couldn't. If you had to go up to a hundred and fifty, why not two hundred?

About that article, which I haven't read in a long time, my friend Basil Reeve, who was also very much into international ways of thinking about playing—that is, he likes oboists from all different countries. When he read my article, he said, "You know, I don't think you were fair to Lothar in that article." This might be because I was already changing my embouchure. I wrote it when I was studying with Bloom. During my first year with Mr. Bloom, I had been kind of a resistant student because I had a different sound in my ear. But I did change my embouchure, also because I did not want to go to Vietnam. After my first year of studying with him, I went to the Yale summer school and went totally back to my old way of playing and people seemed to like it. When I had my first lesson back with Bloom, he said, "Sometimes my colleagues hear my students play and they tell me that it sounds very good, and then I hear it myself and it's not so good." He said to me, "You don't have to study with me; we'll still be friends." And I saw myself going off to Vietnam, so I changed my embouchure fast! These days, I don't try to sound like any of my teachers. I'm happy when my worst notes sound closer to my best notes.

With Gillet, what was so compelling was the idea of the art of practicing and the wonderful attitude he had about it. When I first studied with him, all I wanted to do was play fast. But he admonished me, saying, "I practiced in this room for my 30 years with the Boston Symphony and not once did I practice fast. Not once!" A musician, of course, plays a lot of concerts, hopefully, but he spends much more time practicing. Also, people practice before they know they're going to be musicians, and before they have jobs. And now that I'm no longer in the LA Chamber Orchestra, I still like to practice. From an oboe point of view, Mr. Gillet emphasized technique and flexibility, tapering notes, and finesse. He was a wonderful, refined musician, and analytical in a very wonderful, charming, European way. I heard an anecdote from Mr. de Vergie that a guest principal oboist asked him, "How am I doing?" And he answered, "You made more mistakes in three hours than Mr. Gillet made in thirty years!" I found that story very amusing until I myself was a guest principal in the Boston Symphony with the same results!

With Koch, he was just a total genius. He was principal of the Berlin Philharmonic at age twenty-one. In my lessons with him, he would sit at the piano and play. He would inspire you to play as if you were playing with the greatest orchestra. He would encourage you, saying "good," "beautiful," and this would make you play your best, because you were the happiest playing. It was all that kind of stuff.

One thing that Koch said about that article was, "All those things you wrote about me in your article weren't true, were they?" That's why I don't read it. I'm afraid of what I wrote. That probably wasn't fair to him; Basil didn't think so. Maybe I said he bit the reed. When I was finally converted by Bloom to playing on the tip of the reed, I realized it was the best way to play, and I had started out that way with Maly and Gillet. But also Koch wasn't reading it in English; someone translated it for him. It could have gotten a little mixed up with that.

With Bloom, at the beginning, the sound he made was different from the sound I wanted to make. But I studied with him three years, so I definitely adopted all of his techniques in breathing and blowing and embouchure and

I was able to make my own sound better with those techniques. Then there was also reed making. Bloom married my fellow student Sally, but I didn't know that they were friends or anything. I think he deputized her to show me reed making, and she was very interested in showing me, in trying to convert me to the American way of playing. I guess he probably told her to. Bloom was extremely wise and friendly and natural. I'm always finding more meaning in things he said to me many years ago. One thing he said was, "Take your work seriously, but don't take yourself seriously." What he said resonates in one's mind because it's wisdom expressed in a very simple way. Of course, his Bach playing, his phrasing, and his artistry were also incredible.

I feel very lucky, especially as a teacher, to have had such a variety of teachers, different in not only in technique but also in personality. For example, with Gillet and with de Vergie (a French teacher also) it was all etudes and scales, and we hardly did any music. Once, when I won this competition, I had to work on the Telemann Concerto with Gillet. I put in one ornament and he said, "That's jazz! If you ornament, I'm running out. I'm leaving the hall." (He was kidding.) Then he said, "The only good thing about a harpsichord is you can't hear it." He was still in the nineteenth century in a way. He discouraged me from memorizing. He said, "As a wind player, even if you play from memory, have a music stand out there because it looks silly for an oboe player to stand there without a music stand." I stopped memorizing immediately, but in the review, I was criticized for it.

Your playing basically comes from yourself, fundamentally, or should. But I teach more in the style of my teachers than I play in the style of my teachers. I would never understand how my students relate to me if I didn't realize how I related to my teachers. Although I'm not by nature a bossy person, none of my teachers were, either, but I always worked anyway. With my students, I've tried to get results without being mean, and none of my teachers really were with me, either. Nevertheless, Koch once said to me, "Please, play one good note so I can send you home." But he probably said it knowing I couldn't understand German. I didn't know what he was talking about!

On Practicing

First of all, on warming up, I've expanded on and developed my teachers' ideas and take it very seriously. I don't even like to call it warming up but developing fundamentals. We should work on our fundamentals seriously every day. When I want to warm up, I put the oboe under my arm! Even though this is Los Angeles, it's cold here in the morning. When I was in New York and Boston, they had better heating. I have a whole set of fundamentals—practicing oboe fundamentals—as I figured out [see Appendix]. I practice pretty much half an hour of them every day, almost by the clock, because otherwise, I would practice them too much or too little. After a half hour, you do some music. I structure my practicing, basically a half hour of fundamentals, from the sheet: fifteen minutes from the slow section, and fifteen minutes of the fast. Well, actually not fast—moderato. Obviously, you can't do all of this in fifteen minutes or a half hour, but I try to cover the main things over the course of a week. I concentrate on a different scale a week. I happen to be on E♭ this week (in the 2019 update, I'm in G). I do these exercises on a different scale every week.

The great flutist Marcel Moyse lived in this house for a week because my wife's a flutist and she had arranged classes at Cal Arts. Moyse was ninety years old and when he arrived, he said, "My tooth fell out. I have to change my embouchure." And when he started doing this, all he played were just very short notes. When you heard them, you could how great a flutist he had been. So I don't play long tones until I've played short notes, because I don't want to play a long tone with a crappy embouchure. When you play short notes then you focus and you can tell how good your embouchure is. You can tell whether the note came out, for one thing. If the note doesn't come out at all, it's probably a wind issue. If it comes out the wrong octave, it's probably an embouchure issue. The other reason I like short notes is because if you play a long tone, you don't get enough practice taking breaths.

The first side of the sheet is tone production, but fundamentals also have to do with finger fundamentals. On the other side of the page are all the Gillet things or Salviani—working on my half hole technique, etc. I think all that stuff comes from Georges Gillet, because I notice how Mack's students do the same thing. Mack studied with Tabuteau and Tabuteau studied with Georges Gillet, like Fernand. They work the left hand—skillful use of the half hole, stuff like that. Fundamentals have to do not just with wind but with embouchure and with the fingers, especially over the break. The break and register changes are so much harder than everything else. Gillet has a book called *Vingt Minutes d'Etude*: twenty minutes of studies, but he meant play four exercises for five minutes each. He loved efficiency. Five minutes is a long time if you're practicing one thing. Too long. I could run down to the park in five minutes!

On Support and Preparing to Play

I think of the word expansion, which to me means support. When I breathe in, I think mostly in the front, but also a little bit in the back and sides. With my first breath I expand and stay expanded. I love to breathe in rhythm with the piece I am playing. This way I know the tempo and I can clean my lungs with the breath. Posture, of course, is very important and I do some yoga, good posture. A lot can be done during the first three minutes, while the reed's soaking.

Playing on the reed alone is very good to do, long tones on the reed, beginnings and ends of notes on the reed. You can even breathe in and out between the notes, keeping that support/expansion. In other words, if I'm playing a legato line and take another breath, I'm still expanded. With this expansion, you almost can carry the musical line in your body. I don't know if that sounds too spooky but I like it. Being expanded puts the wind under a certain kind of pressure.

Inhale. Relax. Relax your shoulders. Clean your lungs. Clean your mind. And then when you breathe in, keep your shoulders low. Breathe low, not a lot, because you know you'll have to get rid of it later, but all around, strong. That's how I think of support.

On Current Trends

I've become very conventional in my technique. I think my technique and reeds are completely American by now. As we have all these connections across the country and across the world, there's cross-pollination. When I was a kid, you'd always be able to hear who the oboe player was, but it was always kind of by their bad qualities. Every school had its own flaws. The French do this, the Germans do this, maybe the Americans do this, but now everyone's hearing each other on CDs all the time. We have the International Double Reed Society and recordings in high fidelity and people constantly listen to each other. I started early on this because I actually had teachers from different countries. You don't have to have teachers to do that now.

You can listen to great players all over the world. There are a lot of them. It's wonderful.

On Meditation

I'm a freelance Buddhist. I'm very much into Thich Nhat Hanh and his style of meditation, which focuses on breathing. It comes very naturally to me. He's wonderful. He's a wonderful teacher.

Reminiscence

I've played so many memorable concerts with so many great ensembles. But if I was picking out one that was big in my career, I think it was when the LA Chamber Orchestra played Symphony 96 of Haydn in Carnegie Hall—the Miracle Symphony. Which has an incredible oboe solo. I had played that under Casals in Marlboro when he was aged 96. That was also a career-changing experience. But in Carnegie Hall, I played that. And I was hired by a New York management just from playing in the orchestra. That's how my solo career got started. I've never played lots of concertos every year, but I've played enough that I've had to keep practicing! That's how that started and that was a great experience. That's a memorable concert because I had never aspired to be a soloist. I never had any real career ambitions, but practiced a lots and drifted into a lot of things like the LA Chamber Orchestra, where I played forty-two years. I was lucky to get a great teaching job right out of school, at Cal Arts, then later at USC and the Colburn School.

On the Oboe

There are so many personalities. There are only a few instruments and there are millions of people. There aren't millions of oboists but there are thousands of us, but there's only one oboe. I'll always remember, after a lesson with Robert Bloom, we opened the door of the studio and he looked both ways down the hallway to make sure no one was there and then said, "Always remember; the oboe is the greatest of all instruments!"

22

David Walter

After obtaining first prize in oboe and chamber music at the Conservatoire National Supérieur de Musique de Paris, David Walter won international prizes in Ancona, Prague, Munich, Belgrade, and Geneva. He is a founding member (1980) of the Quintette Moragues. He played as a soloist with the Simón Bolívar Orchestra, the Stavanger Orchestra, Guildhall String Orchestra, the Sofia Soloists, l'Orchestre d'Auvergne, l'Orchestre de Chambre de Toulouse, Lithuanian Philharmonic, le Filarmonica et l'OSSDRE from Montevideo, etc. At twenty-nine years old, Walter was appointed the youngest-ever oboe and chamber music professor at the Paris Conservatoire. He also taught at the Guildhall School of Music and Drama from 1997 to 2010. Walter has transcribed and arranged hundreds of musical works and often conducts. This interview was conducted by Michele Fiala in July 2011 in the countryside of the Burgundy region in France while Walter was teaching and conducting at a festival in nearby Autun.

On Being a Conductor and Performer

To me the most important thing is the music; it doesn't matter the way of doing it. My first pull into music was of course the oboe, but also arranging and conducting. It's another way. My only goal is to try to bring something new to the music and if I'm using the oboe, or if I'm singing (well of course I'm not singing as a professional) or if I'm conducting, it's the same goal.

At this festival I've been mostly conducting but also teaching the winds how to react in the orchestra. What to do, how to arrange the sounds, how to tune a chord. All those things you have to do to get a job. In France it's different now than it was twenty years ago but still it's not focused on orchestra like it is in the US. Sometimes in small conservatoires they don't have very much of an orchestral music program. I like to do this kind of summer

Great Oboists on Music and Musicianship. Michele L. Fiala and Martin Schuring, Oxford University Press (2021). © Oxford University Press. DOI: 10.1093/oso/9780190915094.001.0001.

program because the students really enjoy learning how to play in the orchestra deeply, more than in music school.

On Ensemble Playing

Playing a solo and playing in a team in the orchestra, it's the same instrument of course but I don't think it's the same use. You have to forget yourself. You have to turn the instrument and the intonation in a special way to fit the ensemble. You don't have to do those things so much when you are doing a solo so I think it's a different knowledge, another approach to the instrument. It's very important to know the two ways. Otherwise you have a problem, especially for an instrument like oboe, which is mainly in orchestra. It's very important to know how a chord is built and how to react to it. That being said, you need to know what note you have in a chord and how to react and also how to use the sound to fit with the other instruments, especially when you have passages with flute and clarinet and many other instruments. It's not the same position of the sound and so it's very important, very interesting to have your students do just that.

On Chamber Music

Thirty years ago we didn't have an orchestra program in the conservatoire; it was mainly soloists. I stopped taking oboe lessons very early when I was twenty-two. Afterward my teachers were my colleagues in the quintet and all the pianists I played with—people I could listen to and to see how I could, with my oboe, join this kind of music, which was impressive to me. It just came to me. So I forgot the oboe as a goal itself and tried to reach something wider in music, not oboe.

On Competitions

Since I had no teacher, the international competition was kind of a goal program for all year and it was my goal to be able to play all of the program—that means to go to the final. After that, it's so subjective. You hear the people playing, in such different ways. I could see in serving on juries myself that sometimes you can have some decisions so impossible to understand. I was lucky several times to have the prize but it didn't mean that I was the best at this area and I respected all of the other candidates. Of course I was happy to go to the finals sometimes and to come back and win the prizes, but it didn't change my way of feeling music. It just challenged me to work, to study deeply. I suggest the same approach to all of my students. Otherwise, you are going to fight against the others and I think the music is going away when you do that.

On Teaching

The best teacher teaches the student to go without teaching. That means week after week, month after month, and year after year, the student must think, know, and do the things by himself. You are giving the key. You explain things, but it's not to put him down; it's to make a new generation who is set to go further on. So, it's to give them the freedom to be themselves completely without you. Of course, if they come back for any advice, I'm still here, but it's a completely free way of relating. I don't think that I'm above others; I'm just what I am. And my goal is to give everything I have for the next generation to bring something new again, something I didn't know I couldn't do. I feel very young. And I have a lot of very good friends in my students because they really become colleagues after being my students and that's good.

On the International Oboe School

You can't avoid taking good ideas when they come from another school. A national school is never complete; it can be very strong but it's not complete. So I think it's very important to capture the good ideas and to keep them. For example, the first time I came to America, I tried the reeds and they're part of the sound itself. I found that it was so easy to blow that it gave me a lot of ideas to change my way of scraping. Not to change to the American one, but to make it wide and easy, just not suffer. It was really good; it was a lesson. I took many lessons in traveling everywhere because there's always something you didn't think about. Or you were around but you missed it. When something is good for the music, it's good for everyone, not only for a national team.

On Artists Who Inspire Him

I think everyone, the good and the bad ones, are interesting to listen to because you can learn in seeing that something is good or you can learn as well in seeing that something is bad. It's important for me to be very careful in listening and showing all musicians—whatever the instrument is, to see when it's connecting with the heart, with the music, with the public. With an attitude that is completely focused and in the mood of the music or if it's only an affect to say look at me, I'm the best. For me, the artist must be there and must forget himself at the same time because he's nothing without the text of the composer. And at the same time the composer is nothing without the artist, so it's a combination. It's also interesting to be able to change your mind in changing the type of music you play. For example, I really have a Baroque mind that means without vibrato or quasi without vibrato. There's a technique to singing the phrase which would be completely different by the time of Schumann and also different in contemporary music. So, it's like theater, an actor being different persons—as an artist that is interesting.

On Finding Your Voice

I would really like to see this kind of teaching go away: I have the truth and you have to follow me otherwise you're bad. I think this is the old world. The real music is in the complete freedom of the other, and the complete respect of this particular thing that we all have [gestures to his heart]. That's why it's also important not to be too fanatic of one player in particular because we are just building a wall around us, not to be able to find something which is different, which is not the exact imitation of this great person. I was a fanatic of Maurice Bourgue when I was very young and, without rejecting him, I understood very fast that I wanted to be myself, not to be only a copy. The copy would have been stupid. And if I'm leading as a musician, my duty, my goal is not to do something again as the "main chief" would have, but to try to bring something, my soul richness, adding to the others. That's why I want to feel free when making music; I want to share that with everyone. When I'm conducting I have to set the work for everyone to be together, but I'm very careful to leave the musicians in front of me to be themselves and to be able to bring something—their own special way of doing it. If it fits to the music, OK I won't change it. I will change only things that are fighting against nature. So, that's very important—the quality of the human relationship. Making music is for me the top thing and I'm sure that we can express ourselves in a better way, a deep way, if we are feeling supported by others even though they are older and have more experiences. It's very, very important. It's a human adventure. It's not only being a musician.

On Rock Climbing

Music is a big effort; to be a good musician you have to spend a lot of time and energy. You're never sure that tomorrow you will find what you did the day before. It's one of the most spiritual things in this way because you have to do it and do it again and you are never sure it stays. Sports have a separate relationship with that because you have to make the effort but when you climb the mountain—you did it—you have the great scenery, the great view. But it's not a goal for me; it's just a hobby I like. It's this kind of effort I like but if others prefer swimming or whatever, running—I do a little bicycle as well—the only thing is to improve what you can do but without being too competitive. We must find a way to make an effort to be better, but not to be the best.

Reminiscence

When I played with my wind quintet with Sviatoslav Richter in the Pushkin Museum in Moscow and when we went to his apartment to rehearse and we saw people like Natalia Gutman coming forth listening to the rehearsal in Moscow. It was . . . wow. And that was natural. It was the Beethoven Wind and Piano Quintet, Opus 16 and he was telling us, "The music is very difficult for me. We must rehearse a lot. I must rehearse a lot." This guy was really genuine. He was with us like a fellow, like a friend. The music was incredible; as a player he was fantastic. He was almost 80 and we were—I don't know, 35, 40? But there was no age, just musicians. French or Russian doesn't matter, just musicians. That's maybe my best memory. I had many others but this one has meaning. I can remember that at his age he was tired of all the public and all the people who wanted an autograph and he was very closed with people from outside but with us he was so warm. We played in France as well and before coming to the stage we made like a basketball team taking a [makes a gesture of putting hands together]. He was smiling big and when he passed the door to come onto stage, his face got very deep and very closed, just because the only thing that was important for him at the end of his life was making music the most purely. Being brilliant in front of the public wasn't interesting at all. When he was playing a solo he used just a little light to know where to put the fingers and see the music—nothing else, him in the dark. For me it was authentic. He was a great player.

On Humanism

My father was a Protestant preacher. I took my own spiritual way but I kept this sharing of things because when I was young I saw many people come in trouble who were helped by my parents. For me, teaching and making music must be a human thing, not only a money, an earning problem. Otherwise it makes no sense.

23

Robert Walters

Robert Walters joined the Cleveland Orchestra as solo English horn in 2004. Prior to coming to Cleveland, Walters was the solo English horn player of the Metropolitan Opera Orchestra (2000–2004) and with the Cincinnati Symphony Orchestra (1997–2000). He has appeared as soloist with the Cleveland Orchestra, Chicago Symphony Orchestra, Cincinnati Symphony Orchestra, Orpheus Chamber Orchestra, Beijing Radio Symphony, Qingdao Symphony Orchestra, New York Chamber Soloists, Philadelphia Chamber Orchestra, and Phoenix Symphony. He performed and recorded with the Philadelphia Orchestra from 1990 to 1996. A native of Los Angeles and raised in Nebraska, Walters is a graduate of the Curtis Institute of Music and holds a Master of Fine Arts degree in poetry from Columbia University. He studied with Richard Woodhams and John Mack. Walters has taught at the Oberlin Conservatory of Music since 2006 and was appointed professor of oboe and English horn in 2010. This interview was conducted by Michele Fiala at Oberlin College in May 2009.

Early Career

As a child, I wanted to play the trombone. My father was a violist in an orchestra and I would go to the symphony concerts and I was just fascinated by the trombone. He did not want to listen to me practicing the trombone for the next ten years of his life, so he kept saying I was too young and maybe next year. Then the St. Paul Chamber Orchestra came to town and they played this concert. It was Bach Magnificat and it had this big oboe solo and I thought it was the most beautiful thing I'd ever heard. It was Richard Killmer playing and I went up and talked to him. I was in third grade and he was really nice to

Great Oboists on Music and Musicianship. Michele L. Fiala and Martin Schuring, Oxford University Press (2021). © Oxford University Press. DOI: 10.1093/oso/9780190915094.001.0001.

me and then he crowed his reed and I got to push the buttons and about three days later, I had my first oboe and an oboe teacher and suddenly I was not too young. That was funny.

Actually, I had a lot of interest in the bassoon for a while but my hands were too small so they said, "Well, you learn the oboe first and then when you get a little bigger you could switch to bassoon," and I never did. Maybe the English horn is a good compromise; it's somewhere between.

My early teachers liked what they were doing. They were enthusiastic about the oboe. They liked it and they enjoyed teaching me. When I got better, they seemed pleased. I liked the whole process; it was a very positive experience. I think because the oboe is a little peculiar and I grew up in Lincoln, Nebraska, it certainly wasn't cool to play the oboe. I did play it in the marching band. I used a fibercane reed and a plastic Bundy. In seventh grade I was in the Panther band!

The teacher I had, Brian Ventura, was principal oboe of the Omaha Symphony (now he's retired from the Detroit Symphony) and I grew up in Lincoln and I would drive once a week for lessons with him. I studied some with Robert O'Boyle, who was the oboe professor at the University of Nebraska. When I was sixteen, he told my parents, "You need to get your kid out of Nebraska. He needs to go study oboe with this man," and it was Richard Woodhams. He said, "Have him make a tape and we'll send it to him." He sent a letter of recommendation and I sent this tape of me playing the Haydn Concerto. Richard Woodhams called up my parents and said, "I'd love to teach your son. Please send him out here." I didn't even know who he was or what the Philadelphia Orchestra meant. I had no idea. I liked the oboe and apparently there was someone who was really good at it in Philadelphia, so that's where I went, and that's all I knew.

Another teacher sent me to the John Mack Oboe Camp when I was fifteen. I didn't know who John Mack was or what the Cleveland Orchestra was or who these Gomberg boys were or Ray Still. It was all foreign to me. But I learned pretty quickly who they were and how they sounded and I wanted to do that, too. It helped, I think, coming from a musical family. I played in my father's orchestra—the Lincoln Civic Orchestra—this community orchestra with all ages from ten-year-old violinists to eighty-year-old cellists. I still remember these retired professors playing. It was a great orchestra; I loved playing in that. I was lucky. My family was very supportive, but I never felt like I had to do it. I wasn't forced into it, but if I showed enthusiasm, the next step was always provided somehow.

In my second year at Curtis, I wasn't doing particularly well on the oboe. It was very difficult and I had a slump in my learning curve. I was considering quitting pretty seriously. The atmosphere at the Curtis Institute wasn't quite right for me. My parents were both academics and I grew up on college campuses and this [Oberlin College] is a much better fit—a place like here. I just was not flourishing in the way I wanted. At the end of the semester in May, I put my oboe in the closet and I was not going to play all summer. I just needed to get away from it and I was going to decide in August if I was going to continue or not.

I didn't play all of May and all of June and then the first week of July at seven o'clock in the morning, I got a call from the personnel manager of the Philadelphia Orchestra. "Could you please come to the Mannes Music Center? We need an extra oboe player for the week. Someone has fallen ill." I stupidly said yes [laughter], got my oboe out of the closet, and I thought I'd be safe. They were doing *Rite of Spring* and I thought I'd play fifth oboe and no one would really hear me. My teacher at the time, Mr. Woodhams, decided to have me play second to him. I hadn't played in two months and there I was sitting in the Philadelphia Orchestra next to Richard Woodhams, sight-reading *The Rite of Spring*. Luckily, during my last couple lessons in the semester, he finished a truckload of reeds for me to try to keep me on track for the summer. They were played in and it was humid out so I actually had pretty good reeds. Somehow with the focus of concentration and the adrenaline of it, I got through it somehow. It was thrilling beyond description to sit next to him and to hear what he produced on the instrument and to sit in the middle of a great orchestra like that. I thought, "Oh, crap, I have to do this for a living. I can't really quit because I love it; it's just too amazing." That put an end to my "I might not play the oboe," just that one concert.

The next two years at Curtis, I started taking English courses at the University of Pennsylvania. They have this exchange program and that fed the academic side of my personality so I had a balance that made my life at Curtis a lot better, that I had one foot in academia. The last two years at Curtis were much better for me. I thrived in a certain way from reading and writing and thinking about literature and then thinking about music. I'd go back successfully between the two and I thought: this is a model for me that works. Where could I do this after I leave Curtis? And the Iowa Writers' Workshop was not such a place because I figured my oboe playing could suffer in the cornfields of Iowa! I thought of New York City. I could freelance; I could play; I could go to Columbia University, which is what I did.

After Curtis, I got into the Marlboro Music Festival and went to Marlboro for five summers in a row. My first summer there, Alex Klein was with me. We had spent our first year at Curtis together and the atmosphere was not right for him and after a year he came to Oberlin. It was interesting: freshmen at Curtis, then five years later at Marlboro, and fifteen years later, here we are teaching these kids together. I met a lot of musicians at Marlboro who lived in New York, who freelanced with various groups: Orpheus, St. Luke's, American Ballet, American Symphony, studio stuff, and some Broadway stuff. I got hooked into New York freelance life and I thought, "I'm going to move to New York and see if I can break into the freelance scene so I know that I'll be playing music." I knew that it was important to me and I didn't want to quit. Then I'd also apply and if I got into Columbia I'd go. I was afraid that if I just applied and went and didn't have a musical life that the subculture of higher education would lure me away from music completely. I was careful about how I struck a balance. It was a two-year program, the MFA program, but I did it in three years to give myself time to practice. I took major auditions, but nothing for regional orchestras because what I was doing in New York seemed more significant to me at the time. I did that for five years, freelanced in New York, and then by the time I got my degree at Columbia in poetry—which was probably the one thing I could do that is less marketable than playing the oboe—the music profession was starting to look pretty good!

On English Horn

After that I thought, "I've been in New York now; I've done this and I really want to get a job in orchestra." There were no oboe auditions that year at all, but there were three English horn auditions. There was one in Minnesota, one in Cincinnati, and one in the National Symphony. They were a couple of months apart and I knew they were coming up. That summer, I took my phone off the hook and sequestered myself in my apartment. I turned myself into an English horn player by doing all the things that I did on the oboe: long tones, slow scales, arpeggios, finding where the pitch center was on the instrument, and trying to understand bocals and reeds and equipment. I listened to all the English horn excerpts I could get my hands on. I'd get eight recordings of Shostakovich 8 and nine *Tristan*s and would listen and think who sounded best to me and why. The principles of wind playing that I was taught on the oboe all applied to the English horn. I took myself through the slow Ferlings on the English horn. The F minor slow Ferling has all the worst notes on the English horn. I wanted to find a reed that allowed me to do that. I figured if I could come up with a style of scrape where there's an actual scale in that key, I would have solved a lot of problems.

I never studied English horn specifically. Lou Rosenblatt helped me pick out my first instrument. I did play one lesson of excerpts before one audition for him. I never tried his reed, but I got to sit next to him and I had his sound in my ear. I was trying to apply the school of wind playing that we had been taught on the oboe to the English horn.

The reed has to be as stable; the tip needs to be as thin. There are a lot of people who think you don't really need to finish an English horn tip. The danger with the English horn is it sounds less bad sooner when you're making a reed. The oboe sounds horrible most of the time and then you luck into a good reed and it's OK. With the English horn, you clip open anything and it sounds and feels OK until you try to play music on it. Then you realize it's not really finished. For English horn, the reeds lie deeper in the cane. Our best reeds are maybe the third-generation scrape. Make a reed, play some tutti stuff on it, practice on it, but then take it down for other solos. For the really big exposed solo, I'll refine that even further. It's ironic that the deeper in I go and the more cane I take off, the bigger the tone gets and the more range is felt. You have to keep scraping longer on an English horn reed.

Intonation is different—where the notes live in each scale. I recommend slow Ferling for anyone who wants to really figure out where the notes are in a given scale. My approach, other than vibrato, is the same on the oboe. It's a different tessitura, a different vocal range, but you can't cheat on the English horn [laughs]. You can, but you have to be really great at it.

I took learning the English horn very seriously for about three months and then took the Minnesota audition and got in the finals. Then Cincinnati was maybe two months after that and I ended up winning. I think the fact that there were three auditions in a row meant I wasn't really all that focused on getting a particular job. I was just focused on becoming a great English horn player and I had three opportunities to do that.

On Auditions

In the beginning, I used to look at auditions as a crap shoot, that it was all luck, where you just show up. If they liked something they heard, fine, and if not, I didn't really prepare all that deeply. It was more like taking a driver's test or a bar exam: you try not to make mistakes. With that way of going about it, I didn't do well for a long time. Then I stopped thinking of them as auditions and started thinking of them as recitals. I stopped thinking of the excerpts as excerpts because there's no composer in Western art music that ever wrote an excerpt. I thought of them as arias. I thought, "All these English horn solos, those big juicy vocal moments, they're arias and I'm going to give a recital." I got excited the way you get all pumped up for your junior recital in college. You pick your music and you take ownership in what you're doing and your family comes and it means more to you. That's how I approached auditions, and once I had that mindset, I did really well.

I was in Cincinnati for three years and I wanted to go back to the Met. I didn't know opera or the operatic repertoire. I didn't really study it in school, so it was a challenge to me to make sense of all this new music. I went to the library at Curtis and I Xeroxed all the piano-vocal scores from these operas and I gave a recital. I got a pianist and I pretended that they were arias for my instrument so that was not about excerpts. It was trying to make music and get the instrument to sound how you wanted it to and then winning the job became secondary.

I got the librettos and was very aware of all the texts and would listen to the singers sing the same lines and the same music but with words, see where the syllables lay, where the gestures lay, and tried to mimic that, to play in a vocal way. In the beginning of the Barret book, it talks about the English horn and they refer to it as *umana voce*: the human voice in Italian. I think that's pretty cool.

I tell my students now to approach each audition as a laboratory to make yourself better. You've got a fixed amount of time, a set of repertoire, and you use it, especially when you get out of school. In conservatory, you've got a weekly pattern of lessons and orchestra rehearsals and all this, but when you're out and it's all up to you, the only real progress I ever made was preparing for auditions because you practice more than usual. You get more discriminating with reeds; you try to raise your level. I'd come back from a recital—not a recital, an audition—and even if I didn't win, I'd have the best reeds I'd had in months because I'd worked so hard. I enjoyed that aspect of it.

I'd spent the first couple of years not really preparing well and getting really freaked out about flying to a strange city and walking into a building I'd never been in and just picking up and playing this way. I found it all very threatening and alienating. There were around 80 people who were all playing my instrument and my music. It was very strange.

Once I took myself out of that mindset and decided it was a recital, that it was music to be made, I did really well. I noticed when I got into these orchestras and then sat on audition committees, when people actually played music, actually performed instead of rendered notation, the whole committee perked up. It wasn't so much style of playing; it was just actual music-making. Hearing that on the other side of auditions convinced me of that even more, so that's how I've approached it with my students. I've had a lot of success helping people prepare for auditions either on oboe or English horn, I'm glad to say. I helped them approach auditions as a musical encounter and to think of it that way. My goal was to save them all a lot of airfare! I was happy to see that they succeeded. They did really well. It felt like all that suffering I went through was worthwhile, as long as I turn it back on the younger generation and keep them from making the same mistakes that I made. I teach what helped me get where I am.

On Teaching

Teaching's been a very selfish pleasure because it makes you think about music and try to articulate it and also be curious as to why a phrase will sound wrong and you work on it with a student and suddenly it sounds a lot better in a short amount of time. It's the same student and the same reed and the same lesson, but it's a whole different experience. That fascinates me. And the basic elements of wind playing, getting control of your attack—I hate the word "attack"—entrance really. And long tones—dynamic range and color. I spend a lot of time on slow scales developing a tactile awareness of intonation. If you're playing in tune, it tastes a certain way or feels a certain way. There's a sensation to it and the tone improves. If you're out of the pocket, if you're riding a little high or if you're a little flat, nothing sounds as good. I'll have them play sharp on purpose just to experience what that feels like and get used to objecting to that, being all tight and tense and pitch being kind of squeezed. Or I'll say, "OK, no support, let's hear it flat." They'll play it and it's all flat and I'll say, "OK, now, let's play it in tune, in the center of the pitch,"

Once I awaken the students to that, they'll get it and all of a sudden they'll smile because it feels better and it sounds better and then they have a sense memory of what the note feels like in tune.

As an English horn player, because most of my solos are slow, I'm obsessed about legato and intonation. If you're out of tune or your legato's lumpy on a slow melody, it's not convincing. That's something I spend a lot of time on. Playing in an opera orchestra certainly influenced my playing—listening to singers, both good ones and bad ones. With really fine singers, there's something about the line that's fluid and seamless and continuous, and the vibrato is within the pitch. It doesn't waver.

Knowing that my students are in the audience affects how I perform. I want to play well anyway, but they are out there listening to you, trying to understand what they heard you talk about in their lesson, and you can demonstrate it. It's made me want to play better not only for myself but for them. I remember as a student the truly great performances that I heard Richard Woodhams give and Lou Rosenblatt give. It's still in my mind's ear to this day. I can recall what that was like; it never leaves you. I give it all that I can. I'm constantly talking about fundamental things like pitch and rhythm and intonation and legato. I become more aware of it in my own playing and I think about it more. My playing has gotten better because I have good students, so there is a definite selfish pleasure involved.

On Musicality

It's like language. I'd like to hear words instead of each note. I just told a girl today it's like you're playing in syllables. She was sort of stuttering note to note and it didn't make any sense. You have to make the syllables into words and then the words become a sentence and the sentence a paragraph. I'll pick up a book and I'll read something with a flat intonation and it makes no impact whatsoever. If I give it some shape and raise my voice here or lower it there or pause at the cadence, it awakens them. It's fascinating. When a student who's here now first came from China he didn't speak any English so I spent a lot of time in lessons drawing pictures and pantomiming. In the second semester, he had a little bit of English and when I was trying to demonstrate some phrasing he said, "Oh, music, it's like the words in Chinese. Same word, different direction—different meaning."

A speech Obama was giving was on the radio a couple weeks ago was on NPR and this guy was talking about what a great orator he was. He read this passage from the speech by Obama. And the radio announcer has a good command of the language and he read it like he does any NPR thing. Then he played a recording of Obama reading the exact same three sentences and it was another world. It suddenly meant so much more and had so much more impact.

That's always fascinating to me, how students will play the same Barret melody you've heard other students play but for some reason it sounds better. I try to figure out why and what they're doing. I tell the students who don't sound as good to try this and it'll help them play better. When I was at the MFA program at Columbia studying poetry, I'd go and I'd hear poets read their work and you could see that they'd be tapping time. There's a meter to it and they would phrase and you would hear a rise and a fall and inflection, change in volume, change in timbre, all these things we use in music. Tabuteau had this number system which was effectively used by many to convey phrasing. I prefer letters over numbers and language is something most people are really good at, even though they don't know it. You awaken them to that fact. I tell people that all day long you speak with a perfect legato. Air's going through your vocal cords and it's vibrating and you're articulating and shaping vowels and consonants and sound and communicating and you're not [in a halting manner] re-di-stri-bu-ting air for ev-er-y syl-lab-le. And then they realize they have a beautiful legato in them as they speak and they try to do the same thing on the instrument and it always sounds better.

On Air Support

The other thing I stress a lot is just trying to get people in touch with the physical sensation of wind through the instrument. Most people are more in touch with their embouchure and it's usually in a more protective mode because their reeds are bad and they're flat and they're trying to keep the sound from getting too ugly or keep the pitch up by biting. It's not a mouth instrument; it's a wind instrument. I ask them what wind is and they'll say, "Well, air." I'll say, "Air that just sits there? No, it moves, it's air that moves." If you just tell someone to blow faster they don't really know what to do but if you tell someone to pretend they're blowing out a candle then they do. The wind that comes out of them is fast and focused and the light goes on. It's the same thing with breath support. If I tell them to take more air into their diaphragms and support more, they may or may not understand, but if I tell them to yawn and then open up, the air goes in deeper and quicker than usual. I'll take a piece of cigarette paper and put it on the wall and make them blow it hard enough to just keep it up and they're surprised at how much air that takes. If they blow to get a pinwheel to spin or a propeller, they realize that's how to do it. I spend a little time trying to develop tactile metaphors so that they get in touch with how it feels and how that's related to how it sounds.

On Vibrato

Vibrato's interesting. It's a touchy subject. My only objection's if it's too fast and too narrow and too at the surface of the tone. That was in style in the thirties maybe, but not so much today. It sounds really bad on an English horn. As long as the vibrato's inside the pitch and doesn't waver out of the pitch center, if it's a faster vibrato for certain expression or lower, slower vibrato for other kinds, I think that's good. Generally, as long as students realize not to go outside of the tone and not to throw on a lot of vibrato in the high register when your reed is unstable and approximate and hope the note's in there somewhere [laughs]. I spend a lot of time making them play slow scales with no vibrato so that the wind is going first and that the pitch is there. Then you vibrate within that sphere and that seems to work. Most of the kids seem to do it with throat vibrato, which is how I did it and how my teacher did it. There's a couple that have diaphragm vibrato and I don't try to change them to produce it in their throat. Usually diaphragm vibrato is a lot slower. I try to get them to have at least the repertoire of speeding it up on occasion so it doesn't sound like a quirk in their playing.

Vibrato is a big difference from oboe. It needs to be slower and deeper. A soprano has a faster vibrato than a baritone and it's tessitura-related. The oboe has a faster spin to the vibrato than an English horn; it sounds kind of silly if you use the same type of vibrato. It's like trying to play the string bass with a violin bow. It's a fifth lower so I think the vibrato should be at least a fifth slower than the oboe.

With English horn, because the bore is bigger and longer, it gets students more in touch with the reality that they're putting air through an instrument. I find that beneficial when they go back to the oboe and they remember to blow. You have to aim the air differently; it's more focused for an oboe than an

English horn but getting them in touch with that sensation of wind usually helps anyone sound better. You get them to blow through it instead of at it.

On Ensemble Skills

It's important to know the entire piece and not just your part because no matter how great your reed or technique is, if you play like a one-line player, you sound illiterate. It just isn't right. I can tell immediately when people play for me if they know the whole piece or not, even a sonata. I'll say, "You haven't played this with piano yet, have you?" And they'll say no. All the answers for playing a solo line lie beneath that solo line in the score, so becoming aware of how the accompaniment changes, how the harmony changes, is the most vital thing. I will not listen to a student play an excerpt if they haven't listened to the score first. That John Ferrillo book is fantastic because it's got piano accompaniment for all the basic excerpts. The harmony is distilled and the kids go to the piano and get a more direct relationship to those things right away. When you get a pianist to play those things, it'll feel like music instead of an excerpt, and that's very important. When you play in an orchestra, if you're a second player, you've got to learn to hide, have incredible low control and incredible ensemble skills and flawless intonation to make a first player really sound good. You have to ghost what a first player is doing often. There are times that you have to step out of the fray, but if it's the solo on English horn or principal oboe, you've got to learn to be comfortable in the limelight. With the students who don't have the personality for that, I try to get it out of them, and if they don't, they generally don't go on.

Artists That Inspire Him

For me it's all those old great violinists, great singers, great pianists. It's important not just to listen to oboe all the time. Often, oboe students limit listening to oboists. If you listen to just the oboe, you'll never really understand what music is. When they ask who I listen to and I say go listen to Oistrakh play this and Gidon Kremer, they say, "No, no, I mean oboe music." I'll say, "No, I mean music. Go listen to that first and then I'll tell you what oboe recording to listen to." The oboists that imprinted me the most were of course my teacher Dick Woodhams.

I listen to a lot of Marc Lifschey, a lot of Robert Bloom, a lot of Al Genovese. There's something about that old-world Curtis phrasing that is really important and special and I try to make sure that people don't lose that.

I don't play piano very well and I wish I did. For the students who do play piano, I encourage them to maintain a relationship to the piano because that makes you a more informed musician and gives you a better sense of harmony. On the oboe, most people will make a living either teaching in a university or playing in an orchestra, and I try to make sure that they have the skills to do both here. I encourage the ones who are very intellectually curious about other subjects to pursue those things. You can see the temperament of a teacher, even as a student. There's a couple of people who I think, "Oh, these guys are going to be great. When they come around and start teaching people, it's going to be really great." Others have a natural way of playing and it's beautiful but I don't think they are really going to convey it well to the succeeding generation and I think they'll be happier just playing.

Teaching is largely thinking out loud. There are people who do that well and people who don't. To do both—that's one thing about my teacher, Richard Woodhams, that I admired so much. His first and foremost thing always was his own playing, his own music-making. But teaching became very, very important for him, even more so as I watched him over the years. I think he considers teaching and playing to be two sides of the same coin and they definitely inform each other constantly. I play out at Aspen with him and I still like sitting next to him on a recital or concert because he's always fascinated about music. I enjoy watching his mind work.

On Writing Poetry

I stopped writing for a while after I got out of the MFA program in '95 at Columbia. It was time to get a job and I just had to focus on winning an audition. I got the job in Cincinnati, and I had to focus on getting tenure and suddenly I wanted to go to the Met and there was all this opera music to learn. I write a sonnet a year for my wife on Valentine's Day and it was about all I wrote for about ten years. But in the last two or three years here, teaching at Oberlin, and with my life settling in, in Cleveland, I've found the urge to do it again. I started reading and writing a lot more and it does inform how I teach. It awakens my ear. It's something important to me. It's a good way to think about music and the parallels between them. If I'm writing poetry, I feel like I play better because I'm more attuned to the rhythm and the shape of the phrase and the sound of things. It's funny—poetry's kind of an esoteric thing, but for me it's been eminently practical.

In Memory of Louis Rosenblatt

Sibelius Dreams . . .

A single swan
Alone
On water

The curve of a neck ascended
Questioning
The nature of solitude

This liquid wandering
Spinning through answers
Too fluid to grasp

Yet he glides above
Quiet majestic suspended
By the thin glass sheet of the lake

It is (at least) colored glass
As the sun spills its dying
Day's blood upon the water

Tinged with suffering orange
Tossed without thought
By cold lapping waves

A mirror of wet fire
Reflecting the swan descended
His echo an endless returning

—Robert Walters

24

David Weiss

David Weiss performed as principal oboe with the Los Angeles Philharmonic from 1973 to 2003. Prior to his appointment in Los Angeles, Weiss was a member of the Pittsburgh Symphony and principal oboe with the National Symphony Orchestra in Washington, DC. Weiss taught at the University of Southern California and the Music Academy of the West in Santa Barbara. He was also highly respected as a photographer; his pictures of players and conductors have appeared in numerous books and other publications. Weiss died in 2014. This interview took place in Tempe, Arizona, with Michele Fiala at the International Double Reed Society Conference in 2011. Weiss brought his musical saw (on which he had recorded a CD) and played it for me after the interview, including the Strauss Concerto Second Movement! "The Well-Tempered Saw," he called it.

Author's note: At this point, Weiss took out a Stanley Handyman saw and started playing the slow movement of the Strauss Oboe Concerto on it. He said that he had played that particular saw for thirty years and called it "The Well-Tempered Saw." He talked about his experiences playing the musical saw, including on The Tonight Show with Johnny Carson *and on his CD,* Virtuoso Saw. *It was a unique and captivating experience to sit across from him and listen to him evoke music from a piece of hardware.*

—MF

Early Career

I come from a musical family. My mother was a music major at Hunter College in New York; she was a very forward-thinking and pragmatic woman and she knew that her children were all very musically inclined. She felt that

Great Oboists on Music and Musicianship. Michele L. Fiala and Martin Schuring, Oxford University Press (2021).
© Oxford University Press. DOI: 10.1093/oso/9780190915094.001.0001.

music could be of benefit to us in many different ways, partly just as a creative outlet and to satisfy our souls. She was a cellist and a pianist. She's eighty-eight years old and still teaching piano in West Los Angeles.

Her brother did not play a musical instrument but many of her colleagues and fellow students at college did. When the draft occurred for World War II, her brother had to go into combat and nearly lost his life—he was lucky, he survived, and everything was all right, but it really scared her. Meanwhile, she was watching all her friends get into military bands instead of combat, so she thought, "Aha! Well, if I have boys, they're going to play wind instruments so they can play in a band." That was part of her thinking. Her roommate in college was an oboist and she loved the sound.

Her friends at school were getting out of combat. They still did their military service but they got into bands. So she thought, "All right, this is a smart thing to do." There were three of us—two boys and a girl—and I was the oldest. I started piano lessons when I was still in diapers and there were piano lessons in the house constantly—my mother and grandmother both gave lessons. When I was not even a year old, I'd be reaching up and tinkling the notes on the piano, and I started more or less formal lessons when I was about three. She remembered the oboe very fondly from her college years, so when my hands got big enough to hold an oboe—I was about ten, I guess—my mom said, "Let's go take an oboe lesson, all right?" And I said, "Okay." I didn't even think twice about it. She got me hooked up with some good teachers at the USC preparatory department.

We were living in Los Angeles at the time. I was born in New York City but when I was five the family moved to California. We were fortunate that USC has always been an excellent music school and they have a lot of opportunities for young students. I studied with a good teacher—Anthony Desiderio was his name. He got me started and then I switched over to a specialized oboe teacher, Darrel Stubbs, who at the time was the professor of oboe at USC. I was around eleven. He got me connected with a good instrument and proper reeds, and I started making reeds pretty quickly myself. I was with him for a couple of years. He later went on and was principal oboe of the Utah Symphony. When he left California, William Criss joined the USC faculty. He had been principal of the Metropolitan Opera for many years prior to coming to LA, and was a Curtis student for one year himself, so there's a little Tabuteau lineage in my playing, I suppose. So, I studied with Bill Criss, who was my most important influence musically on the oboe.

I started college at USC as a scholarship student but after my first semester I realized that to keep my scholarship I had to play in the band and the wind ensemble and the opera and everything, and I had joined the union the year before and I started to get a lot of freelance work. It was interfering. I figured if I needed performing opportunities I might as well get paid for it and not be obligated to the scholarship. So I switched schools and went to UCLA as an undeclared major. The only music I had at UCLA was oboe lessons with Bert Gassman for one semester. Bert Gassman at the time was principal oboe of the Los Angeles Philharmonic.

At the end of that spring semester I had a complete fluke of an opportunity. Bill had a friend from the Metropolitan Opera. They were looking for an oboist to go on a forty-three-week tour of the US, Canada, and Mexico. They had a principal oboe opening but they could not find an oboe player who could just drop everything and go away for a year—they were really worried. They talked to Bill and Bill said, "I have this student who may be just right for you guys." So I got a call. I was out on a fishing boat at the time with my dad and my hands were full of bait and the harbor-master came over and found us—this is off of Santa Monica Pier. We were maybe a mile out from shore. And they said, "You have an important phone call." And I was thinking, "Oh my God, who died?" It turned out it was my mom and she said, "You know, David, if you can get home right away and wash your hands and change clothes, we have an audition." One of the conductors for the opera was in town, so I went to his hotel room and there was no music or anything. He just said, "Play the solo from Tchaikovsky Four. Play Brahms Symphony. Play Violin Concerto. Play *Tombeau*." So I just, from memory, played through all of the excerpts and he said, "You're our guy, and we can pay such-and-such, and we start in Indianapolis. Six weeks of rehearsals." I was eighteen years old.

It was really a fluke opportunity and Bill Criss said, "Oh yeah, you should do it. Do it for a year, then come back to school." This was 1965. The Vietnam War was going on. Draft age was twenty-one. I was going to turn nineteen soon but I figured, "Piece of cake. I'll do this, I'll get back in school, no problem." So I took the job. And halfway through, when I turned nineteen, the military decided they were going to lower the draft age to nineteen. Of course I got a letter from the draft board: "Come take your physical." And I'm thinking, "Uh-oh. What am I going to do now?" We were performing at Lincoln Center at the time. I was in New York City so I made a couple of quick calls to some relatives. One of them had a car and I called the colonel of the West Point Band and said, "Hey, do you guys need an oboe player for next year?"—just playing all my options. I didn't really see myself going over to Hanoi and fighting the Viet Cong. I scheduled an audition and got a ride up there and played for the colonel and he liked what he heard and he said, "Yeah. We can guarantee you a permanent station playing in the West Point Band but unlike being drafted, which is two years, you'd have to enlist and take on a third year." Given the options I figured that was a better bet but I still had to go through basic training.

They let me finish the opera tour and as soon as that was over I went straight into basic training. Summertime. Fort Bliss, Texas, outside of El Paso. It was brutal. And they didn't cut me any slack for the fact that I was a musician— they made me go through basic as if I was really going to go into combat. It was okay; it worked out well. Being a skinny kid anyway I did better in basic than a lot of the other guys did. And my girlfriend at the time didn't want to see me go away for three years, so we decided we would just get married. After basic training, we got married and we both went to West Point and she finished her degree at New York State University, New Paltz. She got her degree in two years and started teaching the third year, and it worked out really well.

The quality of the band at West Point was amazing at that time because there were so many Juilliard grads and others who had lost their student deferment and didn't want to have to go into combat, so the band was exceptionally fine. We formed a Wind Quintet on the side there, and we rented Carnegie Hall and gave performances, actually three performances at Carnegie Hall during my years at West Point. After those three years I thought, "Well, I should get back in school anyway. I should get a degree, right?" But some auditions were coming. I thought, "Well, maybe I'll take an audition or two. See what happens." And, sure enough, I got into the Pittsburgh Symphony straight out of West Point as associate principal. Elden Gatwood was principal then, and Tom Fay was second oboe. I learned so much from them, being in the orchestra. William Steinberg was the conductor. I was learning good rep and it was just a very nurturing environment for me. Two years after that, James Caldwell decided to leave the National Symphony to go teach at Oberlin and created a vacancy and I took that audition and won it.

I was principal in National for two years, and then Bert Gassman decided to leave the Los Angeles Philharmonic. For me that was always my dream job, because I loved living in Los Angeles, and even though the job started out as co-principal with Barbara Winters, it was great.

I got it . . . It was a hairy audition. There were sixty applicants for that, and in the finals were myself, Dick Woodhams, my teacher Bill Criss, and Sally

Watkins. I can't remember if Dick Killmer was there, but it was just really intense. We got down to the final two; it was me and Dick Woodhams, and I think he was sort of taking the audition for practice because he really had his eyes set on Philadelphia for a couple of years later. Anyway, one thing led to another and I ended up getting the job. The committee was split—half of them wanted Dick and half of them wanted me, and they didn't know which way to go. And Dick made it easy for me. He told them, "You know, I probably won't go even if you offer it to me." You need to be a little bit lucky in this life and I certainly was lucky then.

I was in the LA Phil for thirty years. After a while, Barbara Winters left and they made me full principal and hired an associate. So, it worked out. And it was a great ride, because at that time Zubin Mehta was the music director and the LA Phil was not at the top level of orchestras, but he was building it like crazy and really hiring some great new musicians and recording. A lot of recording sessions. European tours. Then when he left, Giulini came. Carlo Maria Giulini had been the principal guest in the Chicago Symphony. When he came to LA that really brought an extra sheen and stature to the orchestra, and again, with attrition and better replacements the orchestra really started sounding like a world-class band and it was great. The elevator ride up with that orchestra was wonderful.

I was also able to use my other skill, which was as a photographer. After my first year in the orchestra the management had noticed that I was taking a lot of pictures and they were asking to purchase them to use for their brochures for the following season. One thing led to another, and for my second year they made me the official photographer for the orchestra, so I was able to document all of the guest artists, guest conductors, tours. I had to do stuff like visa and passport pictures too. But photography has been a really important part of my overall career as well.

Teaching

Visual images are very important for being able to phrase properly and really communicate a mood and a feeling. Vision. I never really specifically thought about how the two connect—my photography and the music. But I do know that I always appreciate a conductor who doesn't just say, "Play louder here, play softer there," but will actually give you some visual image and say, "It really should be more mystical here, like water evaporating." Sometimes that can be a bit hard to take if a conductor only talks into those terms. But there is the relationship, visual to musical. I know that with my students there are times if I describe a picture they get it much more quickly than if I just write crescendos and diminuendos—how do you explain color change to a young student? Sometimes giving them an image helps.

I've been teaching all along with my orchestral career. When I started in Pittsburgh I was the professor at Duquesne University for those two years. And when I was in the National Symphony I was hired on by Catholic University in Washington, DC. When I got to Los Angeles I started teaching part-time at USC, on and off, and of course all this time I had a private studio as well. When Bill Criss passed away in the mid-eighties they offered me the professorship, full professor, which I had to turn down because I had three children at the time and I liked to have enough time to go fishing and enjoy all that Los Angeles has to offer. So I decided, "Look, I'll stay on a part-time basis but I wouldn't be able to take on the full teaching responsibility." They hired Joel Timm and later Allan Vogel came on. The three of us are continuing—we still are involved a lot with the oboe stuff going on at USC Thornton School of Music.

Auditions

Before we get to the skills required, what I tell all my students is they better love the oboe because the chance of winning an audition is such a long shot. No matter how brilliant and talented you are, there's somebody else out there who is maybe even a little better than you. And you need to be lucky at auditions, too. First thing, you have to love the instrument and make a decision that no matter what, you're going to really enjoy what you do. Because if you're thinking about it as a meal ticket, forget about it. It's not going to pay the rent unless you are very, very lucky as well as being extremely good.

To win an audition you have to have great technical skill. But that alone won't do it. You have to be able to convey some special feeling that's compelling to the ear of the judges. There's got to be some feeling of spontaneity and naturalness, and you telling the story. You're really being an entertainer. Too many people enter auditions as a test. They go in with this mindset that it's an examination and they have to get all of it right. What I tell my students is that you are entertaining that committee. You need to go in there and get their ears to perk up. Not from technical perfection but from some sort of musical *je ne sais quoi*. Because after all, you're number thirty-seven out of a list of a hundred and seventy players, and they've heard it all done before you get there, and they've heard it done really well. You've got to do something to tweak their imagination a little bit. It's the idea of an audition being a real entertaining performance. Even if you make technical mistakes you have to not let that get to you because everyone's going to have flubs. You've got to do something that's compelling enough that you get past that first round, where the judges will say, "Well, they messed up here, or this was a little bit out of tune, but man, did you hear how they did the solo in *Don Juan*?" Or, "*Tombeau*?" And "there was something really magical about that." If you can get that across in the preliminary round, then you are much more likely to be given a second hearing. When you get into the semi-finals and you're only up against ten players instead of sixty, then you've got your toe in the door.

Tone

One of the most important things for a student to know is that there is no correct conception of tone. If you were to listen to the twenty best oboe players here at the conference in Tempe right now, every single one of these great artists has a different quality of sound. And yet they have all made very successful careers and are gods in the eyes of all of us here. Sometimes I'll get a student and they're just fixated on a specific line in the spectrum of darkness to light or bright or from shiny to chocolate. We can admire our heroes out there that have a particular quality of sound but you always have to keep in mind that everyone's physiology is different. The shape of the jaw, the cavity inside the mouth, the sinuses, all of these things have a bearing on how a person sounds. And it's a mistake for someone whose physiology is so different from, say, a Tom Stacy or a Harold Gomberg—you know, where the jaws are really big—it's easy for them to get a certain kind of tone. If you're not built like that, you're going to have to play on extra-heavy reeds to sound that way and it can do physical damage to you. I've seen it happen, where people are trying to get that sound and they develop really bad headaches or they have problems with their esophagus or they have no endurance—they can sound great for five minutes but after that they totally lose it and they can't control the reed and their intonation is out the window. So, the advice I have is, yes, develop what you think is an ideal conception of tone but then blend that with your own physical capabilities and don't be too obsessed. Allow your own voice to come out of your oboe.

The other thing: are you going to become an orchestral oboist or more of a soloist or chamber music player? What is it you really want to do? For those who want to go into orchestral playing, it's so important to find the right combination of reed style and instrument so that you're able to have a good dynamic range without forcing. Here at the exhibit hall there are hundreds of instruments to try, and they all feel a little different, one to the other. And you might feel that one feels really great. But then you take it on a stage and what if it doesn't project as much and you're in a situation where the conductor is always looking at you, trying to squeeze more sound out. You know, "Play out, play out." It's a problem in a lot of orchestras and in halls that are kind of dead where, rather than get the rest of the orchestra to play softly, they're always looking at the oboe: "Come on, play louder." So for this reason, you want to take that into account when you buy an oboe. You need to have one that really has a good focused sound and projects well without you having to force. And that may not be the oboe that feels the most comfortable in a small space.

Be forward-thinking about your reed style and your oboe before you buy something. Too many times I've seen oboists buy something that felt so good at home or in the shop where they're testing it. But the acid test is to take it onstage in the hall where you expect to be playing and have people way out in the audience, two hundred feet away, listening to see which one maintains that focus of tone without spreading when you start playing forte or fortissimo. Because you need to know. Conductors are really brutal, and seldom will you find conductors that will make the orchestra soft enough to really let your sound be on top during the solo passages. That's one of the key things that I have my students give serious thought to. For me personally, I find that a good Lorée works the best for that sort of orchestral situation. I love some of the other instruments that I've tried, the Marigaux and the Howarths. There are so many great brands . . . the Josef oboe. They feel and sound so great. But anyone contemplating putting that kind of investment in a horn needs to really think about how they're going to use it. If it's going to be in chamber music or solo playing, then it's a whole different set of considerations. But orchestrally, you never want to force the sound because it spreads. The louder you try to play, the worse things get. You want your oboe and your reed to work for you so you don't have to be distracted by that and you can just think about the musical phrase and the fantasy and imagination and all those things that really are going to captivate the ear of the conductor and your audience and the audition committee.

25

Randall Wolfgang

Randall Wolfgang studied with John de Lancie at the Curtis Institute of Music. He has performed as a member of the Orpheus Chamber Orchestra, New York City Opera, and New York City Ballet. He has performed on more than thirty recordings for Deutsche Grammophon, including the Mozart Oboe Concerto. This interview was conducted with Michele Fiala in December 2011 in Wolfgang's New York apartment and was updated in October 2018.

Author's note: When I arrived at Wolfgang's apartment, he and his daughter were choosing a piece of cane "for today." "I do it by color," he told me. "This one is too yellow. On another day it would work well, but not today." He asks his daughter her opinion. Together, they select the correct color for today, "creamy with just a tinge of gold."

—MF

Early Career

I grew up in a small town in Pennsylvania where my father was a band director. I had an older brother and sister who were already playing instruments. We all started playing the piano at six years old. My father needed an oboist for his band and gave an oboe to a girl who was about fourteen, but she brought it back after a couple of days and said that it was too difficult for her. Dad thought that maybe she just bumped the reed. He put the oboe together, put on a reed, and then someone distracted him so he left it on the kitchen table. I came home from school, picked it up, and started playing it. Because I was seven years old, he said, "Oh, no. You're too young." I said, "I am going to play it," and he didn't put up too much resistance. He didn't teach me right away but my sister [Bonnie Wolfgang, retired principal bassoonist with the

Great Oboists on Music and Musicianship. Michele L. Fiala and Martin Schuring, Oxford University Press (2021). © Oxford University Press. DOI: 10.1093/oso/9780190915094.001.0001.

Phoenix Symphony] worked with me. Dad was a tough taskmaster and I saw how he treated my older brother so I avoided lessons as much as I could. My plan was to excel so that he couldn't criticize me. By the time I was ten or twelve, Dad needed me, and I became his child prodigy. I was this little kid playing in the senior band, and I would go to all these district and state music festivals. When the orchestra would stop during rehearsal, I'd just keep playing, to show off, and everybody would be looking around at me. Nobody seemed to want to scold me because I was so young, so I got away with a lot of things. I got a lot of attention. By the time I was twelve or thirteen, I had decided I was going to be an oboist. It came naturally to me and I excelled in my little sphere. My sister got into Oberlin and then she got into Curtis.

By that time, I was studying with Laila Storch in Wilkes-Barre, Pennsylvania. I studied with her until I was fifteen and then she left the area for the Soni Ventorum Quintet, at that time in Puerto Rico, and then Seattle, Washington. So, at fifteen, I was playing all her gigs. I was principal oboe at the Wilkes-Barre and Scranton orchestras. Bea Brown, who conducted in Scranton, used to love to call me "Vulfgahng!" like I was young Mozart.

I didn't get into Curtis on my first attempt after high school, so I went to Temple University and studied with Louis Rosenblatt, but I did get in the next year. At Curtis I studied with John de Lancie. He was a notoriously tough teacher like his teacher, Marcel Tabuteau, was. A lot of people didn't make it past the first year. If you didn't get kicked out, you were going to be alright and I didn't get kicked out.

My first job after Curtis was playing with Richard Woodhams in the St. Louis Symphony. I played English horn for the summer season and then I got a job playing principal oboe in the Charlotte Symphony in North Carolina. I was there for two years. During the summers I studied with Robert Bloom in Sarasota, Florida. Then I went to Aspen where I made many New York contacts. After that I came to New York. I found a place to live and I started freelancing. I starved for a year, but by the end of the year I already had enough work to know that I could survive. I arrived in New York in September of 1974 and by December I was already subbing in the New York City Ballet, where I became principal in 1982. In 1975, I started playing with Orpheus. By playing with the ballet and Orpheus, I established myself for the next twenty years. However, with Orpheus I was on the road a lot. Right before I got married I was on the road a hundred and eighty days a year. We'd go to Europe twice a year and we'd go to Japan sometimes on nine-week tours. It was a lot of fun, but once I got married and had three children, it was not what I wanted for myself. I decided that Orpheus and all the travel had become too much for me, so I left Orpheus. Not long afterward, I started playing with the New York City Opera. Even as a child, I loved opera so City Opera was perfect for me.

I became a teacher in ninth or tenth grade because I had to help my father teach, especially in summer band camps. Then my father challenged me. He picked out two oboe students and he said, "I'll teach one and you teach the other, and we'll see how they turn out." My first student was Barbara Herr [Orland]. She eventually ended up in the St. Louis Symphony after studying at Oberlin with Jimmy Caldwell.

I had a great teacher: Laila Storch Friedmann. Everything I learned, I passed on to my students. I always had four or five students. That was a good load. I started teaching at Queens College. I wanted to have my own class at the college level. I taught my students Barret and Gillet and especially slow Ferlings. I also taught chamber music at Manhattan School of Music, because I played in the Windscape quintet and we had a residency there.

My father always liked the challenge of working with students who had lots of problems. He would work and work with them. The townspeople in Catawissa used to say that old Wolfgang could make a musician out of a jackass. I always admired that about my father. So I like to do that too. I like teaching kids. I've had most of my success with kids who are fourteen or fifteen, where they're just beginning and you get them to be really serious about being an oboist. I have had many successes.

Reeds

When I was at Marlboro Music Festival, I would make a new reed every day. I would put the cane to the light and choose the one that had the most beautiful color. The point is, you have to make a reed every day. If you don't make a reed for two weeks, you're no longer an oboist. I started making reeds when I was ten years old. I learned it from a picture book. I didn't have a teacher and I just had pictures. No explanation, no words. You have to keep an open mind, be willing to make mistakes and discover what works for you. A reed vibrates and you have to learn what kind of vibration you want to play with.

Motivation

Once I decided I was going to be a musician, I put everything into it. There was no B plan. I love reading and I love good writing. I wish I could write the way I'd like to. I have a hard time writing a letter but playing the oboe, I can do that. Even when I was a small child, if I had problems in other areas, when I played, it made sense to me. That's where I could express myself. That's where I could excel. I had a teacher once who used to say, "You're an artist when you're in your studio. And when you're playing the show, that's not as important as what you are in the studio." It's not a matter of communicating with the universe. It's a matter of communicating with yourself, saying things that you couldn't say any other way. It doesn't matter if anybody else hears it or not. Although, you'd like them to.

If you have good teachers, they will help you but to be a good musician it has to something from within. You'd like it to be good and to get better. It's something you can work on; no one can take away from you. And you can build on it.

Teaching Philosophy

It's important to get some technique. As soon as you can get your students into the Barret, get them doing the scale articulation studies, before the second articulation studies and the progressive melodies. You start teaching the right notes and the right rhythm, right articulation, and phrasing right away. Barret is written so well for the oboe; the notes and the keys and the style throughout the whole book. Also transposing: I tell the kids it's not a matter of reading it. You have to read it, you have to hear it, and you have to feel it in your fingers.

Skill Sets for Diverse Ensembles

It takes a different set of skills to play the ballet and the opera. With the ballet, you need to play energetically. The dancers need to hear and feel the music. At the opera you need to play under the singers: softer, warmer, and a different kind of reed. When I recorded the Mozart concerto with Orpheus, I played it every day for a year and recorded it and listened to it. That's a different skill. With ballet it is opposite. There is never enough rehearsal and certain dancers dance faster or slower or something happens and in a way it's not wise to know things too well because if you are half sight-reading all the time, you are really on your toes and it is more alive.

De Lancie used to say all the time that he played for seventeen years without using a pencil. He would never mark anything. But in the opera, I always felt, because it's so long, if I made a mistake and I didn't mark it, I'd make the same mistake again and again and again because there's just too much to remember. So at the opera, I always make lots of marks so that I don't fall into the same mistake twice. I like the drama in the opera. At first it seems a little overwhelming. Somebody dies every night, and you have to be there for it. But then the ballet seems light after that. I feel very lucky that I have both the dark and the light. The more you play the operas, the more you love them. You never get tired of *Figaro*. You look forward to the next time you can play *Rosenkavalier*.

The ballet repertoire at City Ballet is different than most ballet companies. Balanchine really took a lot of the best pieces from the orchestra literature and then created ballets to them, so the repertoire is fantastic. Balanchine and Stravinsky were good friends, and the collaboration is amazing: *Orpheus* and *Firebird* and *Agon,* etc.

Phrase Shaping

Laila Storch was my oboe teacher and before I knew what was happening to me, I was learning the number system and where the high point of each phrase is. To make visual images with numbers is something I learned when I was quite young. Then I studied with de Lancie and I had that number system drilled into me. I think that now it's kind of a lost art.

I used to be able to tell every orchestra by the oboe player. You could tell this was Philadelphia, this was Chicago, this was Gomberg, this was Ralph, this was Harold. You could tell this was Cleveland Orchestra. We'd hear the piece of music and we would have to guess who the composer was, who the orchestra was, who was the conductor and who the pianist was. What the style is, what the touch is. You could certainly identify these things. I still can. That was part of the fun of listening to classical music: the contest, to see what it is, who it is, who the composer is, who the performer is.

26

Omar Zoboli

Omar Zoboli is professor at the Musikhochschule Basel, Switzerland. He won first prize at the International Competition of Ancona and at the Italian Television (RAI) Competition for Young Performers in 1978. He has performed with festivals and orchestras in Berlin, Rotterdam, Paris, Warsaw, Lugano, Geneva, Zurich, Basel, Milan, London, Japan, and the United States. He has recorded a DVD (Lebrun Concerto, Frans Brüggen conducting) and about thirty LPs and CDs for Accord, Claves, Divox, Ex Libris, Harmonia Mundi, Jecklin, Koch Schwann, Stradivarius, Teldec, and others. Zoboli has been oboe soloist of the Radio Orchestras of Lugano (RSI) and Naples (RAI), the St. Gallen Symphony Orchestra, and the Kammerorchester Basel. He has played Baroque and Classical oboes with Concentus Musicus Wien (Nikolaus Harnoncourt), Il Giardino Armonico (Giovanni Antonini), Scintilla Orchester Zürich, and I Barocchisti (Diego Fasolis). This interview took place with Michele Fiala at the 2009 International Double Reed Society Conference in Birmingham, England, and was updated in 2018.

Early Career and Meeting Holliger

I was thirteen when I started. It was because there was no possibility to play piano or violin. But the teacher was a very good one, Sergio Possidoni, first oboe of the Radio Orchestra Milano. I was very good in mathematics, so I decided I wanted to study mathematics. But the destiny was different for me. My teacher brought me to play in the orchestra of Lugano, Switzerland, because he was playing sometimes there. The first oboe of the orchestra was playing two years in La Scala at the time, so I arrived in Lugano and I stayed two years. In the meanwhile, I heard some famous oboist playing—[Heinz] Holliger of course—and I decided

Great Oboists on Music and Musicianship. Michele L. Fiala and Martin Schuring, Oxford University Press (2021). © Oxford University Press. DOI: 10.1093/oso/9780190915094.001.0001.

I wanted to start again to study. I wasn't quite three years in the orchestra and then I gave up and restarted to study again because I wanted to understand what he did. He was, of course, a very special teacher, mostly not interested in reed making, but basically in analysis of the scores. He played the piano all the time with his students, played the oboe as well. We played much modern music. I got from him some Pasculli scores, and one was "Le Api." But the most impressive thing I heard was contemporary music concert with him where I heard the music of Niccolò Castiglioni, "Alef"—one of the first performances. I recorded with my cassette recorder and I heard many times and I was very impressed with the music of Castiglioni.

Once, I played the low C♯; instead of pianissimo I played mezzo-forte. He said to me, "Why don't you play pianissimo?" At the time I was a little angry. In his life, he wanted to play this note and he found out the technique. For him it was probably normal. It was not for him to understand another who is fighting with his low C♯. But this was also the spirit: he was always looking for finding something over the limit. To find out, if you want to play B5 or C6, is it possible? Perhaps you can try it upper teeth. The note plays. Find something to extend the possibility. All these composers, Lebrun, Pasculli, they did the same: they extended possibilities.

Through Holliger, I arrived to many things. The way he played the Baroque music, even if in not a Baroque way (because the Baroque [performance practice] was not still started), but he played with ornamentation and improvisation and the door that opened for me was the door of the old music. I started also to play the Baroque oboe, even if he didn't. I had the chance to hear Paul Dombrecht once in a concert. I liked very much his way of playing. Through the Baroque oboe, I arrived to play with Harnoncourt in the beginning. It was a good chance for me because it opened to me to another way of making music, which is not forcing the body, just to find expression in the rhythm, in the color, and not in the Romantic way of expression. I made one recording where we improvised the adagio in the style of Corelli, Geminiani, the ornamentations. So I developed more and more interest in improvisation. Now I am playing very much also with some jazz musicians. We play some Baroque trio sonatas, Bach, for instance, with improvisation. This is now many interests I have to develop in the improvisation—free and also with chords.

Sound Concept

Playing the Baroque oboe changed my perspective because one of the things that I like is to experiment with the sound. I don't play one instrument with one sound. I like to find the sound for each piece. In many kinds of music there is not a fixed sound. In jazz, each musician has his sound and his vibrato/non vibrato. I like very much to play also without vibrato, to experiment with colors and with reeds.

I spent years to make reeds with the book of Ledet, *Oboe Reed Styles*, with the measurements. It was for me the Bible. I copied all reeds in this book. All. From the Dutch with very short staples. I also tried all the oboes it was possible to try. There was a big difference some years before in the making of oboes. Now mostly people try to go in the same direction, to make an oboe which is blending. At the time was not this way. It was each oboe with a personality and each player had a really personal sound. This I enjoyed very much.

Sometimes I try to play with another embouchure and change reeds. When I play Berio "Sequenza" and Castiglioni, I change the oboe and I change the reeds, which is a big job, to find the balance with different kinds of reeds. But I like this idea that I can find for each music another way. At that time that this music was composed, probably there was no one playing it the same way. The Italians in Lombard played like Sammartini; they played differently from Lebrun in Germany, and this was very fascinating. In the book of Bruce Haynes and Burgess, you can read many statements about this way of playing. This is also for me a Bible, these two books, *The Eloquent Oboe* and *The Oboe*. It's a fantastic book. This, today, I think is a little lost. It's a pity. But there are still people playing.

Performing on Period Instruments

Now, with the professionalization and the higher standard of the Baroque and Classical orchestras, the people have very few rehearsals, must play very, very precise. There is no time to make experimentation. When I played with Harnoncourt and also with Il Giardino Armonico, in the beginning there was one, two weeks' rehearsal for making a program. This means there was money to pay for the musicians for one or two weeks. And there were state subventions for the groups. Now it's quite impossible. So, the tendency is to play the Baroque standardized. No Baroque player will play similarly to the reed we have in the Baroque because the sound is not acceptable. And the same with the Classical. Even Holliger had this problem because he was playing quite differently. For a German oboe player, it was not acceptable, but it was accepted because he could play at a level that nobody could. I liked him because of this, because it was somebody going his way very, very, very strong.

Pasculli's Instrument

One thing is sure when you take this instrument in your hand, you don't feel that you can play with vibrato that you use with a modern one because the instrument is 300 grams. The reed is so easy; you don't need breath pressure which is so high, so you can really blow very free. It's more naïve, the feeling of naïve. If you play with continuous vibrato, you feel I am playing something strange, big. He bought the lightest instrument from Triébert and the shortest and the highest pitched. I was discussing with Alfredo [Bernardini] about the pitch, and with Burgess also. When I tried to play, I never managed to play it at the normal pitch of Triébert, which is 435 [Hertz]. It goes over 445 and we discovered there were some special high-pitched instruments that Triébert made, probably at 450. This probably is one of those instruments. I don't understand what happened with tuning in Italy. He was playing mainly with piano, but even with piano . . . I am looking if there are some writings about this matter of tuning because I have some more Italian instruments of this period, instruments that were probably played in La Scala by Yvon and they are all 435. Not so high-pitched. And the English horn of Pasculli, when you play with the reeds also of the Barret school, it is playable lower, anyway, probably manageable to play it sharp if the oboe was sharp. I have another Triébert of the same period which is 435, 438, it depends.

The question is, so what did he do with the pitch? And if the reeds that I found in the reed case are his—because the oboe, after he was dead, the daughters told me they gave to a student. And this student didn't do the music too much, and he was making many duels. The daughters said they were afraid the oboe would disappear, so they asked him to give the oboe [back]. So I don't know now if the reed that I have found is one of Pasculli's or one reed of Triébert bought by this student. I tried to go down, but the oboe wants to play sharper, 445, 447; when you play at this pitch, it is perfect. With other Triébert [oboes], I can play lower.

I don't know if it is because he played all his life with this oboe and after time it is going up like many oboes, and after it was not played until I got it, I don't know if something was changed in the bore.

Tone Production

When you play a hard reed with a big, dark sound and you want to play a Bach sonata or Zelenka, you really force over the limit and you don't have flexibility. This does seem to be a problem for many oboe players. Mostly for the orchestras they want this kind of sound. Many students tend to play very, very hard reeds in Europe, mostly in the last ten years. There are also oboe players that can play with a big sound and very flexible, but they are exceptions. This for me is one difficult challenge because I like the idea of playing one hour through with no problems. So, my training is to find the material that you can play continuously through and not stop and make [panting noises]. I try to bring the students to breathe in a way that they can play this way.

My first exercise is to observe yourself. What happens when you play a long note? Before doing something, see what happens. I focus more on the effect. I don't teach how to breathe in, in order to breathe out, but I do teach a long note, crescendo-diminuendo, with stable tuning. The reference is the tuning and the dynamic. It is time to learn how much pressure to use, how much embouchure, which kind of reed for your lips. I don't start the long note with tonguing; I start without tonguing. To start and to realize where the reed is stable and where your support is and your embouchure. Find the focus. I start a long note without tonguing, mezzo-forte, until it is stable. Then I go diminuendo and I go again crescendo and diminuendo. This gives me a feeling of where is the air, where is the support? Then you can go more deep inside this. You can start fortissimo, go diminuendo and go crescendo-diminuendo. The second time, you can start tonguing. Doing air exercises brings very much information to the student.

Teaching Philosophy

When I see someone play an oboe that could be not the best, I take one of my collection, or we go to a shop and we try another one, but I never oblige anybody to play an oboe of one kind, like many teachers may. This is normally an advantage because you can do standard reeds; you can teach very exact. For many students, this is very good. When I hear somebody playing with a sound that is not their sound, even if the sound is good, I don't feel good. For me, the important [thing] is to find out how to help the student to express himself.

My aim is to help the student to find a sound, very simple technique. I learned this way mainly playing with Baroque orchestras, where the discussion is more on the rhythm or the quality of the rhythm or the dynamic than on the technical means to do it. At the beginning, we discovered how we could make this. Now there is a standard also there. But before, it was more coming from the practice, from the experiment. This I like very much. It is like Alexander technique. The first thing you do is not do. You learn to stop. This idea brought me very far. Not many students like this way of teaching; many students need precise advice because they want to be sure. I cannot force anybody to play in my way. This is my style of teaching. Some students go because they don't like this. But I cannot do it any other way.

The students that I have are very good. I am very happy because they go on developing themselves and each time I hear them, I see things that I opened there but they developed. Mostly the students that I have today play different kinds of music; they are not the orchestral type. It's more chamber music, modern music, self-organizing groups, or making projects. This is more my kind of student that I can also help find repertoire or to find ideas of programs. They teach also; some teach very good. I went to hear the lessons and they were very good. Better than me! Some are very methodical. I like to improvise very much—to discover each time. Somebody said [to] me, "It is too much information. Too much. You have to lead your students more; you have to give the limit." This may be true. It is what I studied from Holliger also: it was a big amount of information.

Repertoire

The thing is to find for each student the right material, so it is not the same for everyone. If you want to learn Berio or Castiglioni or Yun, you need the time to learn the style, to find the sound. It is a pity that mostly the students play maximum one piece so they don't have an idea. This is a big, big challenge so they cannot do three, four, five contemporary pieces to understand what that is. When I was studying with Holliger, I got so much information that I took a very long time to digest. But I had also enough time to make enough repertoire. In the Baroque, you need to know at least an Italian sonata, a French sonata with ornamentation, a German sonata, some outstanding piece, experimenting, so you need at least four Baroque. You need at least one or two Classical concerti. You need to play Mozart right away, then you need at least a different [one].

Solo Playing

Yesterday was a good example. Nicholas Daniel played a Thea Musgrave piece. He had something to say with the piece. It was like his piece. Nicholas played a good piece and he was convinced it was a good piece. I like very much when I hear somebody who is feeling the rhythm, the quality of the rhythm of the piece. So yesterday I was very impressed, even if, I must say, it was very challenging to hear Nicholas. For me, it feels the music is there; I make the execution. I am neutral. For Nicholas it is very personal, but in a way, there are two ways to take a position, no? It is interesting. It is mostly interesting when I hear new pieces. I find it very good that there are so many world premieres; this is a very good point of the conference. I like very much people playing new music when it is good music also.

Holliger as an example, the important [thing] is what you have to say about the piece. There are many, many ways. In the jazz workshop, there was the same matter: "What do you want to say? What is your point of view on this music?" Important to have your point of view. Sometimes the point of view is, "I show you that I can play faster than the other one." Which happens, for instance, with the "Four Seasons" interpretations after an Encore '73 recording. All tried to imitate this, and there was more and more fast until some groups played it again with some nice sound. Not very original; there was nothing after Encore because all there was that Encore could discover in the score was there before, but it showed.

On Improvisation and Jazz

To make improvisation is a very important method because improvisation makes you more conscious of what your instrument [does]. In Baroque music, to improvise very much, especially end-of-sonata Adagio, for instance, is very good. I take the Partita for flute and I take the chords and [create] another line over the same [chords] to discover that the music has other potentials and that you can do something else because this, from Bach, is one version that he could have played. He could have played another one on the cembalo or the organ. All the music that exists is one version of a project piece. You have a project when you make improvisation. This project develops in one way, but it can be different. The music of Bach is one possibility. He was also soloist, of course, and an improviser. To make improvisation is very important. To make jazz improvisation, you need very much work, to play on standards. But to play on Baroque music, the harmony is not so extended. It is a good thing that anybody can do.

Composing a little is important. You can make things. I don't do complicated things. We mostly do in the group some pieces improvised and then we write the project—which things happen here, eventually which course and if there is a melody, that will come. You have a little project. Then you can really discover many things.

My inspiration is Paul McCandless because he was the first oboe player that I heard playing jazz. It doesn't matter if you play the oboe or anything else. If you are interested in improvisation you can go in different ways. There are not only jazz standards, there are many, many kinds of music. Even in jazz, there are very many styles. There are complicated chord changes like Thelonious Monk or there is funky jazz; there is Latin Jazz. Jazz is a project of improvisation in different styles. Baroque music is, in a way, also jazz because Baroque music had a big part improvisation.

Pasculli probably was improvising and then writing. It was not writing and then playing. We read and play. But he was feeling the music; the music was there. If you look at the scores, there is no correction, like Mozart, like Bach. All these cadenzas, is always a structure. There is not one note too much in Pasculli. They are very long and there is no correction. The music was clear. This is the spirit of Chopin or Liszt also, the pianists. He was thinking, of course, harmonically, melodically, but you see all the cadenzas; there are chord changes.

Sometimes I think we are very closed. The oboe is really a very difficult instrument. You need so much time to reach the standard level of the tuning. You can't play a bad reed. A too bad a reed, I mean. [Laughter] Like every oboe player, I started to play the music without understanding what I played. I started to play the notes that belonged to this chord. And this was not the way that people before went. They learned to play the chords that they needed to play and the people then, the musicians, they were a composer, player, they organized. Mozart had to meet impresarios for the stage costumes, for the light, to see how much money, to make the liaisons with the singers, the *prima donna*, to make the rehearsals with the orchestra, to find the tuning, all of this, more aspects of the music. Very modern in a way. Today again you have to do all of this stuff.

Inspirations

Improvisation, jazz music, Baroque music with improvisation. If I hear some-body playing very free and very good, I get inspired. Normally I go home and practice to catch this feeling inside me. Sometimes I go to people or master classes of other instruments. I played also recorder a while in my life and also viola da gamba. I was in the summer courses in Urbino, Italy, where, at the time, it was Frans Brüggen teaching. The way he played in the class was fantastic. I get very much inspiration from this, also for the oboe. Also from cello players. I recorded last year one cello suite with English horn, the Partita, and some Bach solo pieces. I have some colleagues that play Baroque cello very good and we discuss it hours, trying to get these things. When you hear a cellist playing very nice, Baroque cellists, you get the feeling of the breathing inside them and you go home and try to match this. You work on the reeds, you work on the position, how you hold the oboe, to go continu-ously through without cutting the air, which is the feeling when you hear a cello player. These ideas I like very much. Sometimes I succeed in playing in this way. But in the oboe, you are always on the edge, the razor's edge. Either you go really very good and you can be free, otherwise, you become tense and the moment in music disappears for me.

For an oboe player, it is important to hear very good string players—Baroque—and also to hear piano players for contemporary music. To hear many things that are not oboe. To take this energy, to create a new language, and to play good music. Many people play pieces because they think it must be good, not because they feel it is really good. Play music because you feel it is good. And because it is great.

Practicing Oboe Fundamentals

by Allan Vogel

I. Tone Production

A. Breathing/posture exercises. Work with reed alone.
B. Four exercises for tone production: Clean your lungs. Take a good breath and use it.

   1. Breathe in tempo.

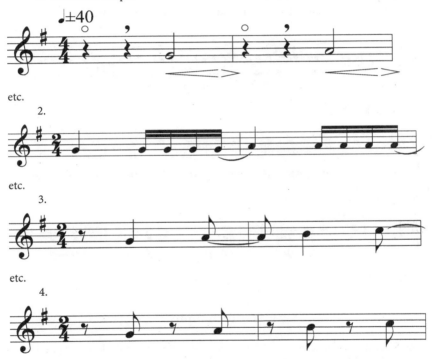

etc.

   2.

etc.

   3.

etc.

   4.

etc.

Pick a key each week and work in the following ways:
- Monday: Perfect intervals and major scale
- Tuesday: Minor scale (melodic and harmonic)
- Wednesday: Scales in 3rds
- Thursday: Major arpeggio
- Friday: Minor arpeggio
- Saturday: Broken major arpeggio (also minor if Sunday is off)
- Sunday: Broken minor arpeggio (or rest)

C. Long Tones
1) Hold *forte* note as long as possible. Check posture, support, relaxation, and hand position. Add vibrato and legato tonguing.
2) *Piano* note, otherwise as in #1.
3) *pp* 4 beats, crescendo 8 beats, hold, cue end
4) *ff* 4 beats, decrescendo 8 beats, hold, cue end
5) *pp* 2 beats, crescendo 8 beats, *ff* 2 beats, decrescendo 8 beats, *pp* 2 beats, cue end
6) Express melody on a single note

D. Sonority and Control Exercises for the low, middle, and high registers

continue to low F#

continue to high D

continue to low E♭

II. Technique

A. Salviani scale pattern. (See Vol. II, exercise #1.) Practice in the key of the week, also with double tonguing and circular breathing.
B. Fernand Gillet: *Vingt Minutes d'Etude*. "Practice four exercises for five minutes each. Practicing is an Art in itself."
C. Vade Mecum exercises 1 and 2.
   Nancy King scale compilation.

D. Monday: none (because of double work in tone production)
  - Tuesday: slow scale in eight notes
  - Wednesday: triplets with upper and lower neighbors
  - Thursday: 16th notes (see Salviani p. 2 #5) all articulations. Other Salviani exercises.
  - Friday: quintuplets (see Gillet p. 5)
  - Saturday: sextuplets—twice as fast as Wednesday
  - Sunday: rest or septuplets (see Gillet p. 6) and trills (Gillet p. 2)

E. Barret
  Ferling
  Georges Gillet
  Bozza
  Silvestrini
  Loyon
  Luft
  Brod
  etc.

F. Fast orchestral solos or concertos from memory

Index